I-MARY

Mary Austin in Santa Fe, probably in the mid-1920s

I-MARY

A Biography of Mary Austin

Augusta Fink

THE UNIVERSITY OF ARIZONA PRESS
TUCSON, ARIZONA

About the Author...

AUGUSTA FINK is the author of a number of books about California and the American Southwest, including histories and a historical novel. With Morley Baer, photographer, she authored *Room and Time Enough: The Land of Mary Austin.* In 1982 she received an Award of Merit from the California Historical Society for outstanding contributions to California history. In 1972 her book *Monterey: The Presence of the Past* won the Commonwealth Club of California's Silver Medal. She is a resident of Carmel, where she has taught classes in contemporary literature and California history.

Quotations from the following publications and collections have been reproduced by permission:

From *Earth Horizon* © 1932 by Mary Austin. Copyright © renewed 1960 by Kenneth M. Chapman and Mary C. Wheelwright. Excerpts reprinted by permission of the Houghton Mifflin Company. From *Experiences Facing Death* © 1931 by Mary H. Austin, used with permission of the publisher, The Bobbs-Merrill Company, Inc. "Love Coming Late," by Mary Austin, published in *The Nation*, July 11, 1928. From *Mary Hunter Austin* © 1965 Twayne Publishers, Inc., and reprinted with the permission of Twayne Publishers, a division of G. K. Hall & Co., Boston. From *Mother of Felipe and Other Early Stories* © 1950 The Book Club of California. From *My First Publication* © 1961 The Book Club of California. From *The Seacoast of Bohemia* © 1966 The Book Club of California. From The Bancroft Library, University of California, Berkeley. From The Huntington Library, San Marino, California. From Mills College Library, Oakland, California. From Special Collections, University of Arizona Library, Tucson. From the Department of Special Collections, University of California, Los Angeles.

THE UNIVERSITY OF ARIZONA PRESS

This book was set in 11/13 V-I-P Baskerville
Manufactured in the U.S.A.

Library of Congress Cataloging in Publication Data
Fink, Augusta.
    I-Mary, a biography of Mary Austin.

    Bibliography: p.
    Includes index.
    1. Austin, Mary Hunter, 1868–1934—Biography.
2. Authors, American—20th century—Biography.   I. Title.
PS3501.U8Z59   1983   818'.5209 [B]   82-21807

ISBN 0-8165-0789-9

For Margaret Marshall, who gave the most—
of time, and thought, and love.

Contents

ILLUSTRATIONS

A Word From the Author

It is Mary Austin's personal story that I have felt it most important to emphasize. All of her writings are in a sense autobiographical. Even when she wrote of the land, she reflected the despair and ecstasy of her own experience. However, in her formal autobiography, *Earth Horizon*, she presented only those aspects of her life about which she wanted the world to know. It is in her novels and short stories, as well as in her letters to those with whom she was on most intimate terms, that the rest of her story is revealed.

The material presented in this biography stems from Mary Austin's personal papers—correspondence, diaries, and notebooks—or is extrapolated from her published writings. The characterizations are based on interviews or careful research into biographies of the persons portrayed. Some of the incidents are taken from reports of individuals closely associated with Mary Austin; others are fashioned out of fragments in her writings. The collections of Austin material at the Henry Huntington Library, the Bancroft Library, Mills College, the University of California at Los Angeles, the University of Arizona, and the University of New Mexico have been thoroughly explored and utilized.

Every attempt has been made to depict Mary Austin faithfully, to re-create her as the person she really was. Her story offers much to assuage the thirst for deeper meanings in today's world. She emerges as a symbol of the universal struggle to know the self, to answer the question, "Who am I, and why am I here?"

To the many people who have made this book possible, I am deeply grateful. I am especially indebted to Peggy Pond Church for giving me access to her research material, to Ansel and Virginia Adams for sharing their personal correspondence and recollections of Mary Austin, and to Lawrence Clark Powell for motivating me to write the biography and for providing encouragement throughout the ten years of its preparation. I am also grateful to the University of Arizona Press for effecting publication.

Enough appreciation cannot be expressed to Elsie Martinez, Kathryn Frazer, Mr. and Mrs. Frank Lloyd, and Mr. and Mrs. Francis Duveneck, from whose reminiscences came many significant insights into Mary Austin's personality as well as the basis for invaluable interpretations of her story. Among the numerous other persons who gave of their time and assistance are Thomas Matthew Pearce, Richard Dillon, Dudley Gordon, Mrs. Harold Sterling Gladwin, Jean Kellogg Dickie, Mr. and Mrs. Francis Herrick, and the staffs of the Henry Huntington Library, the Bancroft Library, and the libraries of Mills College, the University of New Mexico, and the Southwest Museum.

My profound thanks are due Mrs. Peter Cook for granting permission to reprint excerpts from her mother's biography of Mary Austin and to Agnes de Mille for permitting quotations from *Dance to the Piper* to be included.

For permission to reprint other material of prime importance, I am grateful to the following publishers, institutions, and individuals: Houghton Mifflin Company, The Bobbs-Merrill Company, Twayne Publishers, The Book Club of California, the *Nation*, the Henry Huntington Library, the Bancroft Library, Mills College Library, the Research Library of the University of California at Los Angeles, the University of Arizona Library, Peter Steffens, and I. Milo Shepard for The Trust of Irving Shepard.

Finally, I wish to express my gratitude to Mary Hunter Wolf, Mary Austin's niece, who graciously gave her support to the biography.

AUGUSTA FINK

Mary Austin

THE WOMAN AND THE WRITER

MARY AUSTIN'S LIFE AND WORK (1868–1934) have a startling relevance for the late twentieth century. Feminist, naturalist, mystic, writer, she was involved with aspects of the human condition which are ageless. In an era when minority groups were despised and dispossessed, she carried their cause to the highest offices in the land. In a society in which women were treated as chattels, she spoke out for their right to self-realization with candor and eloquence. In a country where natural resources were taken for granted and the land ruthlessly exploited, she interpreted man's abiding relationship and responsibility to the earth with a depth and understanding unsurpassed by later environmentalists.

Dedicated to her writing career, Mary Austin was always also a woman, aching for emotional fulfillment, yearning for the simple joys of hearth and home. Eager for admiration from the opposite sex, she did not disdain to reveal the feminine side of her nature, but intellectual prowess and the exercise of her gifts as a writer were more precious to her than any possible human relationship. Though she knew many degrees of involvement with men, her hunger for a deeply passionate experience was never completely satisfied. Of this need she once wrote, "A woman whose love life has

[1]

been as unhappy as mine, who had no religion, would have gone mad or bad or committed suicide. I have been very near the last many times."[1]

Her religion was eclectic. She explored all traditional systems of belief and forged her own creed. Two powerful ontological experiences which occurred before she was six expanded her consciousness to a different perception of reality. Practicing the absorbed contemplation of the mystic, she developed methods of meditation through which her creative energies were channeled into insights and expressions of great beauty. The best of her writing is unforgettable.

Rooted in the earth and related to its creatures in profound and subtle ways, she was attentive to an inner reality more compelling than the world around her. Of this perception she wrote, "All that I know has always been known by me." And she knew more than she could ever express, despite twenty-seven books and more than 250 articles, stories, poems, and other short pieces. Her writing ranged in subject matter from history, anthropology, and folklore to metaphysics, natural science, and the arts. It delved into such diverse areas as politics, ecology, and the theater. It took every literary form from the novel to scholarly dissertation. It reached its most memorable levels of expression when she wrote of the earth, recreating in metaphor and poetic prose not only the landscape but the spirit of the Southwest.

Though she was raised in Illinois, spent almost a third of her life in the East, and kept a pied-à-terre in Carmel, her heartland was in that vast country of limitless horizons stretching from the glacier-studded bulk of California's Sierra Nevada to the great, broken barrancas and soaring mountains of New Mexico. This land of awesome beauty, "sublime in its immensity of light,"[2] came alive for her as a presence with whom she sought intimate communion. Of it she wrote, " . . . where I came wholly into the presence of the Land, there was a third thing came into being, the sum of what passed between me and the Land which has not, perhaps never could, come into being with anybody else."[3]

As a public figure, Mary Austin was a forceful personality. Notorious for her egocentricity, she was often arrogant and imperious. But she felt herself the tool of creative forces beyond her control and denied the egotism of which she was accused. Held in high esteem by celebrities both at home and abroad, she became a legend in each of the places where she lived—California's Owens Valley, Carmel, New York, and Santa Fe. Of her, Carl Van Doren wrote, "Everybody who talked with Mary Austin knew at once that there was greatness in her. . . . "[4] To the world, she appeared self-assured and omniscient, possessed of a prophet's wisdom.

Privately she was a lonely, often anguished woman, whose personal story has the drama and pathos of tragedy. An unwanted child, she spent her girlhood fraught with frustration in an environment that gave little sustenance to her eager intelligence. Awkward and aloof as an adolescent, she was disliked and snubbed by her peers. Marriage to a man who could not match her vision of a rewarding relationship brought bitter disillusionment, to which was added the heartbreak of a mentally retarded daughter. Breaking free at last from the strictures that bound her, she was confronted with making her way in a sophisticated society, a venture for which she was inadequately equipped. However, out of the grueling years of deprivation in a desert land that many considered desolate, she had gleaned rare insights and strength to achieve success in a world that granted it grudgingly to women.

Though she experienced close friendships, even amorous involvements, with notable personalities, essentially she walked alone, daring unfamiliar frontiers of thought and endeavor. Courageous in the fight for causes vulnerable to the inroads of contemporary civilization, she was among the first to recognize the threat to Indian and Spanish cultures. Through sharing the way of life practiced by Indian tribes of the West, she absorbed the hidden meanings of their art and verse, then worked to preserve a precious heritage that might otherwise have been lost. Also acutely aware of the need to protect Spanish colonial art and architecture from destruction, she was a prime force in the movement that saved them for the enrichment of future generations.

A complex woman of many contradictions, forged in a crucible of struggle and searing hurt, Mary Austin was both mystic and pragmatist, at times harsh and abrasive, yet always responsive to victims of injustice or intolerance and ready to give generously of herself in their service. She believed that the problems of mankind could be solved by "the spirit of truth and brotherliness working their lawful occasions among men."[5] Moreover, she was not afraid to come to terms with humanity's most enduring questions—the ultimate meaning of life and of death—for she herself had discovered the secret of life triumphant.

Prelude
1868-1888

1

The Two Marys

Before she was six, she knew there were two Marys. And she lived in two worlds. There was the lonely child without grace to please and win affection, yearning for the mother's love denied her. And there was I-Mary, self-contained and secure, who had no need to be loved and could not be hurt.

Mary Austin's earliest recollections were of a coldness in her mother's attitude towards her. Evenings when Mother sat rocking baby Jennie in her lap, and brother Jim snuggled against her shoulder, Mary sometimes "forgot and leaned against her knee." It withdrew. "Hadn't you better get your stool, Mary?" Mother said.[1]

Sharp was the remembrance of a hot Sunday afternoon, when she was very little. Trudging up a long, steep hill, Mary had tried vainly to keep up with her parents. Then, too tired to take another step, she had collapsed on the sidewalk. Father made a move to pick her up. But Mother said, "Let her alone. She'll come when she finds she has to."[2] Watching her family disappear over the brow of the hill, Mary felt sure she had been abandoned. After what seemed forever, Father came back and, taking her in his arms, he comforted her.

That feeling of being comforted never came from her mother. Even when Mary was sick and held close to her bosom, "nothing happened"—there was no warmth in her mother's embrace.[3] The baffled child could only sense that somehow she had antagonized the person for whose love she longed. She could not have understood why. Many years later she unraveled some of the reasons.

Susanna Savilla Graham Hunter was a simple woman, artless and unassuming. Dark brown hair, slicked down from a center part, framed her strong, patient face. Only the deepset eyes, harebell blue and still lovely, lightened the stern expression she habitually wore.[4] Though Susanna was still in her twenties at the time of Mary's birth, the soft prettiness of youth had been erased by years of hardship.

A descendant of French and Scotch-Irish pioneer stock, she had been born and raised in the small community of Carlinville, Illinois; the strict Methodist discipline and mores of the Midwest had been bred into her bones. Intelligent and well-read, she had aspired to being a teacher, even entertained the possibility of a writing career.[5] Instead, as the eldest of three children who survived her mother's death, she had helped her stepmother with domestic chores and devoted herself to the "household arts that were proper to young ladies" of her time.[6] Then, at nineteen, in a roseate aura of romance, she married[7] Captain George Hunter, a Carlinville attorney newly enlisted in the Civil War.

Handsome and auburn-haired, Hunter was nine years her senior. Characterized as being "of noble bearing,"[8] he was also said to have that "much-admired quality of sensibility" which strongly appealed to young ladies. Blissfully in love, Susanna accompanied him to military outposts in the swamplands of Mississippi where she bore two babies, both of whom died in infancy.[9] At last, after three dreary years of existence in army camps, Captain Hunter completed his term of enlistment,[10] and they returned to Carlinville, where he resumed his law practice. In the small house he built on First South Street, Susanna had her first real home. With high hopes, she anticipated a promising future, only to find her husband debilitated by a lingering malaise, the aftermath of malarial attacks he had suffered while in service.[11]

Illness kept George Hunter from pursuing his profession aggressively, and the family income was meager. An additional cause for concern was that a son, James Milo, born on July 25, 1866, developed an incipient lameness when he was little more than a year old. Fearful that her husband's ailment might be hereditary and anxious about their unstable financial situation, Susanna bitterly resented the discovery that she was again pregnant.[12]

Despite the fact that Susanna did not want Mary, she might have learned to love her if she had been a tractable child. Unfortunately, the little girl, born at midnight on September 9, 1868, soon manifested behavior which Susanna found exasperating and incomprehensible. The difficulty began with Mary's inability to distinguish between something she had actually seen and something she had only imagined.

When she innocently described a happening as if she had been present, her mother called it "storying" and wicked. For the child, the pictures in her mind were as vivid as the reality around her.[13] Another problem was Mary's habit of blurting out the very things that everybody else was trying not to mention. When there was company in the house and a lull occurred in the conversation, she would burst forth about what she inexplicably sensed somebody was thinking or feeling. Acutely embarrassed, her mother would exclaim, "I think the child is possessed!"[14]

Punishment did not correct Mary's misconduct. Scolded and sent to her room, she would promise not to repeat her transgression, but the impulse simply could not be stifled. Endowed with a perceptivity that bordered on clairvoyance, the bewildered child could only say that "it was like a little bird that hopped out of her mind, onto her tongue, before she could stop it."[15] Still, she was deeply hurt by her mother's displeasure and often cried herself to sleep. Then, one blustery winter morning, not long after Mary's fourth birthday, something happened that ended the need for tears.

Susanna and the two elder children were gathered around the kitchen table. Two-year-old Jennie played nearby. Outside the wind howled, splattering snowflakes against the windows and shaking the roof corners. In the cozy room it was snug and warm, with a fire in the wood stove and the smell of fresh dough.

Mother kneaded bread at the table. Beside her Jim, who was then six, sat studiously over his primer. Mary was perched on a stool, looking over his shoulder while she rolled a bit of dough in sticky fingers. She was intent on watching the letters in the book as Jim recited them.

"O," said Jim, pointing to the picture of the letter.

"O," Mary repeated and made her mouth into the same shape.

"I," said Jim, and again pointed.

Mary plumped a finger to her eye. "Eye?" she asked, looking up at her mother expectantly.

"No," her mother said. "I, myself. I want a drink of water. I, Mary."

Slowly Mary rolled the grubby worm of dough as she thought about what her mother had said. It was a strange and exciting idea. Then suddenly "something turned over inside her; the picture happened."[16] There was I-Mary inside her! In wonderment she touched the folds of her blue pinafore, gazed at the grimy piece of dough clutched in her hand, looked around the familiar room. Everything was the same; the flurry of snow outside, Mother kneading bread, Jim bent over his primer. Nothing had changed. Yet everything was different. Inside her something very important had happened. I-Mary was there!

The coming of I-Mary was a tremendous discovery. It brought the child "a sense of something assured and comforting" that she had longed for and "never found elsewhere." I-Mary had no need to be understood, to be accepted, to be enfolded in loving arms. Henceforth when her mother rejected or disapproved of her, she could withdraw into this other self and escape from hurt. "To be

I-Mary was more solid and satisfying than to be Mary-by-herself."[17]

Because the perception of I-Mary first emerged from the printed page, the child developed a passion for books. When stories were read aloud to her, she stared hungrily at the print.[18] There was always the possibility that the revelation would happen again. Words had become magic. Even their sound was irresistible. On nights when her father was wakeful from an asthma attack or pain in the leg that bothered him, Mary could hear her mother reading to him, and the rhythmic flow of words drew her out of a warm bed to crouch listening at her parent's door. Often she was found asleep there when her mother came to check on the children, and she was punished. But nothing could keep her from the sound that lured her.[19] She merely tried harder to stay awake so that she could get back to bed before she was discovered.

Mary had evolved an exceedingly pragmatic attitude toward punishment. She simply did as she pleased and took the consequences. Though willing to admit misconduct, she refused to repent. Any emotional display of remorse was abhorrent to her. Moreover, if she was sent upstairs to meditate on her misdeeds, "it allowed time for that swift interior turning...and there was I-Mary, against whose complete detachment" her mother could not prevail.[20] Naturally Susanna was vexed, but apparently she did not realize the potential danger inherent in Mary's deliberate withdrawal from normal emotional reactions. Nor was she aware how much the child actually admired and looked up to her.

It was the example of her maternal forebears that made the deepest and most lasting impression upon Mary as she grew into womanhood. The debt she owed them was succinctly expressed in her autobiography, written when she was in her sixties—"Whatever in Mary makes her worth so much writing about has its roots in the saga of Polly and Hannah and Susanna Savilla, in the nurture of which she grew up."[21]

Highest in Mary's esteem was her great-grandmother, Polly McAdams Dugger. First among the matriarchs who

wrestled cultural amenities from the frontier wilderness of the
Midwest, Polly had come to Illinois in 1833, with her husband, Jarrot, and their nine children. Migrating from Ten-
nessee, the Duggers had been among the earliest settlers of
the embryonic town of Carlinville. In her autobiography
Mary described them as "plain people, neither rich nor poor,
devoid of airs, loving the soil, good bargainers, the women
rather outmatching the men in that quality indispensable to
pioneer society, known as mother-wit."[22] Eloquently she de-
picted her great-grandmother, who arrived "sitting on a
bundle of pieced quilts and blankets of her own spinning
with an unrelinquished claim on all the sanctions of civilization and the preciousness of womanhood in her heart."[23]

Of almost equal intensity was Mary's admiration for her
grandmother, Polly's fourth daughter. Handsome and spirited, Hannah Graham as a bride defied convention by wearing a broadcloth dress made by her husband, whose trade
had been tailoring before he became a pharmacist. For being
photographed in the "scandalous" garment, she was disci-
plined by the Methodist Church. Unbowed, she walked down
the aisle in the very same outfit.[24] Later, when Milo Graham's
drugstore burned to the ground, she sold homemade baked
goods until enough capital was accumulated to rebuild the
business. Then, after bearing seven children in twelve years,
she died in childbirth at the age of thirty-two, a testimony to
"the hazard of early American women."[25]

Mary wrote more casually of the accomplishments of
her male ancestors. She had little to say about Polly's husband, Jarrot Dugger, except that he was reputed to be related
to the inventor of the daguerreotype.[26] She portrayed her
grandfather Milo Graham as a likeable Scotsman who had
aspired to study medicine and settled for teaching himself
pharmacy instead. In 1839, at the age of twenty-two, he had
come to Carlinville, married Hannah, and established a
drugstore in his own building.[27]

To women like Polly McAdams, Mary gave credit for
the success of her own generation's "revolt against the traditional estimate of women." With prodigal praise, she de-

clared "that the hope of American democracy" depended upon the pioneer women's ability "to coordinate society, to establish a civilization, to cause a culture to eventuate out of their wit and the work of their hands."[28] It was in their victories that Mary found the roots of the feminist movement which she would espouse.

There is no reason to doubt that Mary perceived her own mother as having carried forward the proud precepts of intrepid womanhood. In fact, the tension that existed between them may have been caused in part by the ways in which they were too much alike. Both were strong, independent women who had a need to control the situations in which they found themselves. Moreover, Mary could retreat into the aloof and impregnable position of I-Mary, behavior which must have completely exasperated her mother. A neighbor of the Hunters commented that Susanna tried "to get Mary to do what was normally expected of her; to act like other children," but "somehow she expected to be regarded as the Delphic oracle from her birth."[29]

Mary was always more comfortable with her father than with her mother. Many of her happiest hours were spent in his booklined study, where shelves held not only the works of Shakespeare, Keats, and Shelley, but also those of popular American authors such as Melville, Longfellow, and Emerson.[30] Just staring at the colorful bindings was satisfying. Handling the smooth, print-filled pages was pure pleasure. The best treat of all was being allowed to sit on her father's desk while he wrote.[31] There was a special rapport between the precocious child and the scholarly man with a finely honed taste for literature.

George Hunter had long been more keenly interested in intellectual pursuits than in the financial returns of professional endeavor. A native of Yorkshire, England, he had come to Carlinville in 1851[32] at the age of eighteen. While his contemporaries were taking advantage of opportunities to acquire land or build business careers, he had spent time attending college courses in the nearby town of Alton and making a return trip to England. Finally, he had settled down to study law in the offices of a Carlinville attorney, and at twenty-five, he was admitted to the bar.[33] Soon afterward he was drawn into a select local group which assembled to discuss advanced literary and aesthetic ideas. There he met and fell in love with a beautiful and gifted young woman whose intellect and romantic temperament matched his own. When their affair came to an abrupt end because of a tragic misunderstanding, he sought solace by immersing himself in the writings that had brought them together.[34] Then, within a matter of months after enlisting in the army, he married Susanna Graham.[35]

Hunter never regained the well-being with which he had entered the war. Illness had its compensations, however, providing an excuse to neglect his practice for more congenial occupations. Because outdoor activity was recommended to improve his health, he purchased a small farm at the end of Plum Street, on the outskirts of town. There he built a two-story house, adjoining which was the orchard where he spent more time than at his office. He also enjoyed the opportunity to study German, write papers for the county horticultural society, and browse in his books.[36] It must have been gratifying indeed for him to have a daughter who shared his interests.

For her part, Mary thought her papa was perfect. When she misbehaved, he would look a little sad and say she must not make her mother unhappy, but he practically never punished her.[37] And no one had a handsomer father— auburn hair brushed back into a shining pompadour, silken beard, and deep blue eyes that twinkled to let Mary know that he and she shared a secret, something of which mother would not approve.[38]

It was with her father that Mary first discovered the enchantment of the outdoors. Many mornings she played in the orchard while he cultivated his fruit trees. There a myriad of wonders burst upon her senses, making memories that would return "with the shattered brilliance of light through stained glass." She was never to forget "great clumps of frail spring-beauties coming up through the sod; the smell of budding sassafras on the winds of March...sheets of blue violets about rotting tree trunks" and "the hot honey-scent of red clover." In winter she took long walks with her father, finding "green fronds of fern and leafy wild blackberry vines under the edge of February thaws."[39] Most exciting of all were their excursions to the "Bottoms"—the marshland that lay along the river. There scarlet flowers streaked like slender torches out of the black shadows, water moccasins surfaced silently to make eerie rings on the glassy creeks, and an aura of mystery stalked under overarching boughs.[40]

It was always glorious to be with papa, but his recurring bouts of illness often left her on her own resources. Then she either played with her baby sister Jennie, whom she adored, or wandered off by herself.

One summer morning when she was going on six, Mary strayed farther than it was customary for her to go alone, beyond the orchard to the brow of a hill. There a gentle wind rippled through tall grasses, and a solitary walnut tree towered above her, "reaching into infinite immensities of blueness." She stood motionless for a moment. Then, quite suddenly, "earth and sky and tree and wind-blown grass and the child in the midst of them came alive together with a pulsing light of consciousness," so powerful that she would vividly recall the experience more than a half century later.

> There was a wild foxglove at the child's feet and a bee dozing about it, and to this day I can recall the swift inclusive awareness of each for the whole— I in them and they in me and all of us enclosed in a warm lucent bubble of livingness...
>
> How long this ineffable moment lasted I never knew. It broke like a bubble at the sudden singing of a bird, and the wind blew and the world was the same as ever—only never *quite* the same. The experience so initiated has been the one abiding reality of my life....I can recall, even as a child, leaving the companions of my play to bask in it, as one might abandon the shade to walk in the sun....[41]

At a remarkably tender age Mary had made a discovery that would alter the course of her life. Like I-Mary, it would provide a means of escape from the anxieties of everyday existence. Through the awareness of a reality other than the ordinary world around her, she would know moments of pure exaltation. Later, however, this gift would also plunge her into depths of anguish and despair. For the present, the child hugged the experience to her heart and, for want of another term, called it "God."

Because Mary was different from other children, they regarded her with a mixture of awe and suspicion. When she entered school, she could already read and was immediately promoted to the third grade. There she faced a barrage of hostile stares from classmates who resented the intrusion of someone three years their junior.[42] Her air of knowing more than anybody else inevitably aroused antagonism. Before long, though, she had devised a way to earn acceptance and attract a coterie of devoted followers. Storytelling was the magnet which proved irresistible.[43]

She invented tales replete with spine-tingling adventure that held her companions spellbound. Shrewdly she shaped her plots to their level of appreciation. Summer afternoons in the hayloft, or by the fireside on snowy winter days, she was the center of attention.[44] But the newly found popularity did not replace her need for spells of solitude, nor did it diminish her passion for books.

At the age of seven, she encountered *Alice in Wonderland* and begged her father to buy her a copy. Her hopes soared when with shining eyes he exclaimed, "By Jove, Susie, she really has been reading it. We'll have to get it for her."

But Mother gave him the familiar "can't afford it" look and said, "When she's older, perhaps. I can't think it good for children to read so many fairy stories."[45]

Papa did not let her down. The next evening he came home, twinkling in the way that was a sign of surprises, and presented her with both the book and her own card to the library from which it had come. The card became her open-sesame to a world of never-ending wonder.

That same year Mary announced that she intended to write books as well as read them.[46] She began experimenting with putting words together. They were arranged in short phrases and sometimes simple sentences, written on separate slips of paper which she rolled up and hid in secret places around the house. The words she produced were enormously precious to her, not to be seen by anyone. But both her mother and brother took delight in finding the bits of paper she had hidden and reading them aloud, especially to company. Mary was outraged. It was as if an intimate part of herself had been violated.[47]

Only Jennie, gentle and loving, always understood how Mary felt. With the little sister, who seemed almost an extension of herself, she could share her most sensitive experiences.[48] Together they wandered in the woods and meadows, where Mary sat for hours observing the pattern of a leaf or flower, the design of the bark or branches of a tree, the evocative image of how a shadow fell.[49] The presence of Jennie was never a distraction. Upon the lovely, delicate child, she centered the full force of a basically affectionate nature otherwise often repressed.

Despite Mary's preoccupation with ideas beyond her years, the setting in which she grew up provided a ballast of practicality and concern for the commonplace. Susanna did her best to inculcate high standards of homemaking into her daughter's training, and cooking was one area in which the child responded wholeheartedly. Because the best recipes were associated with tales of pioneer days, she eagerly learned how to make Polly's celebrated spiced apples and Hannah's honey-colored quince preserves, as well as the four-layered pies that were a frontier specialty.[50]

Though the Hunters were sometimes in straitened circumstances, Mary suffered no real hardship. Thanks to Susanna's competence, the children were well fed and clothed, and because Grandfather Graham was a pharmacist, they had the benefit of the most up-to-date remedies for illness. Of course, no one escaped the colds and malaria prevalent in their part of the country, and there was a dread of diphtheria, a new disease for which apparently nothing could be done. Problems like these were accepted as part of living, and on the whole the children enjoyed a better life than most of their neighbors. In addition to the fun of participating in community celebrations, picnics, and excursions, they had the advantage of a home in which stimulating discussions of books and current affairs were a daily occurrence. Mary could not imagine a better place to be for the present, and a future filled with dreams beckoned enticingly.[51] Only her father's illness disturbed the calm of her self-centered existence.

She had become accustomed to nights when she awakened to the sound of his labored breathing and the odor of burning pastilles permeating the house. In the winter of 1877 his condition worsened alarmingly. The doctors seemed unable to diagnose the new ailment, or at least the children were not told its nature. Mary did know that her father suffered excruciating pain. It was frightening to see him clumping about on crutches, swearing in strangled gasps, with his leg drawn up in an agonizing cramp.[52]

The prior summer another baby had been born, and Mary was given responsibility for his care. With the crib placed beside her bed, she scarcely slept for fear little George would cry and bother her father. Mornings she fed her brother before going to school and hurried home to take him off her mother's hands. The nine-year-old girl, always slight, became even thinner as the months dragged on with her father better some days, worse on others. There was an operation from which much was hoped, but the surgery did not help. For Mary, the anxiety would have been unbearable but for the source of strength which never failed to sustain her.

The awareness of I-Mary could be summoned almost at will, and through this invulnerable self she was able to accomplish things far beyond the capacity of Mary-by-herself.[53] She also sought moments of communion with the "vast friendly presence"[54] that always brought transcendent peace and joy. Often she stole out to the orchard at dawn, carrying George and a bowl of bread and milk for his breakfast. There she sat amid the aisles of trees and absorbed the still, ordered feeling of comfort. Suddenly a great wave of exaltation would well up inside her—"a sense of innumerable bright events, of tingling and unattempted possibilities...."[55] It was during this time of her father's gravest illness that she began her first serious piece of writing, a play in rhymed verse.[56]

Finally, in the fall of 1878, the ordeal of her father's agony crept to a close. Several times in the days before he died, Mary was seized by a sudden foreboding and rushed home from school, taking Jennie with her. The last time this happened, as they passed the cemetery, she was overcome by desolation. Squatting down on the sidewalk, she wept bitterly, while Jennie snuggled close and tried to comfort her. After that she waited at home, silently struggling to cope with what the loss of her father would mean to her. The end came on the twenty-ninth of October.[57]

She was summoned to her parents' room, where in the big bed Father lay frail and wasted. Mother sat beside him, face worn with grief and watching. Tenderly she moistened his dry, cracked lips with one hand while she wiped her streaming eyes with the other. Mary felt as if her chest would burst.

Then, without warning, she was aware of I-Mary. This second self seemed to stand apart, looking at everything as at a scene in a play. She heard her mother cry out and knew her father was dead, but she shed no tears. Within her she felt only the familiar, shining warmth—the "sense of something assured and comforting." Quickly she hid her face, afraid the others would notice that she was not weeping and think she did not care.

The comfort of withdrawal into her inner self was not without price. Torturing herself with remorse, "she laid herself dumbly against the sharp edge of sorrow, fearful that she would miss...the least aching instant of loss,"[58] as she had failed to react in her father's last moments. The full impact of his death was soon enough felt. Not only would the family have to give up the house and farm, but already the routines that had made it home were broken. An atmosphere of impermanence pervaded the splintered days. There was a constant stream of relatives, helping to dispose of the property and giving advice on how a widow could earn her way. Mother went about with a harried look, paying little attention to any of the children except Jim, who at twelve took on the role of man of the family. Meanwhile Mary grew increasingly dependent upon Jennie for affection and understanding.

Early in December Mary developed a severe sore throat. Her harassed mother did not notice how sick she was, and the child tried not to bother her. No one realized that she had diphtheria. Jennie shared her bedroom, and at night when Mary's throat choked up so she could not swallow, her sister held her close. By the time Mary was better, Jennie fell ill. Still Mother was too distracted to pay attention.

The gentle, little girl sat unobtrusively in a corner by the fire, burning with fever but never complaining. Patiently she tried to answer Mary's questions about how she felt. Then the day came when she could no longer speak. Too late the doctor was called. With Jennie's death, Mary's world fell apart. Naturally she blamed herself. Jennie had caught the sickness from her. She had known how her sister suffered. She should have made her mother notice.

The day of the funeral she stood on the bleak hillside where her father was buried and watched the little coffin being lowered into the ground beside him. Looking up at her mother, white and pinched in mourning clothes, Mary reached out to her, wanting as much to give as to receive comfort. In a paroxysm of grief, her mother thrust her aside and flung herself down upon her husband's grave.[59] That night the desolate child overheard her mother say to a relative, "Why couldn't it have been Mary?"[60]

In time Mary was to recover from the shock of her father's death, but she would never cease to mourn for Jennie. Fifty years later, when she wrote of the tragedy in her autobiography, the words were fraught with agony: "The loss of her is never cold in me, tears start freshly at the mere mention of her name. And I would not have it otherwise. She was the only one who ever unselflessly loved me. She is the only one who stays."[61]

2

Adolescence

THE SEEDS OF REBELLION

In the spring of 1879 the Hunters moved into town. The little rented cottage was far removed from Mary's beloved woods and meadows. Being cut off from the comfort of communion with nature compounded her aching loneliness for Jennie.[1] Even more difficult to bear was the loss of all contact with the inner resources that had once sustained her.

Tormented by guilt and remorse, she could not recapture the awareness of I-Mary, nor could she reach that radiant state of being in which she had known such incandescent joy. Emotional turmoil, aggravated by an early onset of adolescence, would for several years inhibit the mystical experiences for which she yearned.[2] In the meantime, she struggled through a daily round of responsibility too great for a ten-year-old to shoulder.

Susanna had applied for a widow's pension from the army, but until it was approved she had to earn a living for the family. Occupations open to women in her situation were limited to housework and home nursing. She chose the latter, amply qualified by years of experience with an invalid husband. While Susanna was away at work, Mary had to take on all the housekeeping tasks as well as part-time care of George.

Awake before dawn, she scurried to fix breakfast and put up lunch for Jim and herself. En route to school she left her baby brother with a woman who looked after him during the day. In the afternoon she hurried home to fetch him, put the house in order, and cook supper. When the dishes were washed with some halfhearted help from Jim, there was still schoolwork to be done.[3]

Often when Mother was out on a case, Mary lay tense and sleepless, listening to the scrape and creak of night noises and bracing herself against a nameless dread. At such times she sought consolation in the one remaining link with her childhood—a large, wax doll. Propping it up on a pillow, with its blue painted eyes fixed in a beneficent stare, Mary pretended the doll would watch over her until morning. The following summer, one of a group of visiting children stepped squarely on the doll's face, crushing its countenance beyond repair. Quietly Mary laid the broken symbol away at the back of a bottom bureau drawer. Not for anything would she admit how much it had meant to her.[4]

Mary's mother remained markedly cool towards her, but the child was more sympathetic than censorious. She was aware of the hardships and indignities that went with being a widow, and she deeply resented the subservient role her mother had to play in the households of other women.[5] If she could have communicated her feelings, both she and Susanna would have benefited from the exchange. Unfortunately, though Mary identified with her mother, she was incapable of showing it. Already she had begun to develop the defensive shell designed to ward off further rejection.

In the summer when Mary was going on twelve, relatives asked Susanna and the children to spend six weeks with them in Boston and sent a check to cover their traveling expenses. The invitation instantly brought Mary alive with excitement. For her, the New England of Longfellow,

Hawthorne, and Whittier meant pure magic. She could hardly wait to explore the places about which she had read.

The visit more than met her expectations. She astonished her cousins by leading them on sightseeing expeditions to all the important landmarks and relating pertinent historical information with a smug air of importance that irritated Jim. She even fancied that she saw Longfellow walking in the garden of his home. Altogether the interlude did much to bolster her confidence and revitalize her intellectual interests.[6]

That fall Mary entered the eighth grade, still two years ahead of her age in the school curriculum. Although she was highly competent in all subjects which required verbal facility, she had serious deficiencies in other skills. Her penmanship was atrocious, she had no real comprehension of arithmetic, and because she had learned to read by the word method, she could not spell.[7] These shortcomings did not concern her. The enchantment of books continued to be her all-consuming passion, but she missed the stimulation of sharing her enthusiasm. Since the death of her father, there had been no one with whom she could talk about what she was reading. Then new neighbors moved in next door, and wider vistas opened in Mary's world.

The Keplingers were a young couple, lively and well-educated. Mrs. Kep, as she was affectionately called, happened to be a devotee of the Chautauqua movement. Meetings of the local branch of the organization were held in her home. The program of home study, originating in the New York headquarters of the Chautauqua Literary and Scientific Circle, provided a course in guided reading to small groups scattered across the country. Susanna joined the Carlinville branch, and the course materials became available to Mary. To her delight, she discovered that the literature section included a study of Longfellow's poems complete with fascinating footnotes. Though Susanna was too busy to discuss them, Mary found a kindred spirit in Mrs. Kep. The ensuing friendship with an understanding adult brought a much-needed mental stimulus to the eager young girl.[8]

An even more significant contribution of the Chautauqua Circle to Mary's educational development came from a book on the reading list for the geology course. Written by Hugh Miller, who was a mystic as well as a geologist, *Old Red Sandstone* offered a lyrical interpretation of a subject new to Mary. Her imagination was immediately captivated by the singing prose, which conjured images of nature long absent from her daily experience. Fifty years later in her autobiography, she was to describe the evocation of a sense of earth—"transparent, molten, glowing"—which the book brought to her. Even the title had "a calling sound." She defied her mother's dictum that the book was too old for her and unsuitable in any event, as it dealt with the suspect theory of evolution. Saving pennies from her pocket money, Mary managed to purchase a copy. It was the first book she ever bought for herself, and from it she garnered lasting insights—"the feel of the purposeful earth" that would profoundly influence her writing.[9]

Mary was fourteen when the Hunters moved to the house on Johnson Street. Susanna had finally been allowed her widow's pension and, with the family fortunes considerably improved, she felt free to build a house pleasing to her taste. Square, solid, and shiny, it stood at the north end of Carlinville in a newly settled neighborhood near Blackburn College. Mary detested everything about it.

The six small rooms, aligned in two straight rows, proffered no feeling of warmth or welcome. Neatly squared and angular, they seemed to reject all impulses to living within their walls. Parlor and sitting room were made especially ugly by imitation black marble mantels and paneling grained to resemble hardwood. Three bedrooms and a kitchen constituted the rest of the house. Of course it did not boast indoor plumbing or central heating: such luxuries were reserved for the very wealthy.

The first time Mary walked into the house after the workmen had left, she almost became physically ill. Her distress was aggravated by the decor which Susanna had chosen. Chocolate-brown blinds clashed with a combination of red and green in carpet and upholstery. Cheap, contemporary furniture, adorned in cut-out designs of black and gold, replaced the few fine old pieces the family had owned. It was an alien atmosphere in which Mary knew she could never be at home.

The outdoor scene was no more attractive. A scattering of houses, forlorn and naked of greenery, were widely spaced in weed-grown lots, and only a sparse planting of maple saplings broke the monotony of barren prairie. Mary thought the most beautiful sight on the landscape was a nearby foundry, rust-red against a dark blue sky with its long, clean lines in harmony with the horizon. When she made the mistake of saying so, her notion became the family joke. She was careful to keep the rest of her opinions to herself.[10] Any criticism of the house would have branded her as being queer and ungrateful. She was already at odds with her mother in too many areas.

The tendencies towards willfulness and nonconformity which Mary had demonstrated since early childhood became more pronounced in adolescence. She was unwilling to accept a pattern of behavior simply because it was expected of her. Driven by a need to assert her individuality, she insisted that her personal preferences be respected. She especially resented the fact that her mother deferred to Jim as head of the family and assumed that Mary would behave accordingly. The first open confrontation resulting from Mary's rebellion took place at the breakfast table. Her feelings erupted over a ludicrously commonplace issue.

Jim liked his eggs very soft-boiled, but the sight of a loose egg upset Mary's stomach. Her requests that her eggs be put in the kettle ahead of those for the rest of the family were ignored, and her mother would not countenance the annoyance of allowing Mary to cook her eggs separately. The family ritual of all activity being centered on the wishes of its eldest male member must not be disrupted by the smallest divergence. Jim summed up the situation complacently by saying to his sister, "Somehow you never seem to have any feeling for what a HOME should be."[11] Furious, but convinced she could not win, Mary settled the skirmish by refusing to eat eggs. The battle was to break out later on other fronts.

Susanna's well-meaning attempts to inculcate in Mary behavior appropriate for a young lady met with stiff resistance. Mary would not subordinate her ideas and opinions in order to be popular. Most especially she would not tolerate the masculine prerogative to choose the topic of conversation and be the supreme authority, the accepted rule of "affording ample opportunity for His Whiskers to display...those gems of wisdom which only gentlemen could produce."[12] No man would tell *her* what to think, merely because he was a man!

Yet she had some interest in boys and was disturbed when she found it difficult to talk to them. They were bored by everything she considered exciting—books, poetry, and nature. She was incapable of coyness and scorned the dalliances that beguiled other girls of her age. She thought games like post office were downright silly—"if she wanted to kiss a boy she'd just kiss him."[13] In truth, among "the things Mary cared most about, sex never mattered much."[14]

Susanna's nursing occupation had brought Mary an early awareness of the facts of life, as well as of the seamier side of marital relations. Though she did not always comprehend the full meanings of the conversations she overheard, she sensed the anguish of overburdened mothers faced with the onus of too-frequent childbearing. There were allusions to "the horrid appetites of husbands"[15] and the "fearful menace of the middle years."[16] There were whispered confidences and an undercover trade in nostrums to avoid pregnancy. And there was the poor mother of nine who, when she discovered there would be a tenth, jumped off the roof of the buggy-shed. In those decades at the close of the nineteenth century "nobody, positively nobody, had ventured to suggest that women are passionately endowed even as men are. Not *good* women!"[17]

Other forces brought lasting impressions during Mary's formative years. The Woman's Christian Temperance Union had been founded at Cleveland, Ohio, in 1874, and Susanna Hunter was an ardent participant in its activities. From childhood Mary had accompanied her mother to W.C.T.U. meetings held in the Methodist Church. There the horrors of having a dissolute husband were openly discussed. She heard women speak out for "the right of women to refuse to bear children to habitual drunkards."[18] An object lesson was provided when a pretty little woman came to Susanna for help with a bloody bruise on her forehead and three small children in tow. The greatest impact on Mary's sensibilities, however, resulted from a Sunday night session at the church in which a woman stood up and boldly stated that marriage without love was "legalized prostitution."[19]

Concern for the right of women to have dominion over their own bodily functions was one area in which Mary and her mother forged a strong bond. Several years later, when Mary hit a man for abusing his wife because she was helpless to avoid repeated pregnancies, Susanna voiced hearty approval of her daughter's action. It was a rare instance in which she showed "genuine respect for Mary."[20] Early exposure to the temperance crusade and its sister movement, the struggle for the right of women to vote, laid the groundwork for Mary's ardent espousal of the feminist revolt. Stemming from esteem for her maternal forebears and brought to fruition in her adolescence, her firm belief in woman's potential for making unique contributions to society would profoundly influence her life as both a woman and a writer.

Meanwhile, at fifteen, Mary's personality was an amazing mixture of sophistication and naiveté. Her highly developed romanticism, nurtured on books by the Brontes and others in a similar mood,[21] was in conflict with her practicality and fierce independence. She rejected the concept that marriage was the crowning glory for which a woman should willingly sacrifice her person,[22] yet she longed for the tenderness and poetic ardor portrayed in fiction.

Lonely and restless, Mary even sought solace in organized religion, yielding to the fervor of a revival meeting held at the Methodist Church. Somehow she hoped it might lead her to the mystical experiences for which she still hungered. Solemnly she stepped forward to declare she was saved and in due course was admitted into full church membership.[23] But the promise of salvation proved empty. She never really accepted it intellectually and soon discovered that it did not answer her needs.[24] Out of touch with the source of her spiritual strength, she continued to drift and grope. Then, suddenly and inexplicably, the luminous moments of her childhood returned.

Early mornings before she was fully awake, or alone in the translucent hour of twilight, she again felt the billowing sensation of being uplifted, cradled, in a great cloud of knowingness and exaltation. This time there was a subtle difference in the experience. She perceived it as "the pressure of knowledge, all the knowledge in the world, pulsing just out of reach. It came up *inside* her, she was uplifted with it, rocked upon it . . . all the knowledge in the world, hers, aching intolerably to escape through her."[25]

It was at this point that Mary's mysticism merged with an insatiable appetite for learning. Her taste in books broadened to range from Egyptology and Oriental literature to John Ruskin's *The Seven Lamps of Architecture.* Susanna soundly disapproved. She denounced Mary's more esoteric interests as "filling your mind with that truck" and condemned the reading of Ruskin as "trying to be too old for yourself." She laced her criticism with dire warnings. People would think Mary conceited or peculiar. She would be disliked. Mary was not intimidated, but she did suffer a pang of envy when she heard her mother and Jim discussing the books that appealed to them—such as Theodore Roosevelt's

The Winning of the West.[26] Despite a seeming indifference, Mary was distressed by her alienation from the family's community of interests.

When she was sixteen, Mary entered Blackburn College, where Jim was already enrolled. Her attendance was soon cut short. At Christmas a severe cold, from which she was unable to recover her strength, forced her to drop out of school.[27] It was the first of several illnesses, in part emotionally induced, which would plague her youth.

She spent the rest of the school year at home, dabbling in an art course and indulging a yen to paint, but it quickly became evident that she would not earn a living as an artist. Ignoring her mother's advice, she refused to produce the type of art then in vogue for home decoration, the only practical outlet for her endeavor.[28] Concerned about her daughter's future, Susanna decided that she must prepare to teach. Mary had little enthusiasm for the prospect, but it was the only accepted vocation open to women in the Midwest at the time. So in September 1885 she enrolled in the State Normal School at Bloomington,[29] located in central Illinois. For the first time she was to live away from home.

Mary found the curriculum unbearably frustrating. There was no room for individual initiative or freedom of thought. The regimentation was suffocating and the subject matter boring. Moreover, the pressure of work was relentless. For Mary, the situation violated all the ways in which her mind naturally functioned. In the middle of the second semester she had a nervous breakdown.

At home the family physician pronounced her condition to be the result of overtaxing her brain. Pompously he suggested that women should not aspire to activity beyond their capacity and opined that the only work suitable for them was beside their own fireplaces. Mary was outraged but did not argue. Quietly she began planning to get the kind of education that would nurture and release her creative potential.[30] "She thought there might be a great deal to be got out of being a woman.... She meant not to remit a single flash of wit, anger, or imagination. She had no idea of what, in her time, such a determination would entail. She was but dimly aware of something within herself, competent, self-directive; she meant to trust it."[31]

Meanwhile she would concentrate on recovering her health. Her period of convalescence was spent in purely pleasurable pursuits. She began to paint again and to write poetry. She kept several fictitious diaries, making up entries for imaginary characters. She read omnivorously, Byron and Emerson being among her top favorites at the time. She also took classes in botany and rhetoric at Blackburn College.[32] There she met a young man whom she liked, and he seemed attracted to her. Her feelings may be deduced from the fact that a highly romantic episode in her third novel, *A Woman of Genius,*[33] centers on a character obviously patterned after this young man. Because he wore bright neckties and smoked cigars, however, Susanna was averse to him and evidently let him know he was unwelcome in her home. She preferred divinity students and, hoping to have a preacher for a son-in-law, encouraged them to call.[34]

By this time Mary was determined to reenter Blackburn College in the fall and obtain a degree. Undaunted by two academic failures, she still had to convince Susanna. In the end her mother's main objection was that even if Mary succeeded in her educational objective, she would only "throw it away on some man." Mary had no qualms about promising to postpone matrimony. Naturally she expected that someday she would marry, but she was very sure about her primary goal: she intended to have a distinguished literary career. In the meantime, she knew she had to earn a living. She was willing to teach and would prepare to do so, despite the disenchanting experience at Normal School.

Susanna finally agreed to see her daughter through college, provided she would be able to enter as a third-year student. The family finances were still tight, although the fact that Jim was to graduate in June would ease the situation. Eagerly Mary made up through private study the sophomore work she had missed. Then, to insure that her health would not again be a problem, she spent the summer with relatives on a Missouri farm in the Ozark Mountains. She came back in good physical condition and an optimistic frame of mind.[35]

The two years at Blackburn College were on the whole happy and rewarding. Because it was a small school, it provided opportunity for fruitful encounters with the teaching staff and a considerable amount of intellectual freedom. Mary majored in science, shunning English as a subject she could study by herself. She expected no help from the faculty in developing skills as a writer. After all, not one of them had written a book![36]

Surprisingly, mathematics turned out to be Mary's favorite course, though she had no aptitude for it. She could barely achieve a passing grade in calculus. Yet problems she only partially understood brought her a strange "awareness of space as one of the dimensions of reality, the dance of time...a sudden dazzle of the spirit...."[37]

Meanwhile, as a writer, she soon attained a reputation for accomplishment. Her contributions to the college paper, the *Blackburnian*, were enthusiastically received. Eventually she became editor of the journal and also was elected class poet. The recognition bolstered her confidence in her future objectives, and she would have been completely content had it not been for some problems in her social life. Though she had a small circle of feminine friends, she could not ignore her unpopularity with the opposite sex.

The custom of "going together" was firmly established in the mores of the college crowd. To attend any social function, it was necessary to be "going with" someone who served as a permanent escort. Lacking this arrangement, the girl was reduced to the status of tagging along with her brother and his girlfriend or imposing herself on another girl and her escort. Mary's pride was affronted by having to accept either of these alternatives. Moreover, she was not entirely immune to being hurt by the evidence of her undesirability.

At nineteen, Mary knew that her appearance did not meet the prevailing standards of pulchritude. Fashion favored ample bosoms, swelling hips, and a pink and white prettiness. She was thin and pale, and her flat-chested figure was not flattered by the styles of the period, with their close-fitting bodices, pinched-in waists, and great bustles in back. She did have an abundance of thick, wavy hair, brown with coppery glints, falling below her knees when loosed. However, she wore it in two huge, rather clumsily arranged braids on top of her head, with a curly cropped bang in front. Certainly she was not endowed with beauty, but more serious than any inadequacy in physical attributes was her unwillingness to cultivate the kind of charm considered essential in an attractive woman. Susanna did her best to correct her daughter's social deficiencies, admonishing her not to "antagonize people" but to "draw people to you." To which counsel Mary replied, "And what would I do with the people after I have drawn them to me?"[38]

Withdrawn and aloof, she hid her sensitivity to rejection behind a screen of haughty detachment. In truth she was deeply absorbed in herself and attentive to an inner reality that set her apart. Fortunately she finally found someone willing to accept her idiosyncrasies. He was a divinity student, gentle and self-effacing, who gave Mary unquestioning admiration. Because of his devotion, the problems of her social life were solved. She was unperturbed by the possibility that his intentions might be serious; for her the relationship was merely a matter of practicality.[39]

While Mary was involved with her own affairs, Jim struggled to make a place for himself. He soon discovered that a college degree gave no assurance of a job. He could not entertain thoughts of marriage, though he was keeping company with a girl of whom he was very fond. Effie Vancil, whose younger sister Ollie was Mary's best friend, came from a fairly prominent family, and Jim had no career prospects. He would have liked to study medicine to fulfill his dream of being a country doctor and owning a farm, but there was no

*Mary Austin on her graduation
from Blackburn College, 1888*

capital for such ambitions. Eventually he took a teaching position in a nearby hamlet, but he was bored and restless.
Meanwhile, letters from relatives in southern California
painted a glowing picture of opportunities on the West
Coast. Fertile government land could be had for the taking
through the homestead procedure. He decided to make the
move.

In the summer of 1887 he left for Pasadena, where
some cousins were living. He was barely twenty-one.
Susanna, whose life had centered on Jim, was desolate. She
missed him so much that her depression affected the rest of
the family. When word came that Jim wanted them to join
him, she was overjoyed.[40] He had filed a homestead claim for
160 acres of land in the San Joaquin Valley. He asked for
authorization to file a like claim for Susanna on adjoining
acreage and hoped that Mary would also take advantage of
the chance to obtain free land.[41] Susanna announced that
they would leave for California in June, immediately after
Mary's graduation.

Mary had not been consulted, but she persuaded herself that she did not much care. Until she could support herself by writing, she could teach one place as well as another. Other aspects of the move concerned her more. She felt that it would be better for Jim to have a life of his own and for her mother to stay in Carlinville. There Susanna could enjoy the home and activities that had been her world. Against her advice the house was dismantled, tenants found to occupy it, and furnishings sold or shipped.[42] Mary herself was more disturbed than she was willing to acknowledge. On the trip west she almost suffered another nervous collapse.[43]

The Awakening
1888-1905

3

Impact of the Tejon Country

THE TOURIST CAR was stuffy and crowded. Whole families were being transported westward, eager to lay claim to promised land. Amidst the noise and confusion, Mary became increasingly withdrawn and peaked as the days crawled past. Susanna, concerned about her daughter's condition, later wrote to friends that "the trip almost killed her....The doctor says he thinks that there is not much the matter but nervous prostration which rest and change will benefit. She came very near going to school too long."[1]

Very likely Mary's illness was due in large measure to emotional disturbance, but her mother was far from understanding its underlying causes. The shock of being uprooted from a familiar environment might well have appeared threatening to the sensitive girl. Moreover, she probably resented the fact that she had not been consulted about the move. The strain of repressing her true feelings, even to herself, could have led to an inner turmoil that surfaced in physical symptoms.

A five-day stopover to visit friends in Denver gave Mary a respite from the oppressive atmosphere of the train. Then, as the next leg of the journey took the Hunters into Utah, she had her first sight of the desert. It was an overwhelming experience, at once exhilarating and soothing to her nerves. For hours she sat "happily absorbed into its vast space and silence, faintly stirred by the sense of something expected, familiar yet remote...the realization of presence which the desert was ever after to have for her...something brooding and aloof, charged with a dire indifference, of which she was never for an instant afraid."[2]

Fortunately, the other passengers, bored by what appeared to them a barren scene, lapsed into silent lethargy, affording Mary the opportunity to meditate undisturbed. She arrived in San Francisco sufficiently recuperated to enjoy several days of sightseeing. The beautiful city intrigued her, and she resolved that someday she would return. For the present the Hunters proceeded to another round of visiting in Los Angeles and San Diego, then settled down with cousins in Pasadena to wait for Jim.[3]

He was in the San Joaquin Valley, planting a fall crop of wheat and preparing the homestead cabin for the family. Susanna was anxious to see her son but a bit apprehensive about the impending departure from civilization. To friends at home she wrote, "If I do not have the grit to stick it out, you may expect me to inflict Carlinville with my presence without much ceremony provided I can raise the *ducats* to get back on."[4]

Toward the end of September, Jim came to take the family to their new home. Located in the southern end of California's great Central Valley, the homesteads were in Kern County, twenty miles south of Bakersfield, the nearest town. The land was circled on three sides by mountains—the Sierra Nevada on the east, the Tehachapi and Temblor ranges to the south, and the Coast Range on the west. It was thought to be good farming acreage, as the soil was fertile and several mountain streams flowed into the vicinity.[5] Within a week the camping equipment had been assembled and the hundred-mile trek was under way. The family traveled in a covered wagon, while Mary rode alongside on horseback. Alert to the possibilities of gathering material for her writing, she carried a ten-cent notebook in her saddlebag and intended to make careful notes of the trip.[6]

The first day's journey traversed the long San Fernando Valley to the base of the mountains. Thousands of sheep and cattle grazed in the foothills, and the road led past old adobe houses with strings of chili peppers drying on their walls and animal hides fastened over fences. With a twinge of homesickness, Mary noted that the October landscape had little color compared to the autumn glory of Illinois.[7]

On the third day, after a steep climb between narrow canyon walls, camp was made near a spring encircled by tall reeds. That night Mary was startled by the spine-chilling sound of coyotes, who came close to the camp and howled, growled, and shrieked like demons.[8] Already she had found much to record in the little notebook she carried. The next day was to prove the most memorable one of the trip.

Ahead lay another range of mountains, "lifting their bare wind-swept peaks and wrinkled sides without a break, as far as the eye could see."[9] Entering San Francisquito Canyon, the road rose between walls of rock, in some sections roughly tumbled and striated, in others sheathed in chaparral against which shone the dark red bark of manzanita. Slowly the canyon narrowed until the road was forced up along its side at a precipitous angle. To Mary it seemed as if silently and mysteriously the mountains were closing in upon them. There was something awesome that she could only dimly comprehend about the scene that reached out to her.[10] The experience made such a lasting impression that more than forty years later she described it in her autobiography:

> There was something else there besides what you find in books; a lurking, evasive Something, wistful, cruel, ardent; something that rustled and ran, that hung half-remotely, insistent on being noticed.... Beauty-in-the-wild, yearning to be made human. Even in the first impact, Mary gave back a kindred yearning; it was in her mind that all she needed was to be alone with it for uninterrupted occasions, in which they might come to terms.[11]

All of her life she was to seek this illusive communion, and her finest writings would reflect the awareness of presences and powers unsensed by the casual observer.

The rest of the trip was relatively uneventful. Then, on the afternoon of the eighth day, as she rode out of the Tehachapi Mountains through Tejon Pass, Mary saw the San Joaquin Valley. It spread below them in a vast dim hollow. To the right stretched the 100,000-acre Rancho El Tejon, owned by General Edward Fitzgerald Beale, and beyond its lower fences lay the homestead section. Mary gazed down at the narrow, treeless strip of land, shimmering pale gold in the autumn haze, and made out a scattering of a half-dozen tiny dwellings. With a shock she realized that one of these was to be her home.

The Hunters' cabin consisted of one room with bunk beds and a minimum of essential furnishings. Sagebrush grew up to the door, tarantulas inhabited its walls, and the flimsy wooden structure stood exposed to the blazing October sun. Water had to be brought from a communal well, and fuel for the wood stove had to be hauled from nearby mountain canyons. Supplies and mail were fetched from Bakersfield, a two-day wagon trip across heavy sand.[12]

Mary's health deteriorated rapidly in the new environment. Part of the problem was an inadequate diet. The Hunters were too poor to buy fresh dairy products or fruit, and meat was restricted to wild game, mostly rabbits. Mary was sent out to forage for them. She was a good shot and did her job, but she hated to kill the timid creatures and could hardly force herself to eat their flesh. Before long she was so thin that the weight of hair above her wan face gave her the appearance of stooping.[13] Susanna was exasperated by her daughter's squeamishness and lack of energy. "I can't help but think," she said, "if you'd rouse yourself to take some interest in things...."[14]

Actually only Mary's acute interest in her surroundings saved her from complete collapse. She spent most of her time outdoors, avidly studying the habits of wildlife and the unfamiliar aspect of native plants. She slept little, often sitting for hours in the moonlight to watch the frisking of field mice or the mating of elf owls. Early in the morning she was out again, sometimes following a bobcat to its lair, then without fear lying down before its den to contemplate the wild creature.

One day while walking in the rain she came upon the ruin of a settler's shack. Seeking shelter from a heavy downpour, she went inside and there discovered an antelope resting on the grassy floor. At first he seemed afraid, but she sank close to the ground and stayed very still in a way she had learned would relax a timid animal—"You gather yourself in like a veil, a little at a time, and wrap yourself in a cocoon."[15] Soon the antelope forgot her presence and began to nibble the grass. Mary carefully recorded the incident in her notebook, which she always kept close at hand, and later the experience would inspire one of her most moving short stories.[16]

Gradually the intensity of Mary's absorption in her environment, along with the physical distress of malnutrition, began to have a strange effect upon her. She was haunted by premonitions and hallucinations. Once while wandering among the abandoned adobe buildings of Fort Tejon, part way up Tejon Pass, she was overcome with an eerie feeling that the crumbling walls were trying to tell her something. She went from room to room, reaching out for the elusive vibrations that seemed to tug at her consciousness. Then, on her way back, she found a skull in the road, pierced by an ancient bullet hole. In her notebook she wrote,

> ...the strange thing was that I knew several minutes before I saw it what I was going to find....Things like that happen to me here very often. There are times when everything seems to have a sinister kind of life. It shows its teeth to me. And at other times it is merely beautiful and gentle.

> Two or three times I have waked up in the night
> and had glimpses and warnings of what is sure to hap-
> pen to me the next day. And there are times when I am
> called and called. I know just where the thing is which is
> calling, though I do not always know what.[17]

The fact that Mary's condition was precariously close to
neurosis escaped her preoccupied family. Meeting the government requirements for "proving up" on their homesteads
took all of their time and attention. In addition to Jim's land,
Susanna had also filed on a quarter section, and there was a
timber claim in Mary's name.[18] The disturbed young woman
was left for the most part on her own resources.

Late in the fall Mary stumbled upon a remedy for the
part of her illness caused by dietary deficiencies. Walking in
one of the nearby canyons, she found an abundance of wild
grapes, and for a week she ate great quantities of the fruit.
Almost miraculously she began to feel better.[19] At about the
same time, her overly active imagination was channeled into
a definite creative effort. Using the first entries in her
notebook, she wrote a description of the October trip to the
San Joaquin Valley. The essay was a finely wrought account
of the journey, written in a lucid, restrained prose and including beautiful descriptive passages. She sent the piece to
the Blackburn College journal, and it was published in
January 1889 under the title "One Hundred Miles on Horseback." Both the endeavor and the recognition had a wholesome effect on her mental attitude. She began to notice the
problems that confronted her family.

Soon after the first of the year, the Hunters had realized
that their hopes for a thriving farm were doomed. The problem was water. There had been a few mild storms in the early
winter months, but the promise of an adequate rainfall had
disappeared. Doggedly, settlers plowed and planted the
powder-dry earth, only to watch kangaroo rats stalking the
furrows to pick out the seeds.[20] Southern California was in
the midst of one of its worst dry-weather cycles, a climatic
condition difficult for midwesterners to understand.

In the spring of 1889 General Beale, owner of the Tejon
Ranch, arrived to inspect the effects of the drought on his
property. His coming proved a fortunate event for the Hunters. Not only did he offer them an escape from what
had become a critical situation, but for Mary he opened a
whole new world. In her notebook she jotted down after
their first meeting, "General Beale has come back to the
ranch—a charming old gentleman—already told me unforgettable things...."[21]

Edward Beale was an early pioneer possessed of an in-
exhaustible fund of information about California and the
West. He had been involved in important activities in the
area since 1864. Among these was his appointment as
Superintendent of Indian Affairs in California and Nevada.
Initiating a policy of humane dealings with the Indians, he
established the Sebastian Indian Reservation on the Rancho
El Tejon, originally a Mexican land grant. Probably his most
famous exploit was the introduction of a Camel Corps into
the United States Army, for which the animals were im-
ported from the Mediterranean and driven overland from
Texas to Fort Tejon. After his retirement from military service he purchased the Tejon Ranch, as well as several adjacent land grants, bringing his holdings to well over 190,000
acres on which he ran cattle and an enormous number of
sheep. Since 1870 he had divided his time among a residence
in Washington, D. C., assignments such as Minister to Austria-
Hungary, and periodic visits to oversee his California ran-
chos.[22]

The cultivated, worldly man, now in his late sixties, took
a kindly interest in Mary. He was intrigued by the intense
young woman who burned with an insatiable thirst for
knowledge. In long, quiet talks, he told her about the history,
geography, and folklore of the Tejon country. Patiently he
answered the questions that had tormented her during the
months she had observed without recourse to factual information, even making available government reports on
geological and botanical surveys.[23] In addition, he instructed

two of his principal ranch employees, James Rosemeyre and José Jesús López,[24] to help her learn firsthand about the operations of his huge rancho. Mary thrived on the exciting new associations with men whom she admired and respected.

Beale's interest extended to the pragmatic problems of Mary's family. He offered the Hunters occupancy of an old stage hostelry located at Rose Station, seven miles from their land, and arranged for them to run it as a roadside inn. They were only too glad to accept the opportunity. The rambling adobe, with plenty of shade and room, was a welcome change from the cramped cabin. Moreover, they would have a dependable source of income.

Susanna was well pleased. She wrote to friends in Carlinville,

> We shall find it profitable here as there is a great demand for hay, grain and something to eat. I sell all the eggs I can spare at 30 cts per dozen and all the bread I can bake.... I know we cannot make a living [on the homesteads] until water for irrigation is put up but if we can live here until we can secure our land it will be time and money invested that will bring good interest after a while....[25]

The Hunters did manage to hold on to their homesteads. Though Mary's timber claim was abandoned, both Susanna and Jim were eventually to obtain title to their land.[26] For this ownership they worked hard. Susanna attended to accommodations for the steady stream of travelers who stopped at the inn, while thirteen-year-old George helped with the care of their livestock. Jim contracted to cut hay on the Tejon Ranch, clearing sufficient cash to make a down payment on a team of horses,[27] and also kept up his duties at the homesteads and at Rose Station. Meanwhile Mary was immersed in the new experiences which her association with Beale made possible. Except for occasionally helping her mother with the preparation of meals, her time was spent exploring the country and observing the activities of the rancho.

She was out every day, sometimes all day, talking with sheepherders, Indians, and Spanish-speaking *vaqueros*. Rosemeyre and López paved the way for her contacts. She attended roundups, brandings, and dances. She learned about the care of the flocks, the procedures for clipping wool, and the festivities that followed the shearings. And she recorded it all in her notebook, dreaming that someday she would write a book about the ways of sheep and their herders.[28] When she did write *The Flock*, some fifteen years later, she paid tribute to the two men who helped her most to understand her subject.[29]

James Vineyard Rosemeyre was a personable, well-educated man in his fifties, who had come to the Tejon area in 1856, married an Indian, and settled down to sheep-raising. At the time Mary met him, he was manager of the Tejon Ranch store.[30] She admired him greatly and cherished the memento he gave her—a camel bell and cord that once had encircled the neck of one of the animals brought by Beale. Of Rosemeyre she would write, "Jimmy the Ruddy...a handsome figure of a man... who knows the Tejon better than its own master...."[31]

José Jesús López, a descendant of distinguished Spanish landowners in early California, was sheep and cattle foreman at the ranch. Held in high esteem for his proud heritage and personal integrity, he was most admired for the feat of moving 10,000 sheep across the desert, from the Tejon country to Wyoming, in the severe drought of 1879. He was in his mid-thirties when Mary knew him, and she was much impressed by his courtly manners and prepossessing appearance.[32] She listened avidly to his story of the long sheep drive, and in *The Flock* she gave a colorful account of it.[33]

As spring advanced towards summer, the sheep on the Tejon were moved to mountain pasture, but the plight of the cattle was pitiful. It was Mary's first experience with the conditions caused by drought, and she viewed the scene with a mixture of objective interest and an awareness that bordered on empathy. In her notebook she wrote, "The ground is baked hard, the roads are powdery. Buzzards sit on every fence post. A few lean cattle totter in the trails; they lie down and can not get up. The buzzards walk around them and even perch on their backs. But they do not begin to eat until the life is well out of them."[34]

Some ten years later these observations would form the basis for much of the chapter entitled "The Scavengers" in *The Land of Little Rain*. There she elucidated the meaning of what she had experienced in greater depth:

> It is a very squalid tragedy,—that of the dying brutes and the scavenger birds. Death by starvation is slow. The heavy-headed, rack-boned cattle totter in the fruitless trails; they stand for long, patient intervals; they lie down and do not rise. There is fear in their eyes when they are first stricken, but afterward only intolerable weariness. I suppose the dumb creatures know nearly as much of death as do their betters, who have only the more imagination. Their even-breathing submission after the first agony is their tribute to its inevitableness....[35]

Time was to prove the period Mary spent in the Tejon country rich in raw material for her future work. In addition to portions of *The Flock* and *The Land of Little Rain*, two novels were to stem from her experience there—*Isidro*[36] and *The Ford*.[37] Also, out of her encounter with the Walking Woman, "that most wise and insane creature,"[38] would come the short story that "was the means of Mary meeting H. G. Wells."[39] For the present her writing activity was limited to her notebook and a few verses about wild hyacinths which she found on the mesa.

Despite the dryness of the season, there were some spring wildflowers, and Mary delighted in discovering them. One day she was walking along a sandy stretch in a hollow of the hills and saw a scattering of poppies "coming up singly through the tawny, crystal-sanded soil, thin, piercing orange-colored flames." Suddenly all the wonder of her very first mystical experience came over her with a sweeping power she had not known since childhood.

She stood absorbing "the warm pervasive sweetness of ultimate reality, the reality first encountered so long ago.... You walk into it the way one does into those wisps of warm scented air in hollows after the sun goes down; there you stand motionless, acquiescing, I do not know how long. It has nothing to do with time nor circumstance.... It is the only true and absolute."[40]

Such moments gave Mary a sense of security which she very much needed. For although she had the friendship of men like Beale, she was only too aware of her unpopularity with people her own age. The personality traits which had caused problems in Carlinville had become more pronounced. At neighborhood get-togethers she was miserably ill at ease, and when she attended similar events in Bakersfield, she suffered even more.

A center of sociability was the home of Ellen Baker, widow of Colonel Thomas Baker for whom the town was named. Because Mrs. Baker was fond of Susanna Hunter, she insisted that Mary be invited to the weekend parties which her own daughter gave. On these occasions, while the other girls bedded down on the floor and talked far into the night, Mary was given her own bedroom to get her out of the way. Conscious that she was disliked, Mary retaliated by behaving in a critical and superior manner, which worsened the situation.[41]

She was equally unappealing to the young men. Her shabby clothes and scrawny figure obscured the real beauty of her hair and eyes. Moreover, she was convinced that she was hopelessly plain and had no notion of how to make the most of her good features. In an attempt to compensate for her inadequacies, she gave the impression of being overly aggressive. Blunderingly she sought out youths at parties and tried to interest them in conversation, only to have them take the first opportunity to join more attractive company. It could not have helped to know that the other girls referred to her as "boycrazy."[42]

At about this time Mary was startled to receive a letter containing a proposal of marriage from the divinity student with whom she had kept company in Carlinville. It was a boost to her morale, proof that she could "pick up a husband when she needed him,"[43] but she promptly wrote to decline the offer. She could scarcely remember what the young man looked like. A few days later she found her mother weeping. Susanna was greatly distressed by Mary's decision. Tearfully she remonstrated, "Well, I've brought you out here where there is nobody of your sort to marry...besides, I'd know where you were."[44]

Suddenly Mary realized how deeply troubled her mother was about the uncertainty of their situation. It shocked her out of her self-centeredness. For the first time she became aware of how old for his years Jim looked. He missed the girl he had left behind in Carlinville and was urging her to come out for a visit,[45] but he still was not in a position to undertake marriage. During the past year Mary's only contribution to the family welfare had been tutoring George. Now in the fall he would attend high school in Bakersfield. It became clear to her that she could not in good conscience continue to depend upon her mother and Jim for financial support.[46]

In May 1889 Mary applied for a teaching position in the Kern County schools. After an uneasy wait she was given an assignment for September in the Old River Primary School at Mountain View, about ten miles from Bakersfield. The permanency of the post was contingent upon her passing the examination for a teacher's credential.[47]

The dreaming days on the trails of the Tejon were almost over. The stimulating associations had to be broken and the desire to write put in abeyance. Depressed and apprehensive, Mary was ill for several weeks before school started, but she insisted upon reporting for work.[48]

4

A Marriage of Convenience

MARY'S SOJOURN IN THE TEJON COUNTRY left its mark on her personality. Years later she would ascribe the start of her self-styled role as a maverick in society to its influence.[1] This land of curving mountains and glistening sand, "sublime in its immensity of light,"[2] spoke to her mysticism. Its impress widened the gulf that already separated her from her contemporaries. None among them would offer the kind of companionship she had known with Beale, Rosemeyre, and López. Moreover, she had always been more comfortable in communion with the earth and its wild creatures than in her everyday relationships with people.

Fortunately in the fall, despite her misgivings, Mary found lodging with a friendly family who welcomed her warmly. She arranged to stay at the Mountain View Dairy, where the superintendent, Darius Pyle, lived with his wife and three children. The Pyles were well-educated people, both having been teachers, and they were happy to have Mary with them. The children also became very fond of her. Teenage Elmo was admiring, little Elva was captivated by Mary's storytelling, and ten-year-old Dena quickly came to adore her.[3]

In the closely knit family circle there was much to remind Mary of the life she had led before her father died. In the evenings she and the Pyles gathered around a big table, discussing current happenings or reading by the light of the kerosene lamp. She especially enjoyed her rapport with Dena. In the afternoons they took long walks, while Mary taught the child the names of native plants and imparted her enthusiasm for nature. She also introduced Dena to the favorite books of her own childhood and wrote verses for her, some of which were to be included in the collection *Children Sing in the Far West,* published almost forty years later.[4]

Although Mary felt at home in the congenial atmosphere, she remained withdrawn. Dena thought she must be "a very serious-minded person" because "she seldom laughed"; she was never "really jovial or the least 'loosened up.' "[5] She did become interested in the problems of the small farmers of the area, a frequent topic of conversation at the Pyles'. Their desperate need for water was something she had experienced.

Two gigantic land corporations held claim to the distribution of water rights in the San Joaquin Valley. One was the James Haggin combine, whose holdings included the 5,280-acre Mountain View Dairy Ranch as well as twenty-two ranches comparable in size. The other was the partnership of Henry Miller and Charles Lux. The two corporations vied in legal battles for the water that drained from the Kern River. Meanwhile, the settlers who owned small parcels of land adjacent to the land barons' enormous acreage fought for access to the irrigation channels which alone could make the desert land productive.[6]

Henry Miller was a fascinating character who appealed to Mary's imagination. He had arrived in San Francisco from Germany at the age of sixteen with six dollars in his pocket. Through indefatigable effort and a single-minded determination he had acquired more than a million acres of land. Mary admired his sagacity and rugged individualism, as well as the personal interest he demonstrated in his huge estates.

Many years later in her novel *The Ford,* based in part on her observations of the water controversy in the San Joaquin Valley, she patterned the character of the landowner on her impressions of Miller.[7]

Both Miller and Haggin infringed upon what the settlers considered to be their rights. Controlling the flow of water from the Kern River and its tributaries with dams and canals, Miller and Haggin forced the farmers to purchase a supply at their prices. Armed confrontations between settlers and employees of the large landowners were a frequent occurrence. Even young Elmo Pyle became involved on at least one occasion. Sent out by his father to help control a water gate, he encountered a farmer with rifle ready at hand.[8]

Mary was in sympathy with the settlers and their struggle to survive. Still, she respected Miller, though she must have known he was scarcely less responsible for the situation than Haggin. She reacted adversely to the latter in part because he held himself aloof from the land and did not appreciate its intrinsic values. She was also disdainful of Haggin's associate, W. B. Carr, and there is a marked resemblance between him and one of the least appealing characters in *The Ford.*[9]

During the autumn of 1889 Mary saw little of her own family, but she was aware that Jim had become disheartened. Early that fall Effie Vancil had come west for a visit, along with her sister Ollie. The girls were a reminder of the close associations in Carlinville which had meant much to the Hunters. Ollie had been Mary's best friend, and Effie was the girl whom Jim wanted to marry. Mary knew that Effie had discouraged his hopes.[10]

Susanna was also depressed. Homesick for her relatives and old friends, she was situated too far from Bakersfield to participate in the church-related activities that could have assuaged her loneliness. Though Mary was sympathetic, she had problems of her own. As the time of the examination for her teacher's credential approached, she became increasingly uneasy.

In December she took the examination and failed.[11] Not only was this a blow to her ego, but she also lost her job. Hiding her injured feelings behind a brave front, she resolved to try again in May when the next examination was to be given. Meanwhile she eked out a livelihood by tutoring the Pyle children and giving private lessons in the neighborhood.

Then early in 1890 she discovered that her mother and Jim had purchased a forty-acre parcel of land about three miles from Bakersfield, where access to irrigation facilities would make possible a productive farm.[12] Capital for the venture had come from sale of the Carlinville property. Mary had not been included in plans for the project and a bitter family quarrel ensued.

Mary felt that she was entitled to a share of her father's estate. She as well as Jim should have the opportunity for "a start in life." She struck out by describing the partnership arrangement into which Jim was entering with their mother as being "tantamount to his marrying a middle-aged widow."[13] Susanna was shocked but refused to listen to Mary's arguments. To her the situation seemed entirely appropriate.

Mary subsided, but her exclusion from the family interests had become complete. She began to realize that probably the most practical way of building a life of her own was through marriage. Yet she had ample evidence that most young men did not consider her desirable, nor did she find them acceptable. That spring, however, Stafford Wallace Austin, a neighbor of the Pyles, began to show an interest in her.

Austin was a quiet, scholarly man, seven years Mary's senior. Tall and slight in build, with steel-rimmed spectacles and a handlebar mustache, he had a somewhat austere appearance but all the characteristics of a gentleman. Son of a prominent Hawaii family and graduate of the University of California,[14] he was intelligent and cultured in speech and manner. The Pyles spoke of him as being "a very absent-minded but extremely intellectual man."[15] Mary was delighted to find someone with whom she could engage in serious conversation.

At the time their friendship began, Wallace Austin was trying to develop a twenty-acre fruit farm, located about six miles from the Mountain View Dairy.[16] Though untrained for the enterprise, he fancied himself in the role of gentleman farmer because he had grown up on a sugar-cane plantation near Hilo, Hawaii. His father, a descendant of New England Quakers, was an attorney who had emigrated to the Islands in 1850 because of ill health. The elder Austin soon attained a position of political influence and married a daughter of early missionary settlers. Embarking upon the sugar business, he achieved considerable affluence and provided his seven children with a very comfortable life, albeit one governed by strict religious discipline.[17]

Wallace was sent to private schools in Honolulu and then to California for his higher education. In 1885, a year before his graduation, the Austin family lost the bulk of its fortune.[18] For a while Wallace taught school, but he did not enjoy it. Then two of his elder brothers, Franklin and Ephraim, came to California and became interested in buying land for reclamation through irrigation. At the urging of Ephraim, Wallace purchased the acreage near Bakersfield.

Mary's refinement and intellect appealed to Wallace. He saw her as a modest, serious-minded young woman who, with her sturdy pioneer heritage, would make a good wife in the life he envisioned for himself. She in turn was flattered by his attentions. The fact that a man of his caliber found her attractive was a balm to her wounded pride. Moreover, he seemed to appreciate her for her real self.

There was nothing romantic about the courtship that proceeded through the spring and summer of 1890. Wallace came to call regularly and either took Mary for buggy rides or sat with her on the shaded lawn of the Pyle residence. The Pyle family teased Mary about her beau but privately wondered why there was never any demonstration of affection between the two. In the end they concluded that Mary was in love with Wallace "in her own modest way," and that "Mr. Austin was persistent and as ardent as an absent-minded professor could be."[19]

The true nature of Mary's feelings towards Wallace can best be understood through her autobiographical novel, *A Woman of Genius,* and the short story "Frustrate,"[20] also obviously based on her personal experience. There is evidence that not only was she not in love with Wallace, but she did not even know what she should have felt for him. In many ways she was incredibly naive and vulnerable. In "Frustrate" she wrote,

> Sometimes I think if I'd known a little more, just a very little...!
>
> It all began, I suppose, in the kind of people I was brought up among. They'd none of them had the kind of things I wanted, so of course they couldn't tell me anything about the way to get them....They wouldn't have thought that one way of being in love, for instance, was much better or different from another....
>
> I suppose that was what got me to thinking that all the deep and high and shining things that I had a kind of instinct went with being married, belonged to it naturally, and, when you had found a suitable man, came along in their proper place without much thinking....[21]

Mary's upbringing might well have led to the repression of normal sexual impulses. It is probable that she was not even conscious of the need for such satisfaction. The conventions of her time surrounded all female functions with taboos. This attitude, coupled with Mary's failure to recognize the growing demands of her body, may have been one cause of the severity of her menstrual periods.

Usually she had to spend several days in bed and suffered such agonizing cramps that the condition sometimes brought on what Mrs. Pyle termed "spells." Completely distraught and irrational, Mary would run out of the house in her nightgown, fleeing wildly in any direction until she was brought back by a member of the family or one of the dairy workers. When she recovered from such an episode, she was acutely embarrassed and begged the Pyles not to tell Wallace.[22]

In May, Mary again took the examination for a teacher's credential and again failed. Fortunately she did not know all the reasons for her rejection. The superintendent of schools had evaluated her English and language requirements as "well enough" but her mathematics as "deplorable." In addition he had described her as "a most unattractive young woman" whose "personality was anything but appealing.[23] For Mary, it was depressing enough to have all hope of qualifying for a teaching position at an end.

Then, in July, Darius Pyle received word from the Haggin corporation that the Mountain View Ranch was being subdivided and the dairy would be closed. Pyle was out of a job and the family would have to move from their residence.[24] Events were closing in on Mary. She had been rebuffed by the public school system as well as by her family. Now the comfortable living arrangement she had enjoyed was about to be disrupted. Late that summer she accepted Wallace's proposal of marriage.

An insight into what probably happened on the occasion of the engagement may be garnered from a passage in the story "Frustrate": "I'd heard about engaged kisses, but this wasn't anything but just a kiss—like when you have been playing drop the handkerchief. I'd always had a feeling that when you had an engaged kiss something beautiful happened. There were times afterward when it almost seemed about to, and I would want to be kissed again to see if the next time...."[25] She was not too innocent to sense that something was missing and to want it.

Mary went home to her family to prepare for the wedding. By this time the Hunters were living near Bakersfield and planning to build a house on the land they had acquired. Mary continued to give private lessons in the area, while Wallace purchased two additional parcels of land on which he attempted to grow alfalfa and grapes. He also began construction of a home for his bride.[26] It was to be a square, one-story, board-and-batten dwelling, with an irrigated garden for Mary's enjoyment.

Susanna and Jim were pleased to have Mary's future so happily settled. They saw Wallace as an upstanding young man[27] who came from a well-to-do family and had excellent prospects. But Mary became increasingly apprehensive as her wedding day approached. Intimations of what marriage might mean began to break through the aura of excitement that surrounded the preparations. In the novel *A Woman of Genius* she would give a clear indication of how she felt.

> Marriage I began to perceive as an engulfing personal experience. Until now I hadn't been able to think of it except as a means of providing pleasant companionship on the way toward that large and shining world for which I felt myself forever and unassailably fit.... Somewhere out of this prospect of sympathy and understanding... I was aware of an incalculable Force by which the whole province of my being was assailed.... [28]

For an individual who had treasured her independence from early childhood, these misgivings would have been a real cause for concern. How much of her privacy, of her essential self, would she have to surrender to this new intimacy? Moreover, there was the physical side of the impending relationship. When Mary hesitantly approached her mother for information and assurance, she met embarrassed evasion. Susanna thought it immodest to discuss such matters.

In the end practical considerations overcame Mary's doubts. Marriage to Wallace seemed to be the best solution to her problems. He was well-educated and shared some of her interests. She liked him and he seemed to be fond of her. Best of all was the promise of freedom to write. She had been completely frank about the fact that she intended to pursue a literary career, and he had agreed to cooperate.[29]

The wedding took place at the Hunter residence on May 19, 1891, at eight o'clock in the evening.[30] The service was performed by a Methodist minister. Mary wore a plain, brown dress designed for durability. Twelve-year-old Dena Pyle was her only attendant; Jim acted as best man. No one gave the bride away.[31]

Susanna had concentrated on the opportunity for sociability which the occasion afforded. All the friends and acquaintances she had made through her church connections were invited. More than fifty guests attended. Mary circulated among them, proudly displaying her wedding present from Wallace. It was a gold, pearl-handled pen in a velvet case. Some of the guests recalled her saying, "I would rather have this than a pearl necklace, because it means I am to go on with my writing."[32]

The newlyweds took a three-day trip, then settled into the house which Wallace had built. There is little doubt that Mary was immediately disappointed in some of her expectations. Several comments in the story "Frustrate" offer an insight into the bleakness of the marital relationship, even in its early stages.

> And we hadn't any more than got the furniture as we wanted it when I discovered that there hadn't anything happened at all!... There are things nobody ever tells young girls about marriage. Sometimes I think it is because, if they knew how to estimate their experience in the beginning, there is such a lot they wouldn't go on with; and when I was married, nobody even thought of anything but that you had to go on with it....[33]

It is likely that Wallace was also disillusioned. He soon learned that Mary was not exactly the kind of person he had imagined. She hated housework, let dirty dishes pile up for days, and did little to keep their home clean and orderly.[34] She was engrossed in her writing—sorting the voluminous notes she had accumulated, meditating over a possible plot

Wallace and Mary Austin's wedding portrait, 1891

for a story, scribbling single lines of verse to capture a fleeting impression. A whole day might be spent pondering adjectives that would best describe the cry of a mule or precisely differentiate between the sound of ripe figs dropping to the ground and olives shaken down by the wind.

She had a desperate need to discuss her work and to get help with its technical aspects, of which she was completely ignorant. When Wallace came in from a day on the farm, she tried to bring up some of the questions she had been mulling over in her mind. He listened politely but with a preoccupied air. Inevitably the one-sided conversation ended by his saying, "Why talk about it? Why not just enjoy it?"[35]

Absorbed in her inner world, Mary was equally indifferent to the problems Wallace faced. From the start, his inexperience and ineptitude for agriculture had presaged failure for the fruit-farming venture. In addition, he chose to grow grapes in an area where seasoned farmers were having trouble with the crop. By fall it was clear even to Mary that the Austins were in serious financial difficulty.

When Wallace refused the offer of a teaching position in the district school, she was disturbed but refrained from making an issue of it. However, she did insist that he acknowledge the futility of trying to wrest a living from the land and find employment.[36] The couple moved to a small rented house in Bakersfield, where Wallace obtained work supervising construction of an irrigation ditch in the area.[37] Again Mary became absorbed in her writing. Then, in the spring of 1892, she discovered that she was pregnant.

Several years later, in reminiscing about the pregnancy, she said, "I never expected to have a child. When I realized that I was pregnant, I promised myself that I would give birth to the smartest child that was ever born. I doubled my working hours. I hardly ate nor I hardly slept...."[38]

Immersion in work was scarcely a normal reaction to impending motherhood. Once again she may have been withdrawing from a situation which she perceived as threatening. Perhaps she even resented the child, and memories of her own rejection brought an added burden of guilt. Certainly her feelings for Wallace would not have contributed to joyous anticipation of the event.

The neighbors noticed Mary's peculiar behavior and gossiped about it. They thought she was an oddity, arrogant and unwilling to spend time on the duties of a housewife. She was not so much concerned by their criticism as she was with the absence of mental stimulation and the companionship of creative people in her environment.[39] Since it was obvious that Wallace's fortunes had not improved and that another move must be made, she hoped it would be to a place more congenial to her work. When Wallace's brother Franklin suggested that they join him in San Francisco,[40] she was delighted. The elder Austin was working on a land reclamation scheme, and he had a place for Wallace on the project.

Wallace left immediately, while Mary stayed to dismantle the house and pack their belongings. Alone and independent of the daily demands of another person in the house, she concentrated on writing two short stories. Slowly and carefully she felt her way, drawing upon the resources she knew to be hidden in her deep self. Forty years later, in her autobiography, she would recall the luminous quality of the creative effort.

> It came very quietly, this opening movement of an activity that was to mean more to me than anything that was ever to happen to me; quietly as I suppose all growing things begin....
>
> There was that stream of knowingness which ever since adolescence I had felt going on in me, supplying deficiencies, affording criterions of judgment, creating certainties for which no warrant was to be found in my ordinary performance, setting up in me the conviction, which as experience I have named I-Mary, that all I know has always been known by me and used as known. At any rate, it was as I-Mary...that I wrote two slender little sketches....[41]

She had come home to the activity that would eventually be husband, lover, and child to her. In it she found a union of forces that had been the well-spring of her most compelling experiences: a mystical communion with her essential being, the I-Mary who was at one with ultimate reality. For the rest of her life she would strive for those exquisite moments of immersion in the creative act, from which she was to reap the beauty of her finest work as well as great personal torment.

The stories were simple tales based on material Mary had gathered in the Tejon country but given a strong imaginative twist. The one entitled "The Mother of Felipe"[42] was somber in mood, a somewhat macabre story about the death of a Mexican youth and his mother's refusal to abandon him to a desert grave. Set in one of the side canyons opening out of the Tejon Pass, it captured the harsh beauty of the land in the style that was to characterize her later nature writing. "A country to be avoided by the solitary traveler, with its hard, inhospitable soil, and its vast monotony of contour and color. A country sublime in its immensity of light, and soft unvarying tints,—fawn, and olive, and pearl, with glistening stretches of white sand, and brown hollows between the hills, out of which the gray and purple shadows creep at night. A country laid visibly under the ban of eternal silence."

The second story, "The Conversion of Ah Lew Sing,"[43] set in Bakersfield, was a humorous, satirical tale about a Chinese truck gardener. In it Mary reflected a disdain for missionary endeavor and an understanding of the foibles of humanity. In both stories the vivid characterizations and rhythmic prose gave promise of the artistry she was to develop.

No doubt she was spurred to produce these first stories by the fact that she would soon be in San Francisco, where since the 1850s a number of illustrious magazines had been published. Among these, *The Overland Monthly* had enjoyed an enviable reputation when edited by Bret Harte, Charles Warren Stoddard, and Ina Coolbrith. Though Stoddard and Harte had long since been lured to greener pastures, the poet Ina Coolbrith was still in the area, working as librarian of the Oakland Free Library. Although she had been unable to devote herself exclusively to a literary career, she had achieved considerable fame for her poetry. Now in her early fifties, she was known for her generosity in helping aspiring young writers. Mary resolved to seek her out.

Late that spring Mary joined her husband in San Francisco and immediately journeyed across the bay to Oakland. Locating the public library, she approached the tall, stately Miss Coolbrith with some trepidation but was soon relaxed by the older woman's gracious manner. In dealing with Mary's questions, she was kind and matter-of-fact, telling her how to prepare her manuscripts for submission and suggesting that she take them to *The Overland Monthly*.

Though the magazine had fallen from the eminence of its early years, it was still a publication of substantial repute. Mary was elated when both of her stories were accepted.

Now that she knew the mechanics of getting her work into print, she planned in the future to set her sights higher. Basking in the glow of success, she scarcely noticed the passing of time or wondered why Wallace did nothing to establish a permanent residence.

Then, two months after her arrival in the city, Wallace told her that they must move on. Frank wanted him to manage an irrigation project in the Owens Valley, east of the Sierra Nevada. There were prospects of high financial gain in the venture once the land was opened up for settlement. Of the place to which they were going Mary knew nothing other than its location on the map and its name: Lone Pine. There was no reason why she could not write there, however, so she went happily, with no inkling of what awaited her.[44]

5

The Owens Valley

COMMUNION WITH THE LAND

MARY WAS TWENTY-FOUR when she came to live in the Owens Valley—that long, narrow trough of semi-desert land cradled between the towering Sierra Nevada to the west and the massive Inyo Mountains to the east. The name *Inyo,* given by the Shoshone Indians, meant "the dwelling place of a great spirit." To that spirit Mary would surrender. Even at first sight, the splendor of soaring mountains, limitless space, and radiant light struck upon her senses like a resounding chord.

The trip to the Owens Valley took three days by train. The first leg of the journey led through a high pass across the great granite backbone of the Sierra, then plunged abruptly to the desert floor at Reno, Nevada. The next morning the Austins boarded a branch line of the railroad, traveling to Mound House station, where they transferred to the narrow-gauge railway which took them south. That night was spent in the small settlement of Sodaville, still in Nevada. The third day the train took them back into California, gyrating over a zigzag roadbed of tight curves through the White Mountains to emerge in the Owens Valley.

There Mary again saw the jagged profile of the Sierra Nevada, glacier-studded peaks etched against the sunset sky, and to the east the massed silhouette of the Inyos, bare and buff-colored, gleaming with a milky iridescence above the blue-shadowed ground. The train now followed the path of the Owens River, stopping at a series of station houses, their dingy paint sun-baked and peeling. The fourth stop was Lone Pine.

A light wagon transported the Austins the short distance to town. Riding towards the looming, ghost-gray bulk of the Sierra, Mary felt its impact like a powerful presence. The bold escarpment, deeply cleft by canyons, seemed to reach out with giant arms, enticing her to enter its secret recesses. As soon as she was able, she intended to follow that beckoning, into "the streets of the mountains."[1] For the present, her pregnancy would limit her activity to a leisurely exploration of the town.

In the somnolence of the hot summer mornings she sat on the porch of the hotel, absorbing the strange beauty of her surroundings.[2] Lone Pine was nestled at the base of gigantic peaks which rose precipitously from the floor of the valley to well over 14,000 feet. Highest of these peaks was Mount Whitney, its crest flanked by a cortège of needle-like points that pressed into hollows of infinite space. In the forefront towered the awesome face of Opapago, also known as Lone Pine Peak. To Mary it seemed to lower over the town, threatening it with imminent disaster from which the only protection was an intervening strip of contorted, volcanic mounds called the Alabama Hills.[3]

Beneath this overwhelming grandeur huddled the row of ramshackle, frame buildings that made up the main part of town. Huge, full-leafed cottonwoods shaded the unpaved street. Along its sides ran a raised, wooden sidewalk on which fronted a clutch of stores, a couple of saloons, and the two-story hotel. Straggling into the desert were the dusty lanes where stood the dwellings of the townspeople, mostly Mexicans lured to the land by the mining bonanza that had marked the latter days of the Comstock era. In their midst, strolling in the long afternoons, Mary savored the exotic ambience of the place.

The houses were part of the earth, built of mud bricks cemented by the rays of the sun. Strings of reddening chili peppers made bright splashes of color on the white adobe walls. Each dwelling had its garden plot planted in corn and beans, a patch of aromatic herbs, and a trellised patio thickly sheltered by grapevines. Towards evening the thrum of guitars and the sound of singing echoed from recess to recess of the vine tangles, and the pungent odor of sauces redolent of onions and chili filled the air. From the lofty tree arches overhead came a cantata of birdsong, and at Mary's feet the scattering quail greeted her with their gentle cry of "cuidado."

Often she stopped to watch the doe-eyed, impish children, of which every family had a brood of nine or ten, and to chat with their placidly proud mothers, always with a baby clasped to the full breast. She felt a great rapport with these soft-spoken people, so carefree and filled with the joy of living. Even the cemetery, where the pine headboards blossomed with paper roses and prints of Our Lady of Sorrows, had the reassuring aspect of a garden from which the dead would rise whole. Mary luxuriated in the feeling of earthiness, of kindliness, in the even-breathing days. Later she would capture her impressions in the essay "The Little Town of the Grape Vines" in *The Land of Little Rain*. Meanwhile, she waited lazily for the advent of the new life stirring within her.

About the business that occupied Wallace from dawn to dusk she knew nothing and asked no questions. It was not considered necessary for a young wife to be informed about her husband's work. Then one afternoon, when she had taken her daily walk earlier than usual, she returned to find her baggage stacked on the sidewalk. When she demanded to know why, she was told that their bill for board and lodging was unpaid: the Austins had been evicted.[4]

Dumbfounded, Mary shrank back into herself, determined only that she would not show the humiliation she felt. Mustering what dignity she could, she sat down on a trunk to wait for Wallace. She thought the landlady had taken an unfair advantage by bringing matters to a head in his absence. Hours went by while she waited, looking anxiously up and down the road and struggling not to break down.

Finally, a woman she knew slightly happened to walk past. Taking in the situation at a glance, she suggested that Mary might find lodging at a boardinghouse on the edge of town. It was mostly patronized by miners recovering from lead poisoning, but it was a clean place and the food was wholesome. The name of the woman who ran it was Mrs. Dodge. Mary thanked her and started down the road.

It proved to be a long walk to the farmhouse. There she was greeted by a thickset, worn-looking woman who spoke with a heavy German accent. Gruff but kindhearted, Mrs. Dodge invited Mary to join her in a cup of coffee and piece of cake. Then she let loose a torrential tale of woe. Her feet hurt, her cook had left, and too many of her boarders were delinquent in their rent. When she paused for breath, Mary hesitantly told her who she was and that she needed a place to stay.

Mrs. Dodge exploded in another barrage of broken English. She wouldn't take any more boarders. Her situation was bad enough. This minute she should be making pies, but with her aching feet—"besides, everybody was saying the ditch people weren't paying their bills."[5] Mary had difficulty hiding her mortification. She knew that somehow gossip about her predicament had preceded her, but she managed to say quite cheerfully, "Oh, well, I'll make the pies."[6]

Fatigue won out over Mrs. Dodge's wariness and she consented. Then, pleased with the pastry Mary produced, she agreed to let her stay and help with the cooking in exchange for her room and board. Mary put on a brave front while she waited for Wallace to appear.

It was evening before he came, someone having told him where to find her. He stood silently, eyes averted. Realizing that he must be famished, she suppressed her questions and set out some supper for him. At this turn of events, Mrs.

Dodge could not contain her indignation. Angrily, she asserted that Mrs. Austin was in no condition to earn her husband's board as well as her own. With imperturbable poise, Mary prevailed over the woman's protests. She would give full value for what they received.[7]

Alone with Wallace, Mary expected him to apologize, to comfort her, at the very least to explain. He said nothing. In the end, she was able to ascertain that the irrigation project had failed and he was out of work. When she discovered he had known they were to be evicted that morning, she asked why he had not told her. With a look of surprise, he answered simply, "How would that have helped?"[8]

For three months, while Mary worked at the Dodge boardinghouse, Wallace took odd jobs that paid next to nothing and looked for an opportunity that would "lead to something." The day that she learned he had rejected a position as principal of the Lone Pine School she was appalled. He blandly turned aside her accusing questions with the reply that he hated teaching. Still she tried to understand, to find reasons for his behavior, hoping that she might break down the barrier that seemed to shut her out of his life.

Mary knew that in his own way he was devoted to her. Since their betrothal he had not looked at another woman, and there was evidence that he suffered when his actions made her unhappy. Yet he rebuffed all her attempts to discuss their financial problems or his plans for the future. She did not give up hope. Maybe after the baby came, he would feel the necessity for giving his family security.[9]

The summer spent at the Dodge boardinghouse was not wholly unpleasant or unproductive for Mary. In the evenings, when the miners gathered on the porch to trade tall tales, she picked up much rich story material. It was there that she first heard about fantastic silver strikes, hold-ups, lost mines, and murder. She was also exposed to a new vocabulary in which the quaint idiom of the mining camp, interlarded with a unique kind of blasphemy, sounded almost like poetry. One of the boarders whom Mary never forgot was a tall, handsome young woman named Lupe. The common-law wife of a minister turned professional gambler, she had a flamboyance and insolence that was irresistible.

Nights when her paramour was in a neighboring town dealing at the faro table, Lupe entertained Mary with Spanish songs and impromptu dances. Her favorite sport was to beat down bats from the eaves of the barn, imprison them in a shoe box, then jam tiny, lighted cigarettes into their jaws and let them fly away twinkling and smoking. To Lupe's delight, Mary participated in the game.[10] Winning the girl's friendship, Mary garnered many an additional incident which she would later weave into the collection of stories called *Lost Borders*.[11]

As August slipped into September, Mary found it harder to move about her daily tasks. She was increasingly awkward and tired more quickly; soon she would be in the ninth month of her pregnancy. She decided it would be best to go to her mother's house in Bakersfield to have her baby.[12]

The first lap of the trip was by stagecoach, skirting the Sierra southward to Mojave, a distance of 130 miles across barren desert. Traveling over wheel ruts worn deep in the sand, the rickety coach rocked and swayed for a stretch of twenty-six hours, stopping only to change horses at relay stations along the way. Crowded inside the stuffy interior was the usual motley assortment of passengers—a tubercular, a couple of liquor salesmen, a mining expert, and a girl from one of the local bawdyhouses. Fortunately, in deference to her condition, Mary was given the seat beside the driver. The perch could be precarious, and the cold before dawn was numbing, but at least Mary could breathe. At Mojave she boarded the train to Bakersfield.[13]

Susanna welcomed her with an uncharacteristic display of affection, and Mary was glad to relax in the atmosphere of family solidarity. It was good to feel cared for and secure. On October 30, 1892, her child was born, a daughter.

It was an excruciatingly difficult delivery. Mary labored for forty-eight hours. Halfway through the ordeal the doctor was called away to amputate the leg of a man injured in an accident. That the baby was born alive was little short of a miracle.

For more than a week Mary was unable to rise from her bed. Susanna, who had borne her first baby in an army camp, perceived her daughter's behavior as malingering, and on the ninth day she insisted that Mary must get up. The result was a relapse, followed by months in which Mary was wretchedly ill. Driven by pride, she managed to stay up for a few hours at a time and at least take care of her baby.[14] She named the infant Ruth, only because it was a name no one in the family had espoused or opposed.[15]

Then, while Mary was still struggling to regain her health, she was served with a legal notice that plunged her into despair. She discovered that Wallace had incurred a considerable array of debts, both before and after their marriage. Everything that they had supposedly owned had been obtained on credit. The total indebtedness was staggering, especially in view of their utter lack of resources. Moreover, the creditors were holding Mary responsible along with her husband.

To people like the Hunters, debt was a disgrace. Jim and Susanna were so outraged by Wallace's behavior that they put aside their prejudice against divorce and suggested that she apply for one. They were willing for her to remain at home, but Mary realized what this arrangement would mean: not only condescension on their part and abject dependence on hers, but also the absence of any understanding of her goals as a writer.[16]

While she was still sick in bed, the first of her accepted stories, "The Mother of Felipe," was published in the November issue of *The Overland Monthly*. Though Susanna consented to read it aloud to Mary, she offered no comment. Pressed for an opinion, she said, "I think you could have made more of it."[17] Nothing had changed between mother and daughter.

Meanwhile, Wallace was temporarily out of reach. He had gone to a remote mining camp on a venture about which Mary knew nothing. Finally, he wrote and told her to do whatever she thought best about the state of their affairs. She arranged to sell what remained of their property near Mountain View and then to pay off the rest of their debts in installments. Despite Wallace's bizarre conduct, she held fast to the belief that they would be able to work out their problems. At Christmas she secretly sent him the money she had received for her story. It was a gesture of faith in their joint future.

Soon after the first of the year, she received good news. Wallace had accepted a teaching position at the little settlement of George's Creek, a few miles north of Lone Pine. At least there was the assurance of food and shelter. "She would go to her husband and they would talk it out and come to an understanding and began all over again. There was nothing two intelligent people couldn't do together if they set about it."[18] When the winter rains abated, she packed her baby in a market basket and took the long trip by train and stage that brought her back to the Owens Valley.

The reunion proved cruelly disappointing for Mary. The arrangements she had made for handling their debts did not meet with Wallace's approval. He had expected her to file for bankruptcy. From his point of view, the commitment to make payments was a stupid solution that would cause unnecessary hardship. At last Mary realized the enormous difference in their backgrounds. He had never experienced the need to budget a small income and felt it to be beneath his dignity. They could not agree upon common goals or a way of making a life together, yet they felt they must go on with it.[19]

In the little house at George's Creek, Mary scrimped and saved, determined that they would meet their obligations. Much of that first year both she and Ruth were ill, and there was no money for a doctor. Sometimes help came from a kindly neighbor who had a large brood of children and was knowledgeable about the homely remedies upon which pioneer women relied. Then, one day in the winter of 1893, Doctor Woodin came into Mary's life.

The huge, bewhiskered man in his rattling old buggy was a familiar sight on the desert roads. Having heard of "the Austin woman with the sick child," he made an excuse for stopping by. From the first encounter, they related to each other like two lost souls. The bluff physician sensed a loneliness in Mary that matched his own.

Woodin had been forced by tuberculosis to leave a lucrative practice in New York. He had recovered his health but was prone to periodic drinking bouts. A good doctor, with patients scattered over a wide area, he had satisfaction in knowing he was needed. Still, he missed the cultural stimulus of the city. With Mary he found intellectual companionship. He came often to bring a book or magazine, chat a while, and give her some advice about how to care for herself and Ruth. His friendship made Mary's dismal existence more bearable.[20]

When spring came, spreading a shimmering web of misty green over the valley, Mary began to take short walks, carrying Ruth in a knapsack on her back. A favorite destination was the Indian campoody up George's Creek. There a row of wattled huts like wasps' nests sat in the chaparral, dwellings of the once proud Paiute Indians. Laughing children played along the creek borders, and old women sat on the sunny side of the wickiups, their high, cracked voices raised in gossip and reminiscence of the old times. The one called Seyavi, beautiful with the wisdom of her sixty years, took a fancy to Ruth. While she brooded over the frail baby, she sometimes let down her restraint and shared what she termed the "fool talk" of her people. In the slow-moving hours Mary listened avidly to tales rich with legend and lore and gleaned material which she later used in *The Land of Little Rain* and the short-story collection *The Basket Woman*.[21]

Heaped at the opening of Seyavi's hut were the baskets she had woven. Fashioned of willow branches and cedar bark, they were perfect in design and workmanship, seeming to reflect the soul of both the wood and the weaver. Mary touched them with awe and asked if she might learn the art.

Seyavi's smile was inscrutable. Let Mary first go with the women to cut willow, then she would know.[22]

So, with the baby on her back, Mary accompanied the young *mahalas*, absorbing the deeper meanings that went with the motions of their hands. She found healing in the simple activities, gathering seeds or wild hyacinth roots on the mesa, weaving snares out of human hair, catching trout from under stream banks with her bare hands. Best of all was the feeling of kinship with these quiet women who did not give their friendship lightly. The next time that Mary was too ill to leave the house, one of the *mahalas* came to care for her and nursed Ruth along with her own lusty, brown baby.[23]

While Mary was developing strong linkages with her new environment, Wallace knew little about the interests that occupied her time. However, she got to know his boon companion, Alfred de la Cour Carroll, quite well. The charming, indolent Irishman was a frequent guest in their home. A son of landed gentry, he had a small income from his family estate and a large appetite for idleness and adventure.[24] His beguiling manner and talent for conjuring illusive moneymaking schemes captivated Wallace. Among his more frivolous suggestions was that Wallace file a homestead claim on the mesa between the Alabama Hills and the awesome bulk of Lone Pine Peak. There in a one-room shack, on the fringe of the ancient, fire-stained rocks, the Austins spent the summer of 1894.[25]

Despite the hardships and merciless heat, Mary could not but respond to the compelling beauty of the place. The jumbled, deeply serrated rocks, worn by centuries of wind and storm, were "sculptured into strange shapes of weirdness, between which the filmy flame of cactus flowers ran red and orange and apricot, with little patches of a more fiery green and blue pools of lupine wetted by artesian springs." Across the valley lay a cloud-mottled country, "all fawn and red and black with faint tinges of citron." Behind the cabin "in towering blocks of gray and black and white gathered the peaks of Whitney and Opapago."[26] Nearby Mary found an Indian burying ground and an old signal smoke station of the Paiutes. She came there often to commune with "the personalities and powers" she felt "moving in the unshadowed space between the mighty ranges."[27]

One day that summer Mary was brought forcibly aware of the grimmer aspects of the beauty around her. A cloudburst had come roaring out of the mountains, and in the luminous aftermath of the storm she went outdoors with Ruth in her arms. There she saw a large trout thrashing around in one of the pools left in the wake of the rain. Quickly she laid the drowsy baby under a sheltering sagebush and picked up a hoe. She intended to flip out the fish, then catch it in her hands.

Suddenly there was a great rush of wings overhead, and an eagle swooped out of the sky. In the instant that it snatched the trout, Mary struck the bird with the hoe. It dropped its prey but swooped again, this time for the sleeping child. Frantically, Mary beat off the huge, hovering creature. A claw caught her arm, leaving a long gash. Then the eagle soared away, screaming. That night over a succulent supper of trout, Mary refrained from telling Wallace about the incident.[28] It was but one of many worrisome things that she kept to herself, for she had long since discovered he was least helpful about matters which concerned her the most.

Her worst anxiety was about Ruth. Despite a dramatic improvement in her health, thanks to the *mahala's* milk and Doctor Woodin's remedies, she was not normal. Now approaching her third year, Ruth was a beautiful child, round and pink, with fair curly hair and deep blue eyes. But there were days when she cried almost continuously without apparent cause, and the inarticulate sounds she made were not the soft gurgles of babyhood nor the beginnings of speech. They were strange and frightening to Mary, as were the constant restless, uncertain movements of the small body. When she consulted Doctor Woodin, he was comforting but noncommittal. Wallace simply brushed her misgivings aside. Why look for trouble? Why couldn't she just relax and enjoy life, especially now that their fortunes were about to improve?[29]

He had been elected superintendent of the Inyo County schools, with a teaching post in Lone Pine.[30] It meant more money and better living conditions. In the fall the Austins moved into town, renting a house on the main street. It had adequate space inside and a place in back for Mary to have a garden. She renewed her acquaintance with the convivial Mexican women with whom she had always felt at ease, finding occasional relief from worry in the unhurried atmosphere of their homes. From the buxom *señoras* she collected bits of folklore along with cooking recipes, learning about the special flavor that only brooding attention can bring to food.[31]

Mary also appreciated the camaraderie of the men who frequented the saloon next to the Austins' house. Old-timers and derelicts of defunct dreams, they never gave up hope of finding that fabulous vein of silver or pocket of ore. It was from them that Mary picked up the thread of the story she later told in "The Pocket Hunter," one of the essays in *The Land of Little Rain.*

With the semi-annual migrations of sheep, in autumn and spring, another kind of companionship came into Mary's life. As the flocks were driven from and to the upper Sierra pastures, the shepherds camped en route. Often Mary encountered men she had known in the Tejon country and delighted in hearing news of the long trail. With gusto she traded greens from her garden for fresh lumps of mutton meat and even occasionally shared a meal of mutton-cabbage soup at one of the camps.[32]

Such hobnobbing with miners, Mexicans, and herders was sharply criticized by the self-styled respectable women of Lone Pine. To mollify them, Mary took care not to shirk any of the precepts of neighborliness, including nursing the sick and washing the dead. Her single article of finery, a pink plush cape probably given her by Wallace during their stay in

San Francisco, went to cover the pine box in which a neighbor's child was buried.[33]

While Mary struggled to make a life for herself in the Owens Valley, she had little contact with her mother and brother. Most of her activities were not of interest to them, and she was not inclined to write about her problems. Still, there were times when she longed to share her anxiety about Ruth with her mother, to ask for advice and perhaps receive reassurance. Susanna wrote repeatedly that she wanted to see more of her grandchild. There had been a couple of brief visits to Bakersfield, during which the baby's beauty had brought high praise from Mrs. Hunter. She had even excused her tardiness in talking by the fact that she had not been with other children.[34] With each passing day, however, Ruth's behavior became more trying. She seemed unable to coordinate her movements. Toilet-training had been impossible, and she was subject to sudden and inexplicable temper tantrums. In the end, Doctor Woodin confirmed Mary's fears. Her child was mentally retarded.[35]

Despite the kind doctor's assurances that Mary was not to blame for her daughter's condition, she was tormented by doubts. Maybe the baby had not had proper care or food. Perhaps the trouble had started during the pregnancy, when Mary had not eaten or slept enough. She even thought that by working too hard she had taken away from her child's brain.[36]

Wallace seemed impervious to the problem of Ruth's behavior, resisting all Mary's anguished attempts to discuss her feelings. He simply took refuge in the maddening silences which she had learned to dread. Torn between the instinct to avoid her family's pity and a desperate need for help, Mary finally decided to let her mother know about Ruth, but she could not bring herself to do it face to face.

When she heard that some friends were going to Bakersfield, she asked them to take Ruth to her grandmother. She did not know what to expect, but she dared to hope that Susanna would understand and sympathize. At last they might talk as one woman to another, weep together and give one another comfort.[37]

Within the week a letter came from Jim. He was indignant that their mother should be subjected to such an ordeal. Mary must take the child away at once. Heartbroken, Mary made Wallace go to her family. He brought back no message from her mother. In fact, they had not even mentioned Ruth's condition. Later a letter came from Susanna. She wrote, "I don't know what you've done, daughter, to have such a judgment upon you."[38]

6

Writer and Mystic Merge

ON THE SURFACE the story of Mary Austin's life in the Owens Valley is one of hardship and domestic woe, which she later described as "long dull months of living interspersed between the few fruitful occasions when I actually came into contact with the Land."[1] Beneath the stifling frustration, however, the seed of her creativity stored energy from the elements around her. Someday it would burst forth in two powerful channels of expression: a passionate, mystical identification with the land and an outrage against the misuse of women's gifts.

Her marriage had failed in every particular, and the bitterness she felt was to color a large segment of her writings. Women were denied the right to make a life for themselves or to share in their husbands' affairs. They were relegated to roles in which their potential was wasted. The stories in *Lost Borders* enunciate this theme with stinging clarity, especially those in which she blends her personal experience with that of women she knew in the desert country. Her novels also are scathing indictments of the conventions that sealed women into airtight compartments of domesticity, withering their capacity for achievement. Even her nature writings are occasionally tinged with a stroke of her feministic feeling—"I knew a mountain once...which could both glow and pale, pale after the burning, like a lovely neglected woman who burned to no purpose, a dark mountain, whose bareness was like a pain."[2]

She knew that kind of pain. In the fall of 1895 it reached a critical level. The anguish of being saddled with an empty marriage and a retarded child was compounded by the fact that she had neither time nor strength to write.[3] For three years she had accepted events as they occurred, without the will to change her lot. Now a new strength welled up from deep inside her. With a bursting sense of freedom, she was again aware of that invulnerable self, the I-Mary, who could accomplish what was impossible to Mary-by-herself.

If she was ever to extricate herself from conditions which she found intolerable, she must do it on her own. There were plans to be made and things to be done. Money had to be provided for Ruth's care and future protection. For herself, she must have "room enough and time enough"[4] for her creative potential to grow and mature. Moreover, she had the need to get away from Wallace for a while, to sort out her feelings and come to terms with her situation. It was as if she had been on a long, turbulent journey and yearned to come home to herself.

In October she took a teaching job at the Inyo Academy in Bishop,[5] located some sixty miles north of Lone Pine. It was the largest town in the valley, surrounded by fertile farmland and framed on the west by the steel-gray grandeur of the Sierra. The bustling main street, a wide, unpaved thoroughfare, was lined with a variety of stores, a bank, and several hotels. In the least pretentious of these Mary found lodging for herself and Ruth.

They lived in a small room over the cellar of the Drake Hotel. Each morning Mary went to her classes at the academy, where she taught art and English. At noon she conducted a session in calisthenics.[6] Ruth had to be left unat-

Mary Austin around 1895, as she made
the initial move to start a life of her own

tended all day. When Mary returned, she often found the room a shambles and the child filthy from her own excreta. Inevitably, word got around that the new schoolteacher was neglecting her daughter.

Hearing Ruth's piercing wails, neighbors went in and saw the soiled tablecloth and broken dishes, the meager meal of crackers left out for lunch, and the little girl's disgraceful condition. Some of the women, motivated by either indignation or kindness, cleaned up the mess, fed Ruth, and even brought food for Mary. She did not thank them for their trouble. Appalled that they should know about the squalor in which she was forced to live, she scarcely spoke to them. Her aloofness and apparent indifference to her child incurred a fresh volley of criticism and animosity.[7]

There probably were times in those first dismal months when despair almost drove Mary back to Wallace. She craved an outlet for her pent-up emotions, someone with whom she could let down her defenses. Occasionally in the evenings, when Ruth was asleep, she tried to find solace in a return to her writing, but sheer exhaustion blocked her brain. At last understanding came from an unexpected source.

She was invited to spend a weekend with the Wattersons, prominent sheep ranchers in the valley. Two members of the family were her pupils, and they felt sorry for the young woman who looked so thin and weary. Mary was apprehensive about taking Ruth, but the visit proved a delightful experience.

Mrs. Watterson was a generous, uninhibited person who instantly recognized the sensitivity and humiliation hidden behind Mary's shell of reserve. Without a trace of condescension she accepted Ruth's oddities, gently encouraging the distraught mother to relieve her anguish through the therapy of talk. Mary's heart filled with love for the compassionate woman, and she thought Mr. Watterson was the kindliest man she had ever met. Of him she later wrote in *The Flock*, "as I sat by his fire, touching his tempered spirit as one half draws and drops a sword in its scabbard for pleasure of its fineness...I understood why the French herders hereabout give him the name of the Best Shepherd."[8]

After that first visit Mary went often to the Wattersons' home. There she could relax and really be herself. It was a joy to sit beside the huge open fireplace, loosing the long hairpins that held the weight of her hair and letting it hang down her back. Not the least of the pleasures she savored was the food, so abundant and delicious. Completely without self-consciousness, she would exclaim, "I have been so hungry!"[9] More than one kind of hunger was satisfied in that house.

Mary spent the Christmas holidays with Wallace,[10] and early in the new year his mother and sister came to the Owens Valley for a visit. He brought them to Bishop to meet

Mary. She seized the opportunity to raise questions about Ruth that had long troubled her. Was she herself to blame for the child's disability, or could there be some other reason? If the problem was hereditary, she must not risk another pregnancy. Both women were matter-of-fact but decidedly uncommunicative in their response. She learned nothing from them, even though they were aware of her distress.[11] The next contact with Wallace's family was not to come for several years, and it would be much more disturbing.[12]

Meanwhile, Mary gradually came to realize that it was impossible to keep Ruth with her and continue to teach. Impatient from exhaustion, she harried the child, and they made each other nervous. Moreover, it was cruel to leave her unattended all day. An ideal solution presented itself when Mary found that she could board her daughter with the Fragers, a childless couple who lived on a large farm nearby.

Ruth thrived on the wholesome food and freedom to play outdoors. The ungovernable spells, when she screamed and fought like a little animal, had no power to hurt the Fragers. They treated her with kindness and affection but were not unnerved by her behavior. At last Mary had the peace and privacy to go on with her writing. From it she hoped someday to reap the money for medical attention that would cure her daughter's condition.[13]

Wallace did not approve. He urged her not to make any teaching commitments beyond the current semester and told her that Ruth should not be living with strangers. Besides, the house was a dreary place without her. Mary also knew what it was to be lonely. Except for the Wattersons, she had no friends. She even reestablished her membership in the Methodist Church,[14] searching for some sense of belonging, but she found no comfort there. Most of the townspeople thought her arrogant and peculiar, preferring to talk about her rather than with her.[15] Then she met a young woman with whom she immediately felt at ease.

Miss Williams[16] was a teacher at the Indian School, located near a large campoody a few miles from Bishop. She too was trying to write, and the two women with similar interests soon became good companions. Eagerly Mary took advantage of her friend's connection with the school to renew her acquaintance with the Indians, enjoying her excursions to their camp. However, she was greatly incensed to learn about the abuses they suffered. It was Miss Williams who told her of the practice called *mahala*-chasing. Many of the Indian girls worked in the town as household help, and it was not uncommon for them to be attacked on their way home. One of them had been kicked to death for her resistance, and two others had committed suicide after being raped by a gang of carousing youths. It was incidents such as these that kindled Mary's fierce advocacy of Indian rights, which later developed into a lifelong crusade.[17]

For the present, she felt irresistibly drawn to the Indian way of life and took particular pleasure in being given the privilege of witnessing their religious ceremonies. Engrossed in her own affairs, Mary refused to return to Lone Pine when the school term ended. Wallace was deeply disturbed by her decision. Insisting that the family must spend the summer together, he rented a house in Bishop and took Ruth away from the Fragers. To placate Mary, he promised that they would go on a camping trip into the Sierra.[18] On the ninth of July a telegram from Jim Hunter put an end to their plans.

Susanna Hunter was seriously ill in a Los Angeles hospital. Emergency surgery had been scheduled. Instantly Mary knew that she must go to her. All the yearning she had felt for her mother as a child, and which she thought had shriveled under the harsh wind of rejection, welled up inside her. It was too late to catch the tri-weekly stage for Mojave, but Wallace helped her make arrangements to take the morning train by way of Reno.

To Mary, the interminable journey that lay ahead, separating her from her mother's side, must have seemed like a nightmare. Overwrought, she sat on the steps of the porch to rest while Wallace put Ruth to bed. Dusk had

quenched the desert heat, and the soft, scented air was soothing. Mary dozed, then woke with a start.

Her mother stood before her, dressed in white and with
a rose in her hair. Young and smiling, she seemed to be
saying all was well with her. There was no need for Mary to
come. Without question, Mary accepted the vision and was
reassured. She told Wallace, then went to bed and slept
soundly. At dawn she awakened crying. Hours before the
second wire came from Jim, she knew. Her mother was dead.

Susanna's last words had been, "Take care of Mary."[19]
Sobbing hysterically, the bereaved daughter cried out for a
loss that was now permanent. As long as her mother had
lived there had been the chance of reconciliation and understanding. The awareness that something might happen to
her had never entered Mary's thoughts. Wallace could do
nothing to control or console her. He simply asked a sympathetic neighbor to sit with his wife and left the house.[20]

A passage in Mary's autobiography reflects the depth
and lasting quality of the grief she felt. "There is an element
of incalculable ravening in the loss of your mother; deep
under the shock of broken habit and the ache of present
grief, there is the psychic wound, the severed root of being;
such loss as makes itself felt as the companion of immortality.
For how should the branch suffer, torn from the dead tree?
It is only when the tree is green that the cut bough bleeds."[21]

Gradually Mary regained her composure, and through
her sorrow slowly broke a sense of spiritual release. For the
first time, she acknowledged the extent to which she had
been dominated by her mother's beliefs and opinions. Despite gestures towards independence, all her actions had
been tempered by a reluctance to cause her mother distress
and a half-buried hope that she might win her approval.
Now that Susanna was gone, Mary was free to find her true
horizon of reality,[22] the "earth horizon" expressed in the title
of her autobiography.

Within her was a tremendous urge toward some depth
or height which lay just beyond the level of her consciousness. Ever since adolescence there had been that stream of

knowingness, a perception of untold and tantalizing possibilities, but she was unable to take hold of it, make use of it to find a rewarding way of life. The luminous experiences of her early years had been moments of at-oneness with pure Being without thought of practical gain. Now she needed help with the problems that kept her from a full realization of her creative potential. The years of heartbreak and disillusionment had hardened her. Henceforth she intended to take a pragmatic approach to all religious experience. She was well aware that the emotional type of petition taught in the Methodist tradition was ineffective, but she was determined to discover if, and how, prayer can be answered.[23]

It was about this time that the *mahala* who had nursed Ruth as a baby and remained Mary's friend collapsed with a searing pain in her chest. Doctor Woodin diagnosed the condition as a lung abscess, predicting that she would die within a few days. The *mahala* begged Mary to bring the medicine man from Fish Lake, several miles across the valley, as she was sure he could cure her. Though Mary could not afford it, she agreed to pay for him if the Indians would fetch him and take him home.

He came at nightfall, when the *mahala* could no longer talk. He went over her body with a gentle tapping until he located the position of the abscess. Then he ordered that she be warmly wrapped, with a fire at her feet, and began his treatment. It consisted of a monotonous chanting accompanied by a rhythmic dance for which he kept time on a gourd rattle. After about an hour the woman appeared to sleep, and the medicine man himself dropped into a short, trance-like slumber. He emerged to announce that he had met "the Friend" and was sure that the treatment would result in a cure. The chanting and dancing were resumed and went on for another hour or two. Finally the medicine man stretched out beside the *mahala* and slept.

Mary stayed through the night, creeping up occasionally to feel if the *mahala* still breathed. About daylight the woman woke, coughed, and threw off a quantity of bloody sputum. A little later, she sat up and demanded something to eat.

Mary was astounded and immediately resolved to find out how this method worked.

Before the medicine man departed, she learned as much as she could. He said that Mary could not get help from "the Friend" simply by asking. She first would have to get to Him, but, he admonished, "the Friend" was not a person. When she had climbed up to "the Friend" by rhythmic motions and sounds, she could lay hold of Him, and the thing she wanted would happen.[24]

Mary was enthralled. It was as if she had stumbled upon something she had always known. Man was not alone and helpless. He had a relationship with the universe through which he could achieve a remedy for any problem. In the weeks that followed she eagerly sought to know more about this form of prayer.

It was Tinnemaha, the medicine man at the Bishop campoody, who taught her the principles underlying the Paiute practice of prayer. The Indians did not pray to a god. They believed in a principle existing in all created life, accessible and responsive to man. This they called "Friend of the Soul of Man." By an outgoing act of the inner self, man could put himself in touch with this creative force, and it would respond to any emergency, whether it be sickness or the need for rain. The purpose of sustained rhythmic movement and sound was to break the tension of immediate circumstances and their hold on the attention. Absolute freedom from distraction and detachment from habitual modes of thinking were prerequisites to the opening movement of prayer. Only then was it possible to set up in one's inner self a motion carefully timed and tuned with the motion of the universe. Through this act, man became at one with "the Friend" and could bring his desire to pass.

These concepts had a strong appeal for Mary. They were in accord with the mystical experiences she had known and, in addition, offered a practical application to everyday problems. She began at once to experiment with this approach to prayer. To clear her mind of distractions, she tried all of the methods Tinnemaha had suggested—repetition of somnolent phrases, singing, various dance movements, and the drum. She discovered the drum to be especially efficacious because she could beat on it and dance at the same time. She performed these rites in strictest privacy, late at night in the seclusion of her home. It was an exciting quest, though she soon realized how long and hard she would have to work for any tangible results.[25]

The first fruits of her effort became evident in connection with her writing. The discipline of detachment increased her ability to concentrate, and she began to make progress. First she produced a few poems, then a short story which she sold to a popular magazine.[26] With fresh conviction in her creative powers, she devoted more time to the one activity that completely absorbed and fulfilled her. However, she still had to earn a living if she was to remain free of household entanglements.

Despite Wallace's protests, Mary contracted to teach a second year at the academy in Bishop. Additional responsibilities were assigned to her, including instructing in the high school course,[27] and the recognition was gratifying. A new friendship also came into her life. It was with a young woman physician, Helen MacKnight, who had recently opened offices on the main street of the town.[28]

Of their first encounter, Doctor MacKnight wrote, "Before I even met her I heard that she grossly neglected and mistreated her subnormal child, that she avoided her duty to her home and her husband, who was a very fine man, that she was a snob, holding herself superior to the people of the town.

"I was prepared to dislike Mary Austin after all the disagreeable things I had heard and my first encounter with her certainly did nothing to discourage that feeling."[29]

Doctor MacKnight had been called by the Fragers to tend Ruth, who was ill with a high fever. Thinking the child's mother would want to accompany her, she stopped at the academy. It was late afternoon, and Mary was alone.

Forty years later, in a biography of Mary Austin, the doctor recorded her initial impression. "As she rose to meet me I saw that she was a rather short, somewhat dumpy looking woman with a homely, heavy lower face, a sullen mouth, fine eyes, a high forehead and abundant, beautiful gold-brown hair. She looked tired, high-strung and harassed."[30]

Standing behind her desk, as if it were a barrier against anticipated criticism, Mary declined to go to Ruth. "No," she said, "I do not wish to go with you. Ruth makes me nervous and I make her nervous. It is not good for us to be together. You go and do what you can for her."[31]

Doctor MacKnight, who was young and sensitive, reacted strongly: "it seemed to me her action was an offense against all motherhood. And yet, behind her words, I caught a burden of sorrow and frustration, an ache of loneliness, that spoke of even greater depths of emotion than would have been evidenced by a natural mother's response to her child's distress."[32]

When the doctor saw Ruth, she really understood the mother's feelings. While the child's illness lasted, she kept Mary informed about her condition. Mary profoundly appreciated the kindness and uncritical attitude of the comely young woman, and by the time Ruth was well a lasting bond had been forged.

Often in the evenings, Mary came to talk with Doctor Nellie, as she was affectionately called, delighted to have found someone who shared her joy in the awesome beauty of the Inyo country. Pacing the floor of the small office, Mary practiced putting into words the spell of enchantment she felt in the place and its people. She also opened her heart about the distractions and anxieties that kept her from giving herself wholly to her writing. Many times she said, "I can imagine no happier arrangement than to be shut away in a room lined with books from floor to ceiling, and with no opening except some place where food could be brought to me and taken away."[33]

Occasionally Mary also talked about Ruth, revealing something of her grief and disappointment, but she never mentioned Wallace. This reticence may have had its root in envy. Not only was Doctor Nellie exceedingly attractive and successful in her profession, but she was engaged to a handsome young doctor who obviously adored her.[34] Soon they would be married and have a joint practice. In their relationship Mary perceived everything she had always wanted: to love and be loved, to work together toward a common goal, and to have children of whom one could be proud.

This was the pattern, the way of life for which she hungered. She did not see it as being inimical to literary achievement. Her physician friend was triumphant proof that women need not choose between marriage and a career. Of her, Mary would later write, "Say what one may, it is difficult to separate Dr. Nellie's success in a difficult and exacting profession from her success as a woman."[35]

In turn, the perceptive young doctor understood only too well that Mary "was as hungry for a really passionate experience as she was for the other things that life had doled out for her so meagerly."[36] But she also sensed that Mary, being the kind of person she was, might not be able to sustain such an experience. Substantiation for this hypothesis may be found in one of Mary's most moving short stories, "The Walking Woman," in which she wrote, "Well I understand that nature which wastes its borders with too eager burning...and have some inkling of the isolating calm of a desire too high to stoop to satisfaction."[37]

As the summer of 1897 approached, a teaching position for the fall opened in Lone Pine. It was under Wallace's supervision, and he urged Mary to take it. That she agreed[38] may have been due in part to a faint hope that she might yet be able to make something of her marriage. It was a chance for a joint endeavor, and, if she had a place in Wallace's work, possibly there would be more communication and closeness between them.

The experiment started auspiciously, despite Mary's indignation at the comment, made by one of Wallace's friends, that her husband was very liberal to allow her to earn money.[39] With their two salaries they were able to pay off most of the debt which had caused their worst quarrels, and for the first time they were comfortably situated. Wallace was considerate, encouraging Mary to spend her evenings writing, and he seemed genuinely pleased when she sold another story, this time to *The Overland Monthly*.[40] However, Mary was aware of a restiveness in her husband that made her uneasy.

Though Wallace was successful in his work, he disliked it intensely. Several times he refused offers of more lucrative teaching posts in other parts of the state, replying to questionnaires in a halfhearted and even facetious manner.[41] Outraged, Mary felt like applying for the opportunities herself. She was determined to get her husband away from the desert, where the compelling character of the land cast a spell over men who stayed too long. Repeatedly she tried to reason with him, pointing out that they needed specific goals, otherwise they could not build toward the future.

His answer was always the same. "Well, this country is bound to go ahead sometime; just look at it."[42] Once in a while, seeing her distress, he was momentarily shaken out of his complacency. Realizing that Mary might mean to remedy the situation by acting on her own, he would add, "Well, but I'm the one who has to decide that, where we live and everything…I'll get into something."[43]

Finally the inevitable happened. Mary, who had been driving herself too hard, became ill from nervous tension and had to go to Los Angeles for hospital treatment. When she returned, Wallace informed her that he had resigned his position with the schools to become registrar of the Desert Land Office at Independence, county seat of Inyo. He assumed that Mary would be willing to finish his term as superintendent along with carrying out her own teaching assignment.[44] She was furious.

His selfish action had been taken in utmost secrecy. It meant that they would continue to live in a small town and have even less financial security. He had shown no consideration for her needs or wishes. She lashed out at him. Neighbors recalled "how they would see her with her hair down pacing the floor at night and railing at Wallace."[45]

She did not refuse the responsibilities he thrust upon her, but overwork and the emotional upsets brought on by frustration took their toll. In the summer of 1898 she was again forced to seek medical attention in a hospital, this time in Oakland.[46] The trip proved beneficial in ways she could not have anticipated.

While in Oakland she attended a lecture given by the philosopher William James. His subject was "Relaxation," based on a book by Annie Payson Call entitled *Power Through Repose*.[47] As she listened, shivers of excitement ran up her spine. Here were the very same principles she had learned from the Paiutes, clothed in the persuasive, sophisticated words of a Harvard professor. Consciousness was a force, a stream of energy, and the brain its organ of transmission. Relaxation of surface tensions allowed the whole personality to "be flooded by the deep life that welled up from below the threshold of selfness."[48]

Mary left the lecture hall to walk in a daze for several blocks, until she came to the hotel where Professor James was staying. To her great surprise, he agreed to see her. Encouraged by his interest, she told the distinguished scholar what she had learned about the Paiute method of prayer. He confirmed the validity of her perceptions[49] and asserted that "the secret of creative thinking lay in the vast area of the mind which, for want of a better word, we call the sub-consciousness."[50]

She was elated, leaving the interview with renewed purpose and a restored sense of equilibrium. Years later she would credit her encounter with William James as being the beginning of an intelligent method for her work.[51] She re-

Courtesy of the Eastern California Museum

Ruth Austin around 1898

turned to Independence resolved to apply the principles of psychic energy to her writing and to experiment with its relationship to prayer as a creative motion of the mind. Given her mystical inclination, it was natural that she would seek to understand the artistic process through the operation of forces beyond herself, and always she would consider herself as an instrument of that power which she described sometimes as "Mind" and other times as "a substance analogous to electricity or light."[52]

Independence was a town of about three hundred inhabitants, located between Lone Pine and Bishop. Beyond its straggling borders stretched the desert, and to the west the towering Sierra wall plunged in broken ridges to the valley floor. Near the base of the mountains was the Indian campoody where Mary spent much of her time during the next year.

Here she was able to pursue her study of the Indian way of life. She participated in their tribal practices and absorbed the hidden meanings in their art and verse. She struggled to understand the symbolism of rhythm as it affected the interaction of the individual and "the Friend of the Soul of Man." She began to perceive how the creative force was present in all rhythmic movement: "the running of the quail, the creaking of the twenty-mule team, the sweep of motion in a life-history, in a dance, a chant."[53] She sought to capture these perceptions in her writing, agonizing to express them in words, but they eluded her. More and more she felt the need for help with the technical aspects of her craft, and for the stimulus of association with other writers.

The prior year, during her brief stay in Los Angeles, she had established a contact with Charles Lummis, editor of the magazine *Land of Sunshine*. He had been cordial, showing an interest in her work, and Mary had liked his wife, Eve, enormously. In the interim since that initial encounter Lummis had accepted one of Mary's poems for publication, and she knew his reputation for encouraging new talent in all the arts. It would be a great boon to her writing if she could live near him and become part of the creative group who frequented his home. Abruptly she decided to move to Los Angeles.[54]

There were practical problems to be dealt with before the move could be made. Wallace's income was small, and at this point Mary could not hope to support herself through her writing. However, she was confident that she could get a job in Los Angeles. The head of the Los Angeles Normal School, Doctor Edward T. Pierce, was a cousin of Doctor Woodin,[55] and she could count on his providing an introduction. For help in finding a place to live, she wrote to Charles Lummis. When a warm reply came, telling her that she could rent a small house a couple of blocks from his home,[56] she was determined to go.

Any objection Wallace may have raised to her plans was probably overcome by the promise of better medical attention for Ruth.[57] Now in her seventh year, the child was still lovely to look at but obviously mentally retarded. Her speech was halting and broken, she had difficulty coordinating her movements, and her attention span was very limited. Nevertheless, Mary had never given up hope that surgery might relieve her daughter's condition. Wallace did not deign to argue with her.

So in the summer of 1899 Mary left for Los Angeles, taking Ruth with her. She eagerly anticipated the new life that lay ahead, and she was resolved to find a way to make the change permanent.[58]

7

Charles Lummis as Her Mentor

AT THE TIME Mary went to Los Angeles, the elements that would form her complex and contradictory personality were already evident. A chilly reserve coupled with untoward aggressiveness masked the conflict between a strong egocentricity and an underlying insecurity. Mary-by-herself still craved affection, understanding, and approval, but I-Mary had conjured a self-image of independence and invulnerability. Moreover, the determination to use her mystical gifts for the attainment of practical results would intensify the conflict, eventually leading to periods of acute emotional turmoil. For the present, however, she was concerned only with developing her literary skills, and to this end she centered her aspirations on Charles Lummis.

Lummis at the age of forty was a short, sinewy man who dramatized his rather nondescript appearance with a flamboyant style and eccentric apparel. Clad in a corduroy suit, red sash and sandals, to which he often added a soft-crowned stetson, he enjoyed holding court as "Don Carlos." Both his penchant for exhibitionism and his reputation as a womanizer were well established. Vain, egocentric, and domineering, he demanded to be the focus of attention. He was also a dynamo of creative energy who drove himself beyond the point of reasonable endurance.

A graduate of Harvard University, he had first come to California in 1885. He was city editor of the Los Angeles *Times* for three years, until the pressure of a brutal, self-inflicted work schedule resulted in a crippling stroke. In 1888 he went to New Mexico to regain his health. There the invalid engaged in a strenuous program of physical activity and suffered two more paralytic attacks, but eventually he managed to achieve complete recovery. It was during this period that Lummis acquired an intimate knowledge of the Mexican-Indian culture and a passionate concern for defending the rights of minorities. The experience provided him with material for ten books and innumerable magazine articles, out of which came his renown as an authority on the Southwest. In addition, the interlude brought a new love into his life.

Courtesy of the University of Arizona Library, Special Collections

Charles Lummis circa 1900

When Lummis met Eva Frances Douglas, his eleven-year marriage to Dorothea Rhodes, a forceful, strikingly handsome physician, was terminating in divorce. The serenely beautiful, blue-eyed Eve, then just twenty, nursed him through his third illness and captivated his heart. They were married in 1891, and afterward Lummis accompanied Adolph Bandelier[1] on an archaeological expedition to South America that lasted over a year. Upon his return, he and Eve settled in Los Angeles, and in 1895 he assumed editorship of *The Land of Sunshine*, transforming the promotional periodical into one of the most highly esteemed literary magazines in the West. At about the same time, he took steps to realize his vision of a house that would become his personal landmark.

After purchasing three acres of wooded land along the bank of the Arroyo Seco on the outskirts of Los Angeles, he began construction of the great stone house which he called *El Alisal*—Place of the Alders. Built by his own hands, with the assistance of Indian youths from New Mexico, the massive edifice reflected architectural influences of Spain, Mexico, and Peru. Single-storied except for two upstairs rooms reserved as Lummis's sanctum sanctorum, the structure was designed around a huge, interior patio where stood an imposing, four-trunked sycamore christened *El Alcalde Mayor*. The house soon became a celebrated center of old California hospitality famed for its food and sparkling company. There gathered such notables as Mary Garden, Helen Modjeska, John Burroughs, and Joaquin Miller, as well as the aspiring writers, artists, and academicians whom Lummis made it a point to cultivate.[2] This was the charmed circle of which Mary sought to become a member.

Eve provided the entry to El Alisal. The empathic young woman understood Mary's need for friendship. Her own life was not devoid of anguish. Married eight years, with two children and another on the way, she endured the brunt of her husband's egocentricity and was only too aware of his philandering. A deep affection quickly developed between the two women whose experiences had been fraught with disillusionment.[3] Their children bound them even closer together.

The seven-year-old Turbese was in many ways like her father, obviously gifted and as spirited as a boy. On the other hand little Amado, then in his fifth year, was an unearthly child whose gentleness tore at the heart. Generous and self-effacing, his every thought was for the happiness of others. The sweetness of his temperament and delicate physique, along with his great glowing eyes and bright mane of hair, made him seem girlish. But he behaved with all the sturdiness and fearlessness of a young knight. He and Ruth loved each other dearly, and the tenderness of their relationship had a beneficent effect on the high-strung child.[4]

Mary and Ruth soon came close to being members of the family. Often Mary was invited to dinner parties in the long, baronial hall, where above the mantel were inscribed the words, "Gather about me! Who can weld iron—or friends—without me?"[5] Don Carlos, resplendent in a ceremonial costume of white deerskin, presided over the abundantly laden table. Mandolins and guitars rested against the high-backed chairs, and between courses Lummis led his large assemblage of guests in the singing of Spanish ballads. At first Mary felt shy and awkward in this exotic setting and withdrew into a silent aloofness. However, when Eve urged her to contribute to the entertainment by reciting an Indian poem, she forgot her diffidence and repeated several Paiute love songs which she had translated. The vibrant beauty of her delivery was enthusiastically received, and, responding to the approbation, she blossomed and was able to enjoy herself.[6]

It was on occasions such as these that Mary met the people whose friendship someday would open doors. One was David Starr Jordan, prolific writer, scientist, and president of Stanford University.[7] His interest in the geographic distribution of animal and plant species and their relation to environment gave Mary an immediate basis for rapport. Eagerly she told him what she had learned about the desert flora and fauna, testing her impressions against his expertise. From Jordan she also received her initial impression of Carmel, the tiny seacoast hamlet south of San Francisco. He declared that, "Of all the indentations of the coast of California, the most picturesque and most charming is the little bay of Carmelo."[8] Mary resolved that this was a place she intended to see.

Another exciting encounter was with Frederick Webb Hodge. The noted anthropologist and specialist in Indian ethnology suggested a method for collecting material on tribal customs which she found invaluable.[9] In turn, he was keenly appreciative of what she had to contribute to the study of the rituals, mythology, and daily life of the Paiutes, requesting that she send him a summary of her findings and promising to provide an alphabet for her use in studying the Indian language.[10] It was the beginning of a lifelong friendship.

Of the women Mary met at El Alisal, she was most impressed by Charlotte Perkins Gilman. The woman's classic beauty had an irresistible appeal, and her defiance of conventional standards spoke to Mary's condition. She too had suffered an unhappy marriage and was accused of being an unnatural mother. Divorced, she had placed her child in the care of her ex-husband's new wife, who had been her close friend, and continued to maintain amicable relations with both of them.[11] Her life was devoted to an ardent fight for the social and economic liberation of her sex. From the lecture platform and in her writings, she spoke out against the enslavement of women to the washtub and the "Holy Stove."[12] She had just published a successful book[13] and had an enviable reputation in the feminist movement. Mary was filled with admiration, identifying with her views, and an inspiring association ensued.

The change in environment proved even more rewarding than Mary had hoped, but there was still the problem of finding paid employment. Summoning her courage, she approached Doctor Pierce at the Normal School. He received her cordially and arranged for her to visit some of the classes. At one of them she discovered a teacher engaged in a lesson about wildlife. It was obvious that she knew nothing about her subject, and her attempt to describe the habits of coyotes was little short of ludicrous. Acting on impulse, Mary offered to take the class. Effortlessly, she expanded her talk to cover other creatures of the desert, holding her audience enthralled. The next day she was invited to give a course of lectures on Western Nature Study to the teaching staff. She had a job for the rest of the school year.[14]

Assured of an income, Mary resolutely applied her free time to the development of her writing skills. She hounded Lummis for help, consulting him about whatever piece of work she had in progress. He "did not take to her," asserting that she had "talent and industry and a certain kind of knowledge, but little gift."[15] Undoubtedly he found her aggressiveness and lack of conventional femininity abrasive. However, he was intrigued by her familiarity with Indian folklore, and in some ways she became a favored apprentice. About him, Mary had mixed feelings.

Unquestionably he was a romantic figure who appealed to her imagination. At the same time, she "shrank from him a little."[16] Perhaps subconsciously she was repelled by the way he flaunted his sexuality. Moreover, she thought that he was wasteful of his talents, dissipating his energy in self-dramatization and carousing. Her sympathies were entirely with Eve, whom she felt Lummis mistreated shamefully. She also developed a great admiration for his first wife, who, though remarried, remained a member of the family circle. Mary was incensed at how much devotion Lummis had casually accepted from both women,[17] but she knew she must cultivate his goodwill. The influence he wielded in the literary world made his good opinion mandatory.

Mary had set her sights high. Reviewing the magazines for which she intended to write, she listed them in the order of their literary excellence and placed *The Atlantic Monthly* at

*Mary Austin around 1900, on the brink of her
writing career. Photograph by Charles Lummis*

the top. By the spring of 1900 she had sold them her first
story, "A Shepherd of the Sierras," for which they paid the
gratifying sum of thirty-five dollars.[18] The sale of several
poems, mostly to the well-known children's magazine *St.
Nicholas,* further bolstered her confidence. Still, the time approached when school would be out for the summer, and she
had to think of how she would support herself. Then an
opportunity came her way: she had an offer of a teaching
post with one of the normal schools in the northern part of
the state. It was an answer to her prayers.[19]

She wrote to Wallace, urging him to join her in the
venture. This was their long-awaited chance to build a better
life. Her income would be sufficient to support them until he
found a position to his liking. Astounded at her proposal, he
flatly refused. Undoubtedly his pride was offended by
Mary's offer to assume responsibility for their livelihood,

even on a temporary basis. Besides, the Inyo country had too strong a hold on him.

When she returned to Independence, still hoping to persuade him, he realized the depth of her disappointment. In a conciliatory gesture, he suggested that she "try another year" on her own. However, Mary knew that if she left again, she could never bring herself to come back to him, and she was not ready to take the step of a permanent separation. There was the problem of Ruth to be considered and, in that connection, a discovery "that hung like a weight about her knees."[20]

During her absence Wallace's sister-in-law, Frank Austin's wife, had been in Independence and left a note for Mary. The message was brief. The woman believed that, because of traits on both sides of the Austin family, Ruth's condition was hereditary.

Mary was beside herself with rage. Furiously she upbraided her husband, demanding to know why she had not been told. His reaction was one of surprise at her anger. He had been brought up to believe that family matters such as this were not to be mentioned.[21] It had not occurred to him that she had any right to the information. Mary's resentment never abated. She saw Wallace's behavior not only as a personal affront but as an offense against all womanhood. Eighteen years later, in a letter to Charles Lummis, she wrote, "I suppose that many women will have to suffer before society arrives at the place where women who give their bodies to the service of Life can hope to be protected from things like this...."[22]

Despite Mary's bitterness toward her husband, she decided to remain in Independence for the time being. She had to have time to accept the implications of what she had discovered and determine what to do about her daughter. Someday she might be forced to place the child in an institution, but first she had to know how much she herself could teach her. Meanwhile she did not intend to lose the momentum she had achieved in her writing.

In the sunny, smiling days of autumn, when Ruth's morning lessons had been accomplished, Mary often left her playing in a neighbor's garden and went on long, solitary walks. She spent hours on the desert trails, returning to the practices of her earlier years. Patiently she observed the life of plants and animals, recording her impressions with the precision of a scientist and the empathy of a poet. She made the desert her laboratory, looking at its myriad forms with a concentration and a reverence that transformed the looking into a celebration of seeing. When the wells of her perception were overflowing, she began to write *The Land of Little Rain,* a paean to the beloved country that was part of her bone and tissue.

The essays that would constitute the book were eloquently wrought, the words chosen with exquisite care and arranged in a rhythmic style evocative of a place and a way of life that were timeless. Some were drawn from episodes of her life in the Tejon, others from sojourns spent in "the streets of the mountains," hiking the high Sierra trails. Most were laced with the vibrant thread of stories gathered from the people of the valley towns and campoodies. Into her writing she poured not only her love of the land but also the aching loneliness and frustration she had known in her twelve years of wandering in the Country of Lost Borders.

In the opening essay she wrote:

> If one is inclined to wonder at first how so many dwellers came to be in the loneliest land that ever came out of God's hands, what they do there and why stay, one does not wonder so much after having lived there. None other than this long brown land lays such a hold on the affections. The rainbow hills, the tender bluish mists, the luminous radiance of the spring, have the lotus charm. They trick the sense of time, so that once inhabiting there you aways mean to go away without quite realizing that you have not done it.[23]

Mary also was captive to the spell of the land, but in a different way than Wallace. He was mesmerized by its promise: the lure of mining projects, oil prospects, and reclamation schemes.[24] Mary loved the land with a generous passion, wanting only to commune with it and participate in its mysteries. In her writing she sought to share something of the intimacy with the earth which she had experienced—"such news of the land, of its trails and what is astir in them, as one lover of it can give to another."[25]

The book was difficult and exhausting work. Aware of the strain Mary was under, Wallace tried to be considerate. He arranged for Ruth to stay with a neighbor and began construction of a house in a location upon which Mary doted. It was on the edge of town, where a footpath led along the stream toward the awesome bulk of the Sierra. Between the mountains and the house was a field fringed by ancient boulders and brimming with wild grasses, to which she devoted the essay in *Land of Little Rain* entitled "My Neighbor's Field." Entranced with the setting for her new home, Mary gave what time she could to making it a place of comfort and beauty. She built the fireplace herself, using native rock, and selected mission-style furniture for the simplicity of its design.[26]

The winter passed quickly with the excitement of the house under construction as well as a surge of creativity in her work. In addition to *Land of Little Rain*, she began work on a novel, a romantic story of early California set in the heyday of Monterey.[27] She also produced a steady stream of poems, which she had no difficulty selling, mostly to the magazine *St. Nicholas*. Inevitably the pressure affected her health, and there were periods of depression. With the advent of the Christmas season, she yearned for her friends in the outside world, especially Eve Lummis.

Ruth also longed for her friend Amado and repeatedly asked when she would see him. Then, on Christmas day, soon after the child had been put to bed, Mary heard her laughing and talking to herself. Puzzled, she entered Ruth's room and found her giggling with excitement.

"Amado is here," she said in her halting speech. "He want me to go a walk with him, a long, long way off."

Pleased because she thought Ruth was showing an imaginative spark, Mary spoke playfully. "But you wouldn't leave mother, would you?"

She left Ruth still laughing and talking to her imaginary visitor. Two days later, a letter arrived from Eve. At the very hour of Ruth's conversation with her playmate, Amado had died of pneumonia.[28] Mary's heart ached for Eve, but the meaning of Ruth's experience burst upon her with new and dazzling light. Perhaps back of that poor, imperfect mind was an awareness beyond what normal intelligence brought.

The weeks that followed were filled with a lingering sadness, but late in January an influenza epidemic broke out in the valley, taking over Mary's time and thoughts. Compulsively she drove herself to nurse the sick, and though she escaped the disease, she became ill from exhaustion. Then, while she was still convalescing, the Austins moved into their new home.

The two-story, brown shingle house, with its peaked, gambrel roof and ample, south-facing porch, seemed light and spacious. Best of all was the small sunroom that looked out toward the mountains. There Mary sat at her desk, and, gazing at the towering peaks of the Sierra, felt a resurgence of the will to write. The mysterious quality of what she experienced was later recorded at the request of one of her publishers.

> ...I remember the day very well—one of those thin days when the stark energies of the land threaten just under its surfaces, the mountains march nakedly, the hills confer.... There was a weeping willow whose long branches moved back and forth across my window like blowing hair.... I think it was this which gave the reminiscent touch to my mood. For though I was there in the midst of it, I began to write of the land of little rain as of

*The Austins' house in Independence, where much
of* The Land of Little Rain *was written*

something very much loved, now removed. As I wrote,
two tall, invisible presences came and stood on either
side.

    I don't know now what these presences were...are.
For two or three years, until I moved away from that
country, in fact, they were present when I wrote. Sometimes, I felt them call me to my desk—sometimes I
summoned them. I suppose they were projections out of
my loneliness, reabsorbed into the subconsciousness
when the need of them was past. Though I could never
quite see them, almost but not quite, and it is years since
they have been present to the outward sense, I am still
occasionally aware of them inside me.[29]

In the spring of 1901 apparently these "presences" provided
a renewed impetus, as *The Land of Little Rain* was soon completed. Mary then turned her attention to the novel, entitled
Isidro, which she had in progress. The plot of the story was

fairly well worked out, but she needed more background information on the period and wrote to Charles Lummis for suggestions of books she might read. Meanwhile, she had become involved in some of the activities in and around Independence. Principal among these was the organization of a little theater, of which she was both producer and director.

Performances were held in an old, abandoned hall, where the seats were boards laid across soap boxes and sacks of wool were piled in back for the gallery. Miners and shopkeepers, as well as Mexicans and Indians, made up the audience. The repertory consisted mainly of Shakespearian plays, in which Mary and Wallace often took the leading roles while other townspeople filled out the cast. The theater was a huge success. Moreover, it was the only enthusiasm which Mary and her husband wholeheartedly shared.

They had little in common. Occasionally she tried to include him in her work, consulting him about the botanical names of species mentioned in her writing, but his interest was superficial. Their reading tastes also differed, as did their rate of comprehension. Evenings while Wallace slowly read aloud to her from a magazine or popular novel, she would surreptitiously peruse a report from the Bureau of Ethnology or browse in the dictionary, still keeping up with the sense of what she heard.[30]

Prominent people began to find their way into the Inyo country: botanists, geologists, collectors of Indian baskets, writers, and members of the Sierra Club. They were directed to Mary because she knew something of their interests.[31] Wallace was always cordial but soon retired behind his newspaper while Mary talked with their visitors. Even camping trips into the mountains, their favorite form of recreation, did not bring mutual enjoyment.

The trips were planned by Wallace with no regard for Mary's capacities. He liked to break new trails and set his own pace. The hikes over rugged terrain, with infrequent stops for rest, taxed Mary's endurance and took much of the pleasure out of the excursions. Even so, Wallace never willingly went without her.[32]

The townspeople sympathized with Wallace. They talked about how patient and kind he was, how devoted to his difficult wife. Though she treated him with respect, they never saw her show any affection for him. Moreover, they thought her handling of Ruth was shameful. Half the time the child was farmed out to strangers, and when she was at home, she was abused. Hearing Ruth's screams, neighbors would go to the house to investigate. They were shocked to find Mary pacing the floor, hair hanging down her back, apparently oblivious to her daughter, who was strapped to a chair. They were ignorant of Mary's reasons for restraining her and unaware that the distracted woman was trying to concentrate on her work.[33]

Ruth's behavior was a constant drain on Mary's strength and nerves. Now nine years old, the girl was fine physically, and under Mary's assiduous tutelage she had learned to read a little, albeit with excruciating effort. But it was impossible to control her. Without warning she would cause havoc in the house. Even worse was her habit of running away. She simply took off in any direction that struck her fancy. Locked doors did not deter her, and often it was hours before she was found and brought back.

Physical restraint was the only practical means of insuring the child's safety and giving Mary any chance to write. Yet Mary was heartbroken to see her daughter's misery. She resolved to find a place where the girl could live with others like herself, happy and free.[34] For this plan she knew money would be needed, and that it must come from her writing.

Carefully she selected several essays from *The Land of Little Rain*, polishing and perfecting them. Then she sent the sample manuscript to Bliss Perry, an editor of both *The Atlantic Monthly* and Houghton Mifflin, asking if he thought a book of sketches such as these could be published. Meanwhile, she produced a couple of short stories and a half dozen poems, which she had no difficulty selling. Some were placed in Lummis' magazine, now renamed *Out West*, and others were bought by eastern periodicals.

Early in 1902 she received an encouraging letter from Perry, praising her descriptive papers about California and requesting that she send the balance of the material she had ready. Elated, she complied. Five months of anxious waiting ensued. Then came the letter telling her that Houghton Mifflin would publish *The Land of Little Rain*. In addition *The Atlantic Monthly* would publish from four to six of the essays, paying at the rate of $8 a page, and they would advance $150 at once. It was a wonderful moment! At last she was moving toward a real literary career.[35]

When Mary answered her publisher's request for a biographical sketch of her life and an account of her work, the material she provided indicated both the strength of her ego and the depth of her insecurity. A brief typewritten summary, impersonally worded and containing some exaggeration, was followed by several pages of handwritten notes. The latter began with a cry of near desperation.

> N. B. I can't do it...I thought it would be easy to do, but it isn't. There is really nothing to tell. I have just *looked*, nothing more, when I was too sick to do anything else, I could lie out under the sage brush and look, and when I was able to get about I went to look at other things, and by and by I got to know when and where looking was most worthwhile. Then I got so full of looking that I had to write to get rid of some of it to make room for more....
>
> I have considered a long while, to see if I have any interesting excentricities [*sic*] such as make people want to buy books of the people who have them, but I think not. You are to figure to yourself a small, plain, brown woman with too much hair, always a little sick, and always busy about the fields and the mesas in a manner, so they say in the village, as if I should like to see anybody try to stop me.

> ...As for the villagers they have accepted me on the same basis as the weather, an institution which there is no use trying to account for. Two years ago I delivered the Fourth of July oration here, and if, when there is no minister of any sort here, as frequently happens, I go and ring the church bell, they will come in to hear me in the most natural manner.
>
> When I go out of this valley (Owens) to attend or to talk to large educational gatherings I ride 130 miles in the stage across the desert to Mojave, and the driver lets me hold the lines. Once when he said the water of Mojave made him sick, I put him inside and took the stage in from Red Rock to Coyote Holes....You see I was the only one who knew how to drive four horses.

Having belittled her appearance and bragged about her exploits, Mary went on to write of her work: "the best is 'A Land of Little Rain,' and the child verse in St. Nicholas. I think the best and worst of it is that I am a little too near to my material....But I shall do better work, and still better....Whatever you are minded to say of my work say this—that I have been writing only four or five years and have not yet come to my full power, nor will yet for some years more."[36]

Now that Mary had sold her first book, she was impatient to sell another as soon as possible. There were still problems about background material for *Isidro*, so she decided to write a book of Indian tales for children. The work went quickly and easily. Many of the stories were built on the legends Mary had heard in the campoody at George's Creek. A central character was the wonderful old Indian woman whose baskets Mary had so much admired in that long-ago summer. The simple tales shone with a loving spirit and an empathy for all living things. When the manuscript was completed, she sent it to Houghton Mifflin, suggesting that the collection be called *The Basket Maker*.

As always after a sustained creative effort, Mary was nervously tired. Moreover, she had developed a nagging pain in her left arm.[37] Though springtime had come to the valley, bringing the beauty of wild almond in bloom, she was unable to enjoy her surroundings. Most frustrating was her inability to get back into her novel. Somehow the threads of the story had become snarled. Initial inspiration for the plot had come from an incident related by General Beale, taken from the lore of the Tejon country. This idea Mary had expanded into a romance between a young hidalgo, determined to be a priest, and the daughter of a Monterey comandante who had been brought up disguised as a shepherd boy. Mary felt the need for more realism in the settings for the story. Perhaps placing some of the scenes at the Carmel Mission would lend authenticity; a visit to the Tejon area might also revitalize her recollections.

The idea of a trip grew in her mind. Another incentive was the chance to meet her brother's wife. A couple of years earlier, Jim had finally married[38] at the age of thirty-five, and Mary was curious about the woman who had persuaded him to relinquish his bachelorhood. She also wanted to see her old friends the Pyles, who also resided in Bakersfield. Afterward she would travel to San Francisco, where Eve Lummis could provide an introduction to the Hittells, and from there she would make her way down the coast to Monterey and Carmel.[39]

Late in the spring of 1903 Mary left on her trip. She saw it as a brief respite from the monotony of her existence in Independence. It proved a fateful adventure that ultimately would alter the pattern of her life.

8

Infatuation With George Sterling

MARY FOUND COMFORT in renewing her friendship with Mrs. Pyle. To the kindly woman she could be frank about Ruth and discuss the heartbreak and uncertainty about what to do for the child. She also confided her concern that the pain in her arm might be a sign of some serious illness.[1] For the most part, though, her sojourn in the Tejon country was light-hearted.

She revisited old haunts, attended a spring shearing, and again resolved to write a book about the ways of sheep and the men who tended them. An added pleasure came from meeting Jim's wife, whom she thought to be "a lovely woman."[2] Time passed swiftly, and it was early summer before she left for San Francisco, where Eve Lummis was visiting the Hittells.

Though Mary stayed in a small hotel on Clay Street, Eve quickly introduced her into the close circle of distinguished people who frequented the house of Theodore Hittell. Eminent attorney and historian, Hittell had attracted a coterie of devoted admirers, making his home a center for San Francisco's literary elite. There Mary met such celebrities as John Muir and Charles Warren Stoddard and also renewed her

Courtesy of The Bancroft Library

George Sterling, photographed by Arnold Genthe

acquaintance with the gracious Ina Coolbrith, to whom she
still felt deeply indebted. Moreover, the Hittells received her
so warmly that she soon felt like a member of the family and
developed a special affection for Catherine, the daughter of
the house.[3]

The highlight of Mary's stay in San Francisco was her
meeting with George Sterling. He had read the essays from
Land of Little Rain published in *The Atlantic Monthly* and had
written a note, praising her work. Now he called to take her
to dinner, arriving at her hotel with Harry Lafler, literary editor of *The Argonaut*. She was instantly entranced by
Sterling's beguiling personality and appearance. Years later
she described her first impression of him: "handsome as
a Roman faun, shy, restless, slim and stooping," with the
puckish quality of everlasting youth.[4]

At the time of their meeting, Sterling was a central figure in San Francisco's celebrated Bohemian Club, as well as a
poet of rising fame, whose work was being compared to that
of Keats. Son of a solid Sag Harbor, Long Island, family, he
had spent three years studying for the priesthood and another in medical training, only to find that neither vocation
suited him. In 1890, at the age of twenty-one, he had come
to San Francisco to work for his uncle, a prominent real-
estate and insurance broker. Harnessing himself to a dull job,
Sterling had married the beautiful young Caroline Rand
and settled down to a prosaic existence. In his spare moments, to escape unbearable boredom, he began scribbling
verse. Then he struck up a friendship with the influential

The Bohemian Club, 1907. From left to right:
Jimmy Hopper, Herman Scheffauer, Harry Lafler, and
George Sterling, in Bohemian Grove, San Francisco

writer and critic Ambrose Bierce, and under the tutelage of this exacting mentor he made rapid progress. Added encouragement came from association with writers such as Joaquin Miller, "Poet of the Sierras," the short-story writer James Hopper, and the zestful Jack London, a boon companion who introduced him to San Francisco's Barbary Coast. By 1903, Sterling's first collection of verse, *Testimony of the Suns,* had been published to considerable critical acclaim, and he was eager to devote full time to his art. At this point, he and Mary Austin met.[5]

Their initial evening together proved memorable for Mary. Sterling took her to Coppa's Restaurant, a favorite rendezvous for impecunious artists and writers—veritably "the heart and symbol of San Francisco's Bohemia."[6] Its atmosphere must have been astonishing to a person of Mary's provincial background. The walls of the long, high-ceilinged room, papered in brilliant crimson, were covered with huge caricatures in bright-colored chalk, topped by a frieze of black cats. At a large center table sat a boisterous group of doyens of the Bohemian crowd. Among them was the Mexican artist Xavier Martinez, flamboyant in rakish velvet beret and flowing red tie.[7] Also present was Jimmy Hopper, whom Mary later described as "a short man with the face of a Breton sailor and hair like one of Fra Angelico's angels." Dazzled by the excitement of being included in this renowned inner circle, Mary also relished the delicious food. Years later she would recall the succulent sand dabs and fresh shrimp, the profusion of crisp vegetables, and the delectable almond tarts filled with whipped cream.[8]

Regrettably, the Coppas did not take to Mary. Probably she was too preoccupied to notice the signals they exchanged. In the intimate circle of illuminati, it was the custom to cast a secret vote on the admission of any new person brought by a member. This was done surreptitiously by a system of hand and foot contacts under the table. Before the meal was over, Mary had been rejected. The problem, according to Hopper, was that though "she was writing beautiful stuff...she wasn't pretty."[9] Unattractive women, however talented, were not welcome.

Still, much happened following the evening at Coppa's that was deeply satisfying to Mary's ego. The very next day Sterling took her for a walk to Portsmouth Square, where she filled the small bronze galleon atop the Robert Louis Stevenson monument with violets, quite possibly given her by the poet. Then they had tea and kumquats in a picturesque Chinese restaurant nearby.[10] Sterling read her passages from the *Testimony of the Suns*, and they discussed their work in progress. When he discovered that she was planning to go to Carmel, he offered to be her guide.[11]

Sterling was familiar with the seacoast village and had already entertained the idea of settling there. For some time Frank Powers, a San Francisco attorney and early developer of Carmel, had been soliciting colonists for the fledgling town. Clients from the city came down on the Del Monte Express to the depot at Monterey and were transported in an open, two-horse carriage up the old dirt road over Carmel Hill. It was a long, hard pull, taking well over an hour; then, rounding a hairpin turn, the narrow road zigzagged into what there was of a town.[12]

When Mary arrived in Carmel, she saw a handful of stores and one hotel. Trails led from simple cottages through sprays of sky-blue ceanothus to the straggling main street. Great stretches of open ground were covered with shooting stars and wild iris. The air was fragrant with the scent of pine and woodsmoke, and everywhere was the sound of the singing sea. Overwhelmed by the beauty of this place that nestled at the foot of the Santa Lucia Mountains, she later recalled the wonder of that first encounter in glowing phrases.

> The Mission San Carlos Borromeo looks inshore up the valley of Carmel to the lilac-colored crests of Santa Lucia; off shore, the view just clears the jaws of Lobos along the sunpath between it and Cypress Point. Full in the crescent bay the sea lifts in a hollow curve of

chrysoprase, whose edge goes up in smoking foam along
the hard packed beaches.... when I first came to this
land, a virgin thicket of buckthorn sage and sea-blue
lilac spread between well-spaced, long-leaved pines. The
dunes glistened white with violet shadows, and in the
warm hollows, between live oaks, the wine of light had
mellowed undisturbed a thousand years.[13]

During Mary's stay in Carmel, Sterling was an ideal companion. Romantic and playful, he entered wholeheartedly into the game of reconstructing the ambience of early mission life, helping Mary build the background for her novel.[14] Before long, her mind was seething with scenes and story ideas. She was eager to get back to her writing, yet loath to leave the idyllic setting and the man who made it come alive for her.

Upon her return to Independence, Mary found readjustment to daily routine painfully difficult. With Sterling she had tasted the heady wine of intellectual rapport with a fellow artist. In contrast, her relationship with Wallace must have seemed more barren than ever before. A single sentence in the short story "Frustrate" sums up the anguish she undoubtedly felt: "...it had come over me that away deep inside of me there was a really beautiful kind of life, singing, and burning blue and red and gold as it sang, and there were days when I couldn't bear to think of it wasting there and nobody to know."[15]

Wallace was not entirely oblivious to her state of mind. In the face of her irritability or indifference, he was humble and propitiatory, attributing her behavior to nerves. He snatched at any occasion to further the illusion that they had interests in common. Aware of her love for the Inyo country, he brought news that a survey party of the U.S. Reclamation Service had been working in the area for several months. There were excellent prospects that a government irrigation district would be established in the Owens Valley. It would make them rich.[16] Mary did not share Wallace's confidence. Too many times in the past he had been carried away by enthusiasm for projects which failed to materialize.

As an escape from emotional unrest, Mary immersed herself in work. She finished *Isidro* and produced several short stories as well, and the plot of a new novel was "brewing at the back of her brain." Nevertheless, she was not pleased with her accomplishments. The insecurity which always lay in wait had overtaken her. In a letter to Eve she confided that her novel of mission times seemed "stale and thin."[17] Moreover, the publication of *The Land of Little Rain* in October 1903 only deepened her depression.

When she saw the words over which she had labored frozen in the cold finality of print, she felt that she had failed. With "a queer kind of shame" she hid the volume among other books in the house and bristled when Wallace insisted on showing it to casual callers.[18] Apprehensively she awaited the reviews. They were exceedingly favorable, including one in *The Argonaut* and another by Charles Lummis in *Out West*. Even eastern periodicals were enthusiastic in their praise,[19] but nothing could convince Mary that her work had literary value.

Reactions of the townspeople in Independence to the book did nothing to bolster her morale. Unable to see the country as she did, they discredited her version as affected if not downright untruthful.[20] She cared little for their opinions; still, their criticism stung. Insidiously it reinforced the gnawing fear that maybe she had been mistaken in thinking she had any real talent for a writing career.[21]

To a friend she wrote, "...I have not spoken out my message to my satisfaction and cannot therefore call my work successful no matter what the book sellers say."[22] She could not accept the approbation she craved. Her egocentricity demanded that whatever she produced must be perfect, but she was unable to meet her own standards. By December, the tension of anxiety and overwork, coupled with an ever-growing concern about her retarded child, brought on another siege of illness.

As soon as her health improved, she resolved to do something for Ruth. She was convinced that her daughter's happiness depended upon her being in a place where she would not know that she was different. She was beginning to notice the thoughtless laughter and taunting remarks of other children and the curious glances of insensitive adults. People who once had thought her abused now concluded that she was queer. As she grew older, it would be increasingly difficult to shield her from hurt.[23]

In January 1904 Mary placed Ruth in the care of a Santa Clara physician, Doctor R. E. Osbourne, for a trial period of a year.[24] Then she would decide whether it was best to commit the eleven-year-old child to a private institution located in that town. Meanwhile she plunged into her new novel,[25] constructing a plot based on the marital problems of two couples. The setting was a small, contemporary California town which she called Santa Lucia. Into the story, she poured much of the frustration she felt in her own marriage, infusing both male characters with Wallace's most infuriating traits. Many of the scenes were developed around her own intimate experiences. It was satisfying work, therapeutic and absorbing. Before the end of the year, she had roughed out a first draft.

In October 1904 *The Basket Woman* was published, and *Isidro* was in its second installment in *The Atlantic Monthly*. Temporarily, anxiety about her work had subsided. Still, as the time for a final decision about Ruth inexorably approached, she became increasingly disturbed. Wallace was no help. Mary continued to blame him for their child's tainted heredity, though in fact there was considerable reason to believe that the girl had sustained brain damage during her difficult birth.

Finally, Mary took the grim journey to Santa Clara. In January 1905 she signed the papers that placed Ruth in permanent residence at the sanatorium.[26] She was never to see her daughter again. Henceforth, when Ruth was mentioned, she would simply say, "We have lost her."[27]

Before leaving Independence, Mary had learned that her brother Jim's wife had died ten days after giving birth to a daughter on December 4. Empathizing with his grief, Mary went to Bakersfield and stayed with him for several months. The infant, named Mary, soon captured her heart. For a while she was content to be with the baby, who undoubtedly eased the ache she felt over the loss of her own daughter. Then, as spring brought a shimmering beauty to the Tejon country, memories of the days when she had roamed the trails of General Beale's great rancho took over her mind. The need to return to the book she had long put aside became irresistible.

Renting a tiny office in Bakersfield's business district, she spent her daytime hours writing the opening chapters of *The Flock*. The sentences were painstakingly carved out of her nostalgia for a land and a way of life she had known with an exquisite intimacy. Once she told a neighbor that she had worked four hours "trying to get the right word to describe the hills to the East." The townspeople thought her queerer than ever. She shocked them by staying at the Tejon ranch for a few days, alone with a houseful of men.[28] However, her efforts were rewarded. In *The Flock* she succeeded in capturing the unique quality of the country in a poetic prose similar to that of *Land of Little Rain*.

Early in the summer, Mary was back in Independence, putting the finishing touches on the book. She sent the manuscript to Houghton Mifflin in September and received an enthusiastic response from her editor, with the promise of a contract to follow.[29] Meanwhile both *Land of Little Rain* and *Isidro* were selling well, and she had every reason to believe that her writing would be increasingly remunerative. At this point, several factors converged, bringing about what was probably the most momentous decision of her life.

First there was the matter of her health. She was forced "to take heart stimulants every half hour" and feared another attack similar to the one she had suffered the prior winter unless she moved to a lower altitude.[30] Even more important was her feeling of being trapped both by her marriage and by the narrowness of her existence in Independence.

The only interest she shared with either the community or her husband was the desperate plight of the Owens Valley. The high hopes that the federal government would establish an extensive reclamation project in the valley had been dashed by news that an aqueduct was to be built to carry the waters of the Owens River to Los Angeles. Representatives of the city had been secretly buying up water rights and conveying them to Los Angeles. In the face of a fait accompli, the Reclamation Service had abandoned its plans for an irrigation district.[31] Wallace led a valiant fight to avoid the disaster. He wrote letters to the secretary of the interior and to President Theodore Roosevelt, charging collusion between federal agents and city officials. When he was offered $5,000 for transfer of a water right to which he held claim, he refused, presenting it instead as a gift to the citizens of the valley.[32]

Mary heartily approved of her husband's actions and lent what support she could to the cause. It soon became obvious, though, that all attempts to stem the tide were in vain. The Desert Land Office, in which Wallace was employed, closed its doors, and he was without a job. Mary sympathized but was sickened by the futility of the struggle to which he had stubbornly given the years of their marriage. Moreover, she could not bear to watch the decimation of the land she held dear.[33]

In her autobiography Mary stated that she left the Inyo country because of the demands of her career and the instability of her health. She also implied that she had a great need to get away from Wallace.[34] There may well have been still another motive for her move: George Sterling was now living in Carmel, and she had not forgotten the excitement of the interlude she had spent with him.[35] In any event, by the end of the year, she had made her decision. She too would make Carmel her home.

Flood Tide
1906-1923

9

Life in Carmel's Bohemian Colony

IT IS DIFFICULT TO DOUBT that Mary Austin was infatuated with George Sterling. One has only to read the articles and verse she wrote about him some twenty years later to surmise the depth of her feeling. To him she attributed the unique quality of life in Carmel, where he was "easily the most arresting figure." She described him as resembling Dante—"the Roman nose, the beautiful long chin, the forward-jutting brow." For her, his virtues outweighed his faults: "he lived so sincerely with himself and so vitally that even his failings were contributive and informing." She saw him as the soul of generosity, a poetic genius, and a "priest to beauty."[1]

When Mary arrived in Carmel, she was thirty-eight, an awkward, country woman, devoid of social graces and acutely sensitive about her shortcomings. Patently plain, she had a short, stocky figure and tragic, brooding face, to which only her lovely eyes and abundant golden-brown hair lent charm. Starved for affection and the understanding of a kindred spirit, she attached herself to Sterling with an ardor that he found a bit boring. However, his admiration of her work and their mutual appreciation of Carmel's natural beauty "made it easy for him to forgive her pushiness."[2] Furthermore, there was something appealing about her eagerness and naivete.[3]

Sterling's house, situated on an acre of wooded hillside, overlooked flower-strewn meadows sloping down to the sea. A far-flung view swept over the mission, up the winding river valley, and across to the Santa Lucias. The thirty-foot-long, redwood living room soon became a rendezvous for the old Bohemian crowd from San Francisco. Gathered in front of the tall, chalk-stone fireplace, they partook of "Thackeray stew"—a fish chowder named for Thackeray's "Ballad of Bouillabaisse"—and downed great quantities of muscatel and ale. A conversation piece was the sacred grove behind the house, with its altar-like, stone firepit and encircling trees, each decorated with the skull of a horse or a cow. Intended for votive offerings to the forest gods, it became the scene of many a mussel roast in the mellow winter days.[4]

Mary luxuriated in the atmosphere of carefree conviviality, so different from anything she had known. She had rented a picturesque log cabin in the north end of town,[5] but before long she purchased land, hoping someday to build a house of her own. Located not far from her rented dwelling, the property comprised eleven lots at a total cost of $1,612.50. It was payable in three yearly installments, with a down payment of $250. She felt sure she could meet the terms and signed the agreement on March 5, 1906.[6]

A few days later Wallace appeared for a brief visit. He accompanied Mary to a picnic at the Sterlings, followed by a mussel-gathering party at Point Lobos.[7] The gracious Carrie Sterling, now in residence with her husband, must have done her best to put him at ease, but there were some in the group who poked fun behind his back, alluding to him as "Mrs. Mary."[8] Besides, Wallace himself must have felt uncomfortable in the company of such personages as the debonair photographer Arnold Genthe and renowned artist Charles Rollo Peters. There is no indication that Mary gave him a warm welcome. She was much too preoccupied with Sterling.

*Mary Austin's Carmel "wick-i-up," a platform built high in
the branches of a great oak, where she wrote each morning*

In her autobiography Mary recalled that she and
George "were very much alone in that first year."[9] Together
they took long hikes over the Monterey hills, while they conjured romantic tales of forest folk and lost treasure.[10] Of all
their walks, the best was to Point Lobos: "no poet's stroll, but
a stout climb, dramatic, danger-tipped, in the face of bursting spray heads torn up from primordial deeps." After such
excursions, "there would be tea beside driftwood fires, or
mussel roasts by moonlight," and always "talk, ambrosial,
unquotable talk."[11]

It is clear that Mary reveled in these activities. Nevertheless, in addition to an unending round of pleasurable
amusement, there was serious work. Every morning the writers and artists settled down to their creative pursuits, "which
it was anathema to interrupt."[12] Mary's workplace was a platform built in the branches of a huge oak on her property.
She called it her "wick-i-up"[13] and daily climbed a rickety

ladder to write there. She was correcting proofs for *The Flock* and had begun work on a collection of short stories based on her desert years.

In mid-April Mary went to San Francisco to meet with her publisher's representative. She was staying at the Palace Hotel, when, on the afternoon of April 17, she was inexplicably overcome with a premonition of disaster. It seemed as if the walls of the hotel were about to crumble around her. In a state of near panic she telephoned her brother George, who was then an intern at the City and County Hospital.[14] The thirty-year-old, practical-minded physician, who had seen little of Mary since boyhood, told her that she was suffering from claustrophobia. Still alarmed, Mary called her friend Catherine Hittell and asked if she could spend the night with her.[15] The next morning, at 5:13, an earthquake of unprecedented violence shook San Franciscans from their beds.

Damage in the area of the Hittells' house was confined to shattered windows, cracked plaster, and collapsed chimneys. For a couple of hours, the extent of the calamity was not fully realized, but by mid-morning, huge clouds of smoke could be seen rising from the south part of town. Entire buildings had caved into the streets, and fires caused by broken gas pipes and torn electrical wires raged through the industrial district. The flames spread rapidly, eating their way through the frame buildings. Fire crews fought to keep the conflagration from crossing Market Street. Then the water supply failed, and by nightfall the city was doomed.[16]

Refugees streamed into the parks, carrying their scant possessions, and bedded down on the grass. After hoping in vain for a shift in the wind, the Hittells were forced to join them. Mary lay with her friends, jammed in among tightly packed bodies, with scarcely space for the common decencies. In the morning she walked the streets of the ravaged city, a hot, sickish smell filling her nostrils. On every side were the horrible sights and sounds of human tragedy. The scenes were burned into her brain.

Jack London and George Sterling at Carmel, 1906

It was several days before she could secure passage on a ferry to Berkeley and then return to Carmel. There she lost no time in writing up her experiences. Her account, published in *The Argonaut,* is an unforgettable description of California's most catastrophic earthquake. She did not neglect to pay tribute to the triumphant spirit demonstrated by the people of San Francisco, nor did she fail to point out that the disaster was caused in large measure by man-made developments—filled ground, "huddled buildings cheapened by greed," and insensitivity to nature.[17]

In the months following the earthquake many San Franciscans fled to Carmel, where Sterling did his best to divert the dejected exiles. One of the visitors to whom Mary felt especially sympathetic was Nora May French. She had first met the golden-haired girl at the Lummis house and was impressed by the emotional appeal of her poetry.[18] Now in her mid-twenties, Nora May was struggling to make a name for herself as a writer. Possessed of an incandescent beauty, a mercurial temperament, and pixie ways, she had many suitors, but she was involved in a stormy love affair with Harry Lafler, who was already married. Mary sensed that behind the girl's breezy manner lurked a deep-seated depression.[19] She rose to her defense when Carrie Sterling remarked, "She is a freak and has a dozen wheels all going at once. I'd rather read her poetry than have her company."[20] Carrie had also been known to make critical comments about Mary,[21] who by this time had taken to wearing long Grecian robes and letting her hair hang loose down her back.[22]

Under the influence of Sterling as well as the setting that now shaped her days, Mary's personality was undergoing a marked change. Her environment did not provide the solitude or opportunity for the kind of communion with the land that once had been hers. She was engulfed by an atmosphere of intellectual ferment and social festivity which inevitably affected the expression of her mystical gifts. No longer did her surroundings nourish an awareness of the Presence she had experienced among the mighty mountain ranges of the Inyo country. Although she responded to the beauty of Carmel, her new lifestyle left an imprint on both her work and her image of herself.

A sensual quality began to color her concept of I-Mary and may have accounted in part for the unconventional apparel she adopted. In addition, she spent considerable creative energy in lighthearted collaboration with her fellow writers. She and Jimmy Hopper had joined forces to produce a short story,[23] while a fanciful novel was developing out of the treasure-hunting game that she and Sterling had been playing.[24] Soon everyone in their circle of friends had a hand in the tale, and the characters bore a marked resemblance to themselves. George called it "a treasury of beauty," and Mary exalted in the comradeship the work provided.[25]

Meanwhile, she devoted her morning hours to the desert stories entitled *Lost Borders*. Though the tales were taken from situations she had observed or stories she had heard, the interpretation was intensely personal. In the introductory chapter her recollections of the once-beloved land were tinged with bitterness and resentment.

> Riding through by the known trails, the senses are obsessed by the coil of a huge and senseless monotony; straight, white, blinding, alkali flats, forsaken mesas; skimpy shrubs growing little and less, starved knees of hills sticking out above them; black clots of pines high upon rubbishy mountain-heads—days and days of this....[26]
>
> ...Mind you, it is men who go mostly into the desert, who love it past all reasonableness, slack their ambitions, cast off old usages, neglect their families because of the pulse and beat of a life laid bare to its thews and sinews. Their women hate with implicitness the life like the land, stretching interminably whity-brown, dim and shadowy blue hills that hem it, glimmering pale waters of mirage that creep and crawl about its edges....[27]

Her feminism flared in stories such as "The Woman at the Eighteen-Mile" and "The Return of Mr. Wills." In them she articulated her anger at the subservient role forced upon women. Imbued with the anguish she herself had endured, the stories were powerful evocations of emotional deprivation. Only in one, "The Readjustment," did she reflect an insight that Wallace may also have suffered in their marriage. In "The Walking Woman" she laid bare all her pent-up longing for a passionate relationship such as he could never offer.

It was a tale of blazing devotion, celebrating the glory of being intimately involved with a man not only as a woman but as a person—fully accepted and appreciated for what she had to give both in his work and as his sexual partner.

> But look you: it was the naked thing the Walking Woman grasped, not dressed and tricked out, for instance, by prejudices in favor of certain occupations;

"Ambrosial talk" on the beach at Carmel. From left to right:
George Sterling, Mary Austin, Jack London, and Jimmy Hopper

and love, man love, taken as it came, not picked over and rejected if it carried no obligation of permanency; and a child; *any* way you get it, a child is good to have...to have it and not wait upon a proper concurrence of so many decorations that the event may not come at all.[28]

"The walking woman" had freed herself from "society made values, and, knowing the best when the best came to her, was able to take it."[29] In spirit, Mary yearned to be like her, but much as she might have hungered for a satisfying sexual relationship, as well as for another chance to have a child, she was held back by mores inculcated in her youth. Some years later she commented in a letter, "My own love life has been tragic, and I have often regretted the habit of early training which has inhibited me from piecing out my love life with slighter, more transient affairs. I would have suffered much less if I had."[30]

As always when she was "absorbed in the emotional reactions of personal existence,"[31] the mystical side of her nature was obscured. Now, exhausted by an intensive interlude of work and disturbed by a newly awakened sexuality, she became depressed. Moreover, the chronic pain in her left arm was a nagging worry. She tried to return to the novel *Santa Lucia* but could not concentrate. Then, the electrifying arrival of Jack London and his new wife, Charmian, temporarily took over her mind.

London's visit prompted a frenetic celebration that lasted five days. It included a gala at the Rollo Peters home in Monterey, an expedition to the Big Sur country, and a roistering beach picnic.[32] Mary was keenly interested in the man who was Sterling's idol. The thirty-year-old London had just published his sixteenth novel, *White Fang.* Handsome and virile, he radiated physical force, yet his tousled blond hair and huge shining eyes, filled with faraway visions, gave him a boyish look. The combination was irresistible to women. Mary remarked scornfully that they "flung themselves at Jack, lay in wait for him,"[33] but there were some among the Bohemian crowd who thought that Mary herself "wanted London but would not admit it."[34]

In her own words, she and London "had to shake down a bit before we began to get on together."[35] They were often embroiled in heated arguments. She was skeptical of the socialism he espoused, while he made fun of her spiritualism. Moreover, Mary contemptuously rejected London's notion that sexual diversion was essential to the creative artist.[36] "I never needed a love affair to release the sub-conscious in me,"[37] she asserted defensively.

For Mary it was impossible to acknowledge that her work could be affected by such needs. Besides, she was not about to let any man be privy to her feelings. Nevertheless, she thoroughly enjoyed the exchange and usually managed to have the last word. Professional literary men like London held a great fascination for her.[38] She never tired of analyzing their motivations and methods of work.

With the departure of the Londons there was a letdown, and for most of November the Sterlings also were away. Mary became bored and restless. Daily association with Carmel's group of artists and writers began to pall upon her. She cast about for new contacts.

A friend had given her an introduction to Mrs. Herbert Hoover,[39] who was visiting her parents in Monterey. Either David Starr Jordan or Vernon Kellogg could have provided this entrée. Jordan, who had known Mary since their meeting at the Lummis house, was president of Stanford University, of which the Hoovers were graduates. Both he and Kellogg, a professor of entomology at Stanford, had summer homes in Carmel, and undoubtedly they kept in close touch with the Hoovers. In addition, the personable Kellogg was involved in Carmel's Bohemian colony, where he was affectionately known as the only "egg head" in the group.[40]

Lou Henry Hoover was in her early thirties at the time Mary met her. During her seven years of marriage to Herbert Hoover, then a successful young mining engineer, she had traveled around the world.[41] A vibrant, unassuming person, Mrs. Hoover welcomed Mary warmly, and the two women soon discovered that they had much in common. Born in adjoining states in the Midwest, they shared a similar pioneer heritage. Moreover, Lou Hoover also loved the outdoors and had an avid interest in both books and nature. Probably what intrigued Mary most was the fact that Mrs. Hoover had defied convention to enroll in the Department of Geology and Mines at Stanford, where she had graduated as the only woman with a degree in that field.[42]

Mrs. Hoover later recalled that "Mary presented herself and explained that she was anxious to meet men who... were doing things out in the world." Her work required her to know people engaged in "practical things." Lou Hoover arranged for her to meet many engineers and professional people, finding the account she gave of her impressions "most interesting."[43] She also invited Mary to visit at the Hoovers' home base in London, if she should happen to go abroad. For Mary, it was a stimulating encounter that eventually would lead to exciting developments.[44]

Meanwhile, there were increasing financial difficulties. Mary had been unable to build on her property and was living in a room at the Pine Inn.[45] Though she had sold most of the stories from *Lost Borders* to magazines for serialization, publication of the next book was stalled. Houghton Mifflin had responded to the manuscript with high praise,[46] but they had requested editorial changes which she found difficult to make. In addition, royalties from her previous books had been disappointingly meager. Blaming Houghton Mifflin for inadequate marketing of her work, she wrote a stinging letter to her editor, William Booth.

> This matter of the sale of my books is getting to be a very serious one with me. I have appreciated very much the personal interest you have taken in my work. ... But it isn't a question of loyalty any more, it isn't even a question of what will be best in ten years, it is just a question of paying my board here and now.... There are publishers willing to back me for the effort if only they can have book as well as serial rights, and unless you can manage some way to make some money for me, I shall have to close with them.[47]

Another visit from Wallace did nothing to soothe Mary's nerves. He had been trying to find employment in one of the small towns near San Francisco but had "not settled on anything yet."[48] Accompanying her to a couple of parties, he was even less at ease than on prior occasions.[49] For the most part, he was the target of cruel amusement, but there were some who saw him as a gentle, self-effacing man who obviously adored his wife and admired her extravagantly.[50] Unfortunately, Mary could not respond to his seeming devotion. Too many years of frustration and pain had hardened her toward him.

Then, in the late summer of 1907, Mary was suddenly dealt a stunning blow. Concerned about the pain in her arm, she consulted a physician. The diagnosis was breast cancer.

Surgery might delay its progress, but the illness would probably be terminal. A second opinion confirmed the prognosis.

Accepting her fate with fortitude, she decided not to undergo an operation but simply to die when her time came.[51] Undoubtedly she sought refuge in the solace and strength she had always found in I-Mary. Evidence that she did so can be found in the play entitled *The Arrow Maker,* on which she had begun work.[52] The plot may be seen as an allegory for her own experience.

The central character is a *chisera,* priestess of the Paiute Indians, who serves her people as an intermediary of the gods. She falls in love with Simwa, the Arrow Maker, and through her powers he triumphs over his enemies. When he rejects her for another woman, she loses the potency of her supernatural gifts. Tragedy strikes the tribe. Then, the *chisera* appeals to the gods, dancing and singing. As the rhythm of her dance accelerates, she builds a bridge to the power of the universe. Her strength returns, and she is restored to at-oneness with the "Friend of the Soul of Man."

> None holdeth my hand but the Friend
> In the silence, in the secret places
> We shall beget great deeds between us!

Like the *chisera,* I-Mary was invulnerable. A woman possessed of such mystical gifts must give herself to their nurturing: the warmth of human love is denied her. Mary's infatuation with Sterling and the lifestyle he represented had led her far from the source of her spiritual strength. Now she would return to the abiding reality that had once been home to her.

Still, she was unwilling to face death in Carmel, nor did she want anyone to know the gravity of her illness. She had heard of places in Rome "where one in great pain could die quietly." In addition, she had a driving need to see more of the world before she had to leave it. The great art of Rome beckoned her almost as much as its promise of peace.[53] Without dwelling upon the grim future that might await her, she resolved to go to Europe as soon as she could get away.

Fortuitously, friends of Mary were abroad at the time. Vernon Kellogg was in Italy, courting Charlotte Hoffman, a teacher who was a great favorite of the Carmel crowd. She and Mary had been very close.[54] Now she urged Mary to come to Florence for Christmas.[55] It was an invitation that fitted perfectly with Mary's plans, but her precarious financial situation was a continuing cause for concern.

Aware that time was running against her, she wrote Houghton Mifflin, suggesting two books which she wanted published before Christmas. One was a volume of children's verse and the other a collection of three Indian tales. When neither idea was accepted and a publication date for *Lost Borders* still had not been set, she became overwrought. The letter she sent them in September was a tirade that covered three pages. In her agitated state of mind, she did not hesitate to stretch the truth.

> ...You are right in surmising that there is another publisher, I might say several others, willing to undertake the poems and *Lost Borders* for the sake of the novel.... Nothing could be worse than the last two years, that is certain, and unless you see a way to better it, it would be useless for us to continue a relation that proves profitable to neither of us....
>
> If before you decide whether you wish to go on with me (with the understanding that you will so manage my work that I shall be able to live by it), you wish to see the first half of my novel [*Santa Lucia*], which is all I can show to you at present, I am willing to send it to you. Best wire if you so wish, for the time grows short....[56]

Houghton Mifflin's reply was polite but unmistakably plain. The manuscript of *Lost Borders* was returned, and the publishing arrangement was terminated.[57]

The end of a relationship which for many years had represented security was deeply disturbing to Mary. Despite her complaints, she was not unaware of her dependence upon the friendly support she had received from her editors. She had not expected them to respond as they had.[58]

Still, she took her rejection in stride. With the hope that either Century or Harper might publish not only *Lost Borders* but *Santa Lucia* as well, she pushed the novel to completion. Then she arranged to spend several days in New York, en route to Europe, and contact both publishing houses. *Century* magazine had accepted two of the stories from *Lost Borders,* and *Harper's Weekly* had purchased eight. There was reason for optimism.

Her attitude was remarkable, considering the fact that she had been given only a short time to live. Possibly she did not fully accept the diagnosis of her physicians, or perhaps it was the resurgent awareness of I-Mary, detached and invulnerable, that provided a sense of ultimate security. Of the doctors' dire predictions she later wrote, "I didn't care whether they were to be believed or not. I was so convinced of going on after it, that I thought to pass through the experience called dying might prove interesting and even advantageous...."[59]

Late in October, Wallace returned. He had found a good job with a potash and chemical company in Death Valley. It is likely that he tried to persuade Mary to come back to him, but it was much too late for a reconciliation. Whether she lived or died, Mary had become her own person. Never again would she subordinate her needs to husband or lover. Nonetheless it was a painful parting. Wallace was deeply hurt, and Mary grieved to see his sadness.[60] Because of his aversion to a divorce, proceedings were postponed. Meanwhile, Mary had the problem of her illness to battle.

On November 2 she left for New York, going by way of Los Angeles, where her brother Jim was now living. She very much wanted to see her little niece at least once again.[61] As the train pulled out of the station, she settled back with a weary sigh. The two years in Carmel had brought her both joy and sorrow. She could not know what lay ahead. Still, whatever happened, it could only be the beginning of yet another great adventure. She faced the future without fear.

10

Sojourn Abroad

THE HERBERT HOOVERS
AND H. G. WELLS

TOWARD THE END OF NOVEMBER, Mary arrived in New York
and checked into a hotel on East 29th Street. She was in
excellent spirits, except for a lingering concern about her
brother. She had found him not in the best of health.[1]
Moreover, parting from her niece had been especially difficult, and she had longed to take the winsome little girl
under her wing. The fact that Jim was engaged to remarry
did not put her mind at ease.[2] Before long, however, a flurry
of exciting activities took over her thoughts.

In a letter to Vernon Kellogg she wrote, "My business
has occupied so much of my time that I have seen very little
of New York but what I have seen is very fascinating." Her
business transactions had been enormously successful.
Though Century had rejected her novel, *Santa Lucia,* because of the unusual views on marriage it expressed, Harper
had pounced at the chance to publish it. According to their
editors, it would place her "in the first rank of American
writers." Even above Edith Wharton! To her delight, they
also had accepted *Lost Borders.* She could scarcely believe her
good fortune. In addition, the managers of both the Belasco
Theater in Los Angeles and the Empire in New York had

called on her to ask if she had a play available for production.[3] She had begun to make a name for herself. Resolutely, she rejected the threat of an untimely death. She was just beginning to live!

Then, on the steamer en route to Genoa, she met Prince Cagiati, a member of the inner circle at the Vatican. The encounter forged the first link in a chain of events that would lead to her deliverance. She never believed that it had occurred merely by chance. To the papal representative she confided her desire to learn about the practices of early Christian prayer, believing instinctively that through them she would find help in overcoming her illness. He graciously offered to introduce her to Cardinal Merry del Val, Vatican secretary of state and confidant of the Pope.[4] It was a thrilling opportunity, and Mary was eager to accept. She arranged to meet the prince in Rome the following spring.

Meanwhile, she felt well, being untroubled by "anything more annoying than a faint insistent pain."[5] This discomfort she would not let interfere with her enjoyment of the Christmas festivities with Vernon Kellogg and Charlotte Hoffman. They were staying at the Villa Orcio in one of the hill towns outside of Florence. Plans were already under way for their wedding in April. Mary decided to remain with them until after the event and then to go on to Rome.[6]

The months in Florence were well spent. She devoted days to studying the art treasures enclosed in renowned galleries and churches, as well as the magnificent sculpture and soaring architecture in the streets of the city. Gradually she became aware that all the great art of Italy stemmed from the same creative source that the Indian medicine man invoked to work cures, see hidden things, and bring desires to pass.[7] "Sitting in the sun by Giotti's tower, the eye beginning to climb its airy intricacies of inlaid and chiselled stone, the slow caressing sense swept outward into whorls and whorls of light," there was no choice but to believe that "there are Supernal Sources that, when by beauty we are removed a little from ourselves, we know and touch."[8] She also realized "how much like prayer is the attempt to get inside art and

Mary Austin (seated) *in the wedding party of Vernon and Charlotte Kellogg near Florence, 1908*

understand it, and how healing is the power of beauty." By prayer she never meant "the practice of petition, but the studied attitude of the spirit in transaction with the creative attitude working from within."[9]

Mary also discovered that she could not call herself a Christian, at least not in the traditional sense.[10] The images she saw of Christ, wan and bleeding, "the deification of pitiableness,"[11] were completely unacceptable to her. She was contemptuous of a Redeemer who offered nothing but resignation. In the book *Christ in Italy,* completed several years later, she wrote,

> ...I saw him, wrapt, mystic, triumphant on the side to Godward, but mazed and fumbling at the exigencies of our common life....And this is why I am not a Christian, for I have counted nothing so much as to live competently among men, pulse with them, love with them, hate, beget, achieve....[12]

> ...For if the certainty of not having conquered life by living, did not draw that bloody sweat, said I to the makers of Christ, you have made too much of his having conquered it by dying. Betrayed was he, and condemned unjustly? But commonly those so used have found it the root of endurance. A nail for his two feet and one in either hand? But did you ever bear a child, or lie shot-torn on a battle field long hours in the sleety rain? What, man! said I to him, hold up your head, if in three days you hope for the resurrection.... Why so much distress at dying unless there dies with you the hope to live life out...to the stretch of all its joyous possibilities, to the reach of its intelligence, to the satisfaction of its appetites, to the fulness of its affections?...[13]

It was Mary's rage to live that fired her reaction to the artists' depictions of Christ. Haunted by the wasted years, she longed for all that she had missed. Moreover, she had never been willing to accept a religious belief that did not provide practical solutions to human problems. At this point, she had not found such help in Christianity. However, the possibility still beckoned in Rome. There she might find cherished secrets of efficacious prayer: perhaps Christ's message had been misunderstood.

Mary's sojourn in Florence provided ample opportunity for pleasurable diversion in addition to the contemplation of art. The Hoffmans had an interesting circle of acquaintances, and before long she had met several stimulating people. Among them was a Polish antique dealer named Voynich, whose wife was a writer, and an American woman physician, Doctor Harris.[14] Often in the evenings she went with Doctor Harris to attend gatherings of the English literary colony at Voynich's shop, where she enjoyed browsing in his collection of rare, old books.[15] It was probably there that she met the celebrated English stage designer, Gordon Craig, with whom she was much impressed.

Then in his mid-thirties, Craig had already earned an enviable reputation for his innovative stage productions. Tall and slender, he was handsome in a subdued, almost feminine way, resembling his mother, Ellen Terry. To Mary he seemed "gentle, modest...and beautiful," though she was scornful of the "young women hanging on his words," calling them "his prairie dogs...leaning on their wrists...their mouths slightly open to receive wisdom."[16] Yet Mary herself found his ideas fascinating. His belief was that the stage designer must also be director and producer, for to create a work of art he must understand the central idea to be celebrated and be in complete control of the means to express it.[17] These concepts spoke to Mary's developing interest in the theater, and she frequently sought him out for lengthy discussions. Then the occasion arose for her to become more intimately acquainted with him.

One day in the Palazzo Vecchio, Mary caught a glimpse of a lithe young woman who moved with stunning grace. Intrigued by the woman's arresting beauty, she followed her out of the palace into the streets as far as the Via Tornabuoni. There she saw her turn into the building where Gordon Craig was staying. Her curiosity aroused, Mary described the woman to Doctor Harris and learned that she was Isadora Duncan. Immediately, Mary engineered an invitation to meet the noted dancer.

Apparently she and Isadora responded to one another at once, because only a few days later, at a second meeting, the dancer freely confided the heartbreak of her love affair with Craig.[18] She had borne him a child, and they were deeply in love, but there were conflicts between their two careers. Now she feared that she was losing him.[19] Mary took it upon herself to intervene on behalf of Isadora, trying to make Craig understand the complexity of a woman who possessed the quality of genius.[20] The extent to which her efforts were appreciated is questionable. Mary stated that several years later, when they met in New York, "Isadora high-hatted me...forgot who I was and what occasions she had of meeting me before."[21]

Soon after the Kelloggs' wedding had taken place, Mary left for Rome. By this time, she was carrying her aching arm in a sling. True to his promise, Prince Cagiati arranged for her to meet Cardinal Merry del Val. The distinguished prelate received Mary cordially. He had heard of her books and was interested in the connection *Isidro* had with the Mission San Carlos. In response to her request for help in learning about early Christian prayer, he was more than generous, even putting his personal library at her disposal.[22] It was the beginning of a profound experience.

Lost in the avid perusal of ancient texts, Mary traced the origins of the mystic way through the centuries, identifying its roots in practices followed by the Greeks and Romans. Almost at once she recognized how much the rites of the early Christian church resembled the approach she had learned from the Paiute Indians. There was the same reliance on ritual, dress, and symbol to break the tension of immediate surroundings. There was the same concept of prayer, not so much as petition but as a gesture of the inner self, linking the individual mind with the power of the universe. It did not matter by what name this power was called. Something always answered.[23]

After Mary had spent several weeks in solitary research, Cardinal Merry del Val asked if she would like to visit the convent of the Blue Nuns. He thought she would benefit from talking with the mother superior, who was a nun far advanced in spiritual sensitivity. The ensuing encounter opened new vistas of perception.

It was Mother Veronica who taught Mary how to escape from pain, not by praying for relief, but by total immersion in the act of prayer itself.[24] There was also a priest, highly adept in the art, who helped her understand the error of emotional involvement.[25] Anxiety about receiving a specific answer to prayer must be especially avoided, as complete detachment was essential to any possibility of success.[26] Enthralled by the progress she was making, Mary arranged a retreat with the Blue Nun sisterhood.[27] By the time it was over, her pain had almost disappeared. Soon after, it was gone.[28]

The realization that she had been cured was an overwhelming reaffirmation of everything she had always believed. Man was not alone and helpless. He was an integral part of the universe and could connect with forces beyond himself, thereby achieving a solution to any problem. Her deliverance from an untimely death also strengthened her concept of I-Mary. Though she would forever insist that she was only the instrument of a power that shaped her destiny, she began to perceive that power and I-Mary to be one and the same.[29] Out of this perception emerged the overbearing egocentricity which characterized her later years. Her mysticism would assume an aspect of manipulation, as its expression increasingly became a means to an end. Some fourteen years later she would write, "I sit here holding my finger on the mysterious forces that always respond to concentrated pressure, and slowly the stream of events turns my way...."[30]

For the present, she was determined to take advantage of all the exciting possibilities life had to offer. Both her ambition for literary success and her appetite for sensual satisfaction were to have free rein. It would be a long time before she returned to the simple joy of being at one with what she had once called "the only true and absolute."[31]

From Italy, Mary moved to Paris. There she met a charming young man, James Wilkinson, who proved a delightful companion. Artist and actor, he was of French descent and well acquainted with the pleasures Paris offered. Though many years her junior, he was her escort at plays, exhibits, and dances. They visited the famed Jardin des Plantes, attended midnight mass at the Church of Saint Etienne-du-Mont, and climbed the 397 steps to the top tier of Notre Dame, where Mary helped Wilkinson rehearse his role in *Macbeth*. There were evenings at the Comédie Française, a performance at the Gaîté Montparnasse, and two dance recitals given by Isadora Duncan.[32] Mary had embarked full sail on her program of living life to the hilt, but there is evidence that there were intervals of melancholy as well.

During a period of illness, when she was confined to her room, she suddenly became homesick for Carmel. In her luggage were notes for the novel *Outland*, on which she had collaborated with Sterling. To while away the time, she began to work on the book.[33] Almost at once the romance of the story took over her mind. Reveling in the beauty of the remembered setting and the happy memories it evoked, she soon completed the manuscript. In the meantime, she had received copies of her two newly published books, *Santa Lucia* and *Lost Borders*. It was time to move on to London and seek out some of the literary luminaries she wanted to meet. She also planned to follow up on her invitation to visit Lou Hoover.

In the summer of 1909 the Hoovers were established in their new home, called Red House, on Hornton Street near Kensington Gardens. It was a roomy, red brick dwelling of the Georgian period. Tall trees shaded the spacious lawns, and a walled-in garden shut out the roar of the London traffic.[34] Mary arrived on a Sunday afternoon, having written ahead that she would be in London. Mrs. Hoover received her with the informal cordiality which was her custom, and Mary felt at home in the relaxed and unpretentious atmosphere. As later developments indicate, she and Herbert Hoover became friends quickly and easily.

Hoover, at thirty-five, had achieved worldwide renown in his profession. As the chief consulting engineer and managing director of some twenty mining companies, his sphere of activity encompassed the far-flung reaches of the Orient, Australia, and the South Pacific.[35] Still, he was unassuming, reserved, even shy. Only his friends were aware of the warm, kindly, often whimsical side of his personality.[36] This was the person whom Mary came to know and admire.

She was to spend a great deal of time with the Hoovers, being their guest on weekends and excursions, as well as at the dinner parties for which Red House became famous. On this initial visit, however, she had to hurry away for another appointment. It was at the home of H. G. Wells. She had sent him a copy of *Lost Borders,* and he had responded with an invitation to tea.[37]

Wells was two years older than Mary. Slight and short, with a large forehead, heavy mustache, and bushy brows, he was far from handsome. Nevertheless, his "limpid blue eyes" had a penetrating power, and he possessed a seductive charm that had given him a reputation for easy conquests of young women of a rebellious temperament. They were captivated by his iconoclastic views.[38] His wife, Jane, had been one of his students when they met in 1892[39] and he was currently embroiled in an affair with another young protégée, Amber Reeves.[40]

It soon became obvious that Mary and Wells had a broad basis for rapport. In her autobiography she recalled, "In the course of an hour or two's conversation...I was saying freely what I yet hadn't any hope of saying to an American man...." Despite areas of disagreement, she recognized him to be "far ahead of us all...in thinking of woman in terms of her worth to society as against her individual value in terms of her emotional relation to one man!"[41]

Wells had read the stories in *Lost Borders* with much interest and was particularly impressed by "The Walking Woman." How Mary must have glowed with pleasure when he said, "We have no woman in England [who] can write like this...no woman in Europe."[42] However, she was discomfited by a remark he made a few minutes later. "I have just advised my wife," he said, "that a friend of mine is about to have a child by me." With considerable embarrassment, Mary noticed that Mrs. Wells "had a bruised look," although the delicate, little woman only said, "Well, we must be kind to her."[43]

Mary learned nothing more that afternoon, because a neighbor, the noted artist William Rothenstein, dropped in to join them at tea. Before she left, however, she had an invitation to dinner for early in the week. Somewhat disconcerted by Wells' outspoken reference to such a highly personal matter, she told the Hoovers what he had said. Mr.

Hoover was outraged. He felt that the man had shown extremely poor taste. Lou Hoover, who already knew about the scandalous affair with Amber Reeves, counseled Mary against seeing Wells again, as her reputation might suffer from the association. Despite this advice, Mary was eager to keep her engagement. Wells had mentioned that his American publisher, Duffield, would be present, and coincidentally she had already initiated dealings with him about publishing her play, *The Arrow Maker*. [44]

The evening proved both entertaining and rewarding. Stunning in yellow satin and amber beads, Mary quickly became the center of attention. [45] She went in to dinner on the arm of "a Labor Secretary" and was seated across the table from the brilliant essayist, Gilbert Chesterton, who recited poetry to amuse her. Mr. Duffield was not only enthusiastic about her play but expressed a lively interest in the book she was writing about her experiences in Italy. [46] Mary's first encounter with London's elite was a complete success. Then, as the party broke up, Wells took her aside and asked that she go walking with him the next day on Hampstead Heath. She agreed. [47]

It was a meeting Mary would long remember. Wells was in an explosive mood and deeply troubled. As they strode away from his house on Church Row to the gorse-covered meadows of the heath, he told her about the emotional crisis he was facing. He was in love with Amber Reeves, a girl half his age. They shared a unique mental intimacy in addition to being lovers. It was the finest thing that had ever happened in their lives. They had gone to great lengths to avoid a scandal. Amber had married an old friend who was aware of her relationship with Wells and willing for it to continue, if they were discreet. Jane also had accepted the arrangement, though Amber's parents, as well as the public at large, were hounding them to get divorces and marry each other, or to break off the affair entirely. Neither alternative was acceptable. [48]

Mary was more sympathetic than censorious. Still, she could not help but be dismayed at the situation. [49] They discussed the problem at great length, and undoubtedly she tended to agree with many of his radical ideas about marriage and sexual freedom. The meeting ended on a friendly note, but Mary's recollections of it, as recorded in her autobiography, were to cause her much trouble some twenty years later.

Meanwhile, it was quite likely that she did not mention the rendezvous to the Hoovers. They continued to be warmly generous in their hospitality, frequently taking her on short trips into the country. It was Herbert Hoover who drove her down to Kent to visit Joseph Conrad. She had sent the writer a copy of *Lost Borders* and had been invited to Capel House. Conrad was more than kind. He praised her work, saying, "I should have supposed this book written by a man, not because it is unfeminine but because I never knew a woman to write so well."[50] When she left, he plucked a rose from his garden for her. She was always to remember him with affection.[51]

Oddly enough, it was also through the Hoovers that Mary received her introduction to the woman's suffrage movement in England. A college classmate of Mrs. Hoover, Anne Martin, was in London at the time, working with Emmeline Pankhurst, and more than once Mr. Hoover had been called upon to bail Miss Martin out of jail after her confrontations with the police in violent demonstrations for women's rights.[52] Anne's ardent feminism appealed to Mary, and they became fast friends. She even participated with her in parades designed to attract attention to the cause, but she did not share Anne's desire for martyrdom. She really preferred accompanying her friend to the Lyceum Club, where she met such notables as Hilaire Belloc, William Butler Yeats, and the highly successful novelist Mrs. Humphrey Ward. Even more exciting were meetings of the Fabian Society, at which she heard the pyrotechnics of George Bernard Shaw and enjoyed her first encounters with Beatrice Webb.[53]

Early in her friendship with Anne, Mary realized that the young woman had ability as a writer as well as a lecturer. Accordingly, she proposed that they find a quiet spot in the

country and work together. They would write in the mornings and then get together to read and discuss their efforts.
Anne agreed, and Mary located living quarters for both of
them in Bromley, a small town in Surrey. The arrangement
was a dismal failure.

Two strong personalities met head on. Anne thought
the rooms Mary had taken were shabby and comfortless. She
also found the food inedible and the odor from a nearby
tannery objectionable. Mary declared that she had no right to
complain. She should develop character by learning to disre-
gard living conditions.

Though Anne was a fearless suffragette and later would
be the first woman to run for the United States Senate, she
was unable to stand up to the force of Mary's personality. In
desperation, she wired one of her English friends, Lady
Hesketh, appealing for an immediate invitation to visit her.
Anne was never to forget the sense of relief she felt "when
she took her departure on the train and realized that she was
free from Mary." Still, their friendship continued for many
years, leading to a close collaboration in the American suffrage campaign. Moreover, no more glowing tribute would
be given Mary than the one by Anne Martin, which appeared
in *The Nation* after Mary's death.

> Her feminism was active and creative. But even if
> she had never opened her lips for the cause her
> achievement as a naturalist and anthropologist, as an
> original and intuitive explorer into the depths of the
> subconscious...as interpreter of the Indian, of the land,
> of man in his environment, as a profound and versatile
> woman of letters undoubtedly places her in the first
> rank not as a woman but as a human being.
>
> Her life and work like that of Jane Addams and
> Madame Curie and countless lesser women who are
> going forth into the unknown and are holding their own
> in fields formerly monopolized by men, validate the
> rights of women the world over.[54]

In 1909 Mary was just beginning the long climb to worldly achievement. It was *The Arrow Maker* that provided her initial entrée to the literary arena of New York. She had the good fortune to meet the American producer, William Archer, who was in London, and he became sufficiently interested in the play to go over it with her in detail. Then he took her to see the distinguished literary critic Edmund Gosse.[55]

At an informal gathering in Gosse's home the conversation centered on the need for new verse forms in modern poetic drama. When Gosse remarked that perhaps the new medium should come out of America, Mary responded by citing examples from Indian ritual drama which she felt were germane to the discussion. She even quoted several Paiute songs to illustrate the rhythm they employed.[56] Apparently she made a lasting impression, especially on Archer, for the following summer he cabled her to return to New York. He had arranged for her to produce *The Arrow Maker* at the National Theater, under the aegis of Winthrop Ames and George Foster Platt.[57]

The woman who sailed for New York was a very different Mary Austin from the one who had arrived in Europe three years before. An insight into the complex and commanding personality she had become can be gained from a letter Jimmy Hopper wrote to George Sterling, after Hopper saw Mary in London. Even allowing for his characteristically acerbic wit, it is still a telling commentary. He reported that "she looked fat and rubbery and well-kept." She alluded to portentous happenings about which she was most mysterious and implied that she was involved in "a tempestuous romance." To sum it up, he said that she had given him the impression she was "carrying on illicit relations with the Prime Minister of Great Britain," or "had raped a cardinal," or "was in love with and loved by a dashing young matinee idol of the theatre." In a more sympathetic vein he added, "I love Mary, but wish she'd stop piling up all that card-board scenery in front of her face."[58]

11

An Evanescent Affair

LINCOLN STEFFENS

THERE IS AN APOCRYPHAL STORY to the effect that Lincoln Steffens "ran away to Mexico" in order to escape Mary Austin's advances.[1] The evidence from a number of sources supports a somewhat different scenario. Within a matter of months after Mary's arrival in New York, she had begun a diary "at the instance of my friend Lincoln Steffens to prove to him that I cannot write a book about the city as interesting as the Land of Little Rain."[2] In the journal's opening entry she referred to him as "Steffy" and indicated that he had taken more than a casual interest in her.

Corroboration of a blossoming friendship is given by Steffens himself. In a letter to his sister Laura he wrote, "I've been seeing Mary Austin....She is an odd but interesting woman."[3] Also, in an article published in 1911 he lavished praise on her prose, describing it as "the poetry of life, of life lived today; conscious, beautiful poetry."[4] At the beginning of the relationship, at least, it seems that he was as much attracted to her as she was to him. To understand the progression of the affair, it is important to consider the temperament of each of the principals involved, as well as the psychological moment at which they rediscovered each other.

[153]

They had probably first met in Carmel, where Steffens visited briefly in 1907,[5] but this meeting could not have been more than a casual encounter. The circumstances that brought them together in New York are obscure; however, they did move in some of the same circles and undoubtedly had mutual acquaintances.

Mary was living in a furnished apartment on Riverside Drive, not far from Charlotte Perkins Stetson, a friend whom she had known years before at the Lummis house in Los Angeles. Charlotte, now married to the attorney George Gilman, was still an ardent feminist and had recently founded a monthly magazine of social reform—the *Forerunner*. The two women saw a great deal of each other, and before long Charlotte had introduced Mary to Emma Goldman,[6] editor of the anarchist magazine *Mother Earth* and fiery exponent of women's rights.[7] Steffens, who at forty-four was the nation's foremost muckraker and advocate of civic reform, participated in causes that also involved Miss Goldman. Such activities could have brought him and Mary together. Moreover, he was on the editorial board of *Everybody's* magazine,[8] and Mary would have lost little time in making the rounds of the city's leading periodicals.

At the time Steffens became interested in Mary, he was deeply despondent over the critical illness of his wife, Josephine. After nineteen years of marriage, he had come to depend upon her in more ways than he realized. She had been not only an unfailing source of intellectual strength, but his conscience as well. Now she lay dying of Bright's disease.[9]

On December 25, 1910, in a letter to his sister Laura, he said, "...my heart is breaking....I don't know how much of me there will be left after it is all over...."[10] When death came on January 7, he wrote, "The end knocked me out." A month later he found that his grief had only deepened and grown.[11] This was the period when his involvement with Mary began.

It is very likely that Steffens was drawn to Mary for some of the same reasons that had initially attracted him to

Josephine. Both were forceful, independent women. Before his marriage, Steffens had described Josephine to his mother as being "strong in character as a man...my equal in all respects....I find it a never-ending delight to find this strong, gentle woman near me, urging me on by her example and taking and giving help and advice."[12] In addition to sharing an intellectual prowess, the two women resembled each other in personality and physique. Josephine was "a resolute, heavy-set woman with a strong chin, a probing look, and outspoken opinions."[13] Steffens apparently had a taste for large, self-assertive women, especially if they demonstrated an unstinting devotion to his own interests.

From boyhood, Steffens had been spoiled by an overly indulgent mother and three adoring younger sisters. Always "he received more love than he gave."[14] As a college student, he was briefly engaged to a Berkeley girl, Etta Augusta Burgess, whom he called Gussie. Though "he thrived on her love...using her to feed his vanities,"[15] he did not hesitate to terminate the relationship when it no longer met his needs.[16] The marriage to Josephine, which had begun so auspiciously, soon deteriorated because of his neglect. Only after her death did he realize how little thought he had given her during their years together.[17] Now, bitterly remorseful, he welcomed the therapy of talking to a sympathetic listener about his feelings.

To Mary he confided the hollowness of his marriage "and how it had trailed off into nothingness and invalidism."[18] Undoubtedly the pathos in his life evoked a responsive chord as she perceived parallels to her own experience. Besides, Steffens was capable of great charm.

Mary had long cherished the hope of finding a man who could command her unqualified admiration. In the autobiographical short story "Frustrate" she wrote, "I thought if I could get to know a man who was big enough so I couldn't walk around him...somebody that I could reach and reach and not find the end of,—I shouldn't feel so ...frustrated. There was a man there who...made you feel like that,—as if you could take hands with him and go out and rescue shipwrecked men and head rebellions." It was an apt description of Lincoln Steffens. When he "turned the light of his personality upon her,"[19] she fell under his spell.

Journalist, editor, and author of sensational exposés of municipal corruption, Steffens "undeniably had power. He was a public figure whose arrivals and departures were noted in the local press, a name to be invoked in the furtherance of good causes," and "a force in politics."[20] He also had an arresting appearance. Though short and delicately built, his fastidious dress, bristling mustache, and closely trimmed beard gave him a distinguished air. Behind steel-rimmed spectacles, his direct blue gaze sparkled engagingly; he possessed a disarming smile, and his mellow voice was mesmerizing.[21]

Small wonder that Mary was captivated. Steffens also was intrigued. There was an aura about Mary that quickened his curiosity. She had mastered the desert, internalized it, and out of its bones and tissue had created a prose that was poetry. He had read her books with enthusiasm. Now he wanted to probe the secrets of the woman.

During the early winter months of 1911 their relationship deepened. According to one source, Steffens even entertained the idea of marriage, before "his ardor cooled."[22] Mary may well have assumed his intentions to be more serious than they were. It was to please him that she began an organized attempt to become familiar with New York. Ruefully she wrote, "Steffy is saturated with the city...and he can't understand that it will take me more years to learn my way about in it than were necessary to know the trails from Mojave to Lone Pine. And he does not know how slow I am...."[23]

Nevertheless, she was simultaneously caught up in a whirl of activity that centered on her own interests. Production of her play *The Arrow Maker*, in February,[24] proved a grueling ordeal. She had been forced to rewrite large sections of it and was disappointed in the final result. Exhausted

Lincoln Steffens,
the "gentle, little, steel man"

by weeks of bickering, she vowed she wanted nothing more to do with plays.[25] To bring in some quick cash, she wrote several short stories and a couple of articles. One of the latter was "An Appreciation of H. G. Wells," published in the *American Magazine.*[26]

Meanwhile, she had become involved in both the suffrage and labor movements. Among her new friends was the iconoclastic little schoolteacher Henrietta Rodman. Notorious as "a firebrand of extreme dimensions," Miss Rodman was an advocate of free love, women's suffrage, birth control, the right of workers to strike, and even nudism.[27] Mary was quite taken with her, though she described her as living "on the lunatic fringe."[28]

Other women with whom Mary became closely associated were Margaret Sanger, the advocate of birth control and of sex for the sake of enjoyment; Ida Tarbell, esteemed journalist; and the labor leader Elizabeth Gurley Flynn. New York's Greenwich Village was seething with new ideas and emotions, and for a time Mary found the intellectual ferment exciting. She even joined her old friend Anne Martin on several speaking tours. Before long, though, she found the arguments for women's suffrage repetitious and boring.[29] Moreover, the demands of her writing left little energy for other activities.

In addition to completing her Italian book, *Christ in Italy,* she had begun an autobiographical novel. Mornings she was hard at work at her desk, while in the afternoons she doggedly continued her explorations of the city. By evening she was too weary to do more than briefly note her impressions. Frequently she wondered if the effort was worthwhile.[30]

Then, as March slipped into April, Mary's thoughts turned wistfully to California. Jottings in her journal reflected her yearning for home. The "only sign of spring," she noted, "is in florists' and milliners' windows." Seeing a single blackbird, "overhead on a bough, as I walked in the crowded street," was rare enough to record. Just before Easter she made a particularly poignant entry—"boys selling bunches of trailing arbutus on street corners...also great numbers of people going about with potted plants under their arms. Wanted one but couldn't afford the price."[31] To a friend, she confided, "Every letter from California increases my distaste for New York and for cities," but "on the whole, New York has been very good to me...don't feel that I ought to leave."[32]

Letters from George Sterling intensified her nostalgia. He wrote of Carmel's beauty and urged her to come West.[33] To make matters more difficult, Steffens was in California at the time on a trip to visit his sisters.

There is no doubt that she missed him. His reply to a letter she wrote him (apparently not preserved) was revealing of both his feeling and hers. Concerned that he might still be depressed, she had sent him a little book by Brother Lawrence, the noted seventeenth-century French mystic, hoping that it would bring him comfort. He responded from Sacramento early in May.

> You are wrong about me and the sorrow. I do not want to nourish it. I felt the temptation to do so. There was, there is a pull off in that direction. But I didn't want it so, and I don't. No, we shall never talk of that....
>
> There is one passage in your letter which I wish very explicitly to answer or, rather, to respond to. It is that about writing to somebody. I know what that need is. I used to have it. I haven't it now; I don't like to write letters.... But I have left a deep sympathy for the feeling you express, and I wish you to know that I shall read all that you care to write, especially in that mood, with more understanding than may appear. For I think I understand. I certainly want to understand. I'd rather a thousand times understand than be understood.... But I must say to you sincerely, and earnestly, that if you wish to put yourself down on paper you may do so with me and be sure, oh, absolutely sure, that you will be read as I would be read—with the wish only to understand.
>
> And I do not show letters, of course; nor do I keep those that should not be kept. Letters are a place for half-thoughts.[34]

Mary had come out of her protective shell with Steffens, exposing her deep-seated vulnerability. Oblivious to the possibility of being hurt, she trusted him and allowed herself to care for him deeply. The consequences were tragic.

In June, after Steffens had returned, she heard about a double apartment available for rent. Thinking it would be ideal for the two of them, she told him about it. That he did not comprehend the gist of her meaning soon became clear. By disastrous coincidence, when she went to look at the flat, she encountered Steffens there, considering the apartment with another woman.[35] Stunned, she recorded the experience in her journal as "a terrible incident, one that promises to bear bitter fruit in my own life."[36] Apparently she had no inkling that Steffens had already slipped away from her.

Sometime that spring he had renewed his relationship with the fiancée of his youth, Gussie. Though they had not seen each other since 1889, a chance meeting brought them together, and the original attraction was rekindled. In the interim she had married, albeit unhappily, and was separated from her husband—"an invalid, who refused to give her a divorce." Now she and Steffens "took up again where they had left off."[37]

For her part, Gussie had never stopped loving Steffens. He, in turn, suddenly found himself overwhelmed with feeling for her. To his sister Laura he wrote, "I know abler, handsomer women, with whom I can talk to greater heights and depths; just the sort of women I'd have thought I'd prefer. But I don't....I think I could tell what it is in G. that so attracts me, but I doubt if you'd see it...."[38]

Very likely the attraction stemmed from the fact that Gussie was willing to defer to Steffens, represented no competition in his milieu, and exhibited the kind of devotion that he craved. Mary, on the other hand, would not subordinate her interests to his. No relationship could take precedence over her work. She herself admitted there was never any possibility "of giving away her gift to brother, husband, or lover."[39]

Still, she was furious at being rejected. She felt that Steffens had been toying with her affections. She would never forgive him, nor would she let him be the one to terminate their relationship. That was her prerogative. Furthermore, she would find a way to get even.[40]

Meanwhile, only her work provided a palliative for her wounded pride. All the heartache she had experienced, both in her marriage and in the evanescent affair with Steffens, was reflected in the autobiographical novel *A Woman of Genius*. The title itself was a clue to her self-image and why she perceived herself to be deprived of emotional fulfillment. In it she wrote,

> ...I grew barren of manner and was reputed to be entirely absorbed in my profession....All the forces of my

being had been by the shock of loss, dropped into some
subterranean pit, where they ran underground and wa-
tered the choicest product of my art.... The loss of him,
the desperate ache, the start of memory, are just as good
materials to build an artistic success upon as the joy of
having. And I did build. I gathered up and wrought into
the structure of my life the pain of loving as well as its
delight.... Whatever else has happened to me, I am at
least a success.[41]

At this point she was indeed enjoying the sweet taste of success. Under contract to Doubleday, Page and Company, she
had established a most gratifying relationship with her
editor, Harry Peyton Steger. In addition to accepting *A
Woman of Genius* with much enthusiasm, he was eagerly await-
ing another novel she had already begun, entitled *The Lovely
Lady*. Warmly admiring of her work, he urged her to discuss
plans for additional books and was even negotiating to secure
the copyrights to all her previous publications. Financial arrangements had been equally satisfactory. She had been
given a $2000 advance, and her contract specified a gradu-
ated scale of royalties up to 20 percent.[42] She had made
great strides in her career. Despite the exhilaration of
achievement, however, she felt weary and depleted.

Letters from Sterling continued to stir up longings for
Carmel. Affectionate, ebullient, filled with praise, they drew
her like a magnet. His words conjured images of a place still
dear to her heart. Moreover, he offered the added incentive
of participation in activities of the newly founded Forest
Theater.[43] By the end of 1912 she had reached a possible
stopping place in her work. Both *Christ in Italy* and *A Woman
of Genius* had been published, and she had completed *The
Lovely Lady*. The need to get away from New York rose like a
fever in her blood and in December she left for California.

En route to Carmel she spent several weeks with her
brother Jim in Los Angeles. Her niece, Mary Hunter, was
now a lovely, dark-haired girl of eight. She showed indications of being exceptionally gifted, and Mary was concerned
that her education be in keeping with her potential. Jim was

not in robust health, and the attitude of his wife, Georgia, did
not inspire confidence. Still, there was nothing Mary could
do except give advice, which was hardly welcome.[44]

Before leaving the area, she renewed a few old associations. Her visit to El Alisal was clouded by sadness. The
Lummises had been divorced,[45] and, despite a hearty welcome from Charles,[46] Mary missed the loving presence of
Eve. There were also distressing memories of Ruth and
Amado. In addition, she was already depressed by news from
Doubleday about the sudden death of Harry Steger.[47] Eagerly she moved on to the one place that promised a respite
from care.

Carmel was even more beautiful than she had remembered it. Though it had grown a bit in the years she had been
away, its tranquil charm was unspoiled. The property she
had purchased stood secluded under noble pines and
century-old oaks. Wild shrubbery covered the ground in a
tangle of manzanita, lilac, and chamise. To the south a shallow canyon opened to a glimpse of the sea.[48] It was a place
where she could have privacy and peace, yet be close to
people who were cherished friends. She decided to have a
small cottage constructed at once.[49] If her fortunes increased, it could be the nucleus of a more commodious
house.

Both George and Carrie Sterling greeted Mary with an
affection that made her feel instantly at home. However,
George had aged, his tousled hair was now streaked with
grey, and he was drinking heavily.[50] Disheartened because
his work was going badly, he frittered away his time, hunting
and fishing, or dabbling in short-story writing, for which he
had no talent.[51] His philandering had caused scandalous re-
percussions, and for a time Carrie had left him.[52] When she
consented to a trial reconciliation, a vestige of brightness
came back into his life, and, with the stimulus of Mary's return, he almost regained his old joie de vivre.[53]

She had sent him a copy of *Outland*, their joint venture
into fantasy fiction, and he revelled in its beauty, reading it

*Mary Austin's house in Carmel, where the simplicity of life
provided a welcome contrast to the bustle of New York*

aloud as he walked about the woods. Mary herself said of it,
"It was more engaging than anything I had ever written."[54]
She and Sterling spent a great deal of time together. Because
his feelings for Mary were purely platonic, he felt completely
at ease in their relationship. He teased her, play-acted amorous behavior, and pretended the tender verses he wrote were
intended for her. At the same time, he talked frankly of his
affairs with other women. Mary understood that his in-
amoratas were merely the fuel he needed to fire his creativity. Still, she was concerned lest they break up his marriage,
with tragic consequences for him as well as Carrie.[55]

By May, Mary had settled in her new home and was at
work on another Indian play. The drama, entitled *Fire*, centered on a tribal legend of how the secret of fire had been
discovered. Giving it a wild mountain setting and providing
several sensational effects, she built a stirring story told in
rhythmic verse. Now an active member of the Western

Drama Society, producing arm of the Forest Theater, she had no difficulty arranging to have the play put on that summer.

The society included many old friends—the Kelloggs as well as Jimmy Hopper and Sterling. Everyone had a wonderful time working together to make the production a stunning success. Sterling and Charlotte Kellogg took leading roles, and Mary acted as producer. In the women's chorus was a lovely girl in her late teens, Alice MacDougal, a student at Stanford University. It was her father, Daniel Trembly MacDougal, who ultimately would open a whole new world to Mary and become her most intimate friend.

Doctor MacDougal, a distinguished scientist, was associated with the Carnegie Institution of Washington's Department of Botanical Research, as head of its field laboratories at both Tucson, Arizona, and Carmel. Mary was instantly attracted to the charming Scotsman, dynamic and virile, with a subtle sense of humor and a brilliant intellect. Moreover, her longstanding interest in botany brought them into immediate rapport. A friendship quickly flowered, and when MacDougal left for his home in Tucson, they agreed to keep in touch. Meanwhile, she had seen little of Mrs. Mac-Dougal, an artistically talented but self-effacing person who rarely appeared in public.[56]

Mary stayed in Carmel until almost the end of the year. By that time, her eccentric behavior had become legendary. Many of "the newcomers among the Carmelites were inclined to laugh...at her waving her arms in the woods as she talked about a grand passion."[57] Even Sterling tired of seeing her with her hair hanging down to her waist. "Once he took off her shoes and said if she wanted to undress she might as well go the whole way."[58] Tall tales sprang up about her, including the apocryphal story of Mary "in long white gown, leading the villagers on a white horse four blocks to put out a fire."[59] Still, in her own way, she had "a kind of majesty," as famed photographer Arnold Genthe put it. "Her little idiosyncrasies did not prevent her from being a real person and a true genius." Behind the "forbidding surface, there were warmth, loyalty, and a genuine humor."[60]

Carmel had a strong hold on Mary, and she was reluctant to leave it. The simplicity of life in the little seacoast village had been a balm to her nerves. Of it she later wrote, "There was beauty and strangeness to the life at Carmel; beauty of a Greek quality, but not too Greek; 'green fires and billows tremulous with light'; not wanting the indispensable touch of grief...."[61]

It had been an idyllic interlude, but she knew that only in New York could she maintain the connections essential to her career. Sales of her most recently published books had been disappointing,[62] and the felicitous relationship with Doubleday had come to an abrupt end. She must establish new contacts and produce marketable material, or the source of her income would dry up. Early in November she returned to the city, but with the resolve that henceforth Carmel would be her real home.

12

The Dazzle of New York
"THE WORLD IS YOUNGER EVERY WAY"

MARY FOUND A CONVENIENT PIED-À-TERRE at the National
Arts Club on Gramercy Park and Nineteenth Street. The
beautifully decorated main building, formerly the home of
New York Governor Samuel Tilden, provided an elegant
setting in which to relax and entertain. Fabulous fireplaces,
Italian wood carving, and priceless stained glass gave it a rich
ambience. Best of all was the comfort and privacy of her
studio in the adjoining thirteen-story structure that had been
erected as lodging for members of the club.

She had scarcely settled in her new surroundings when
she discovered that Steffens was staying practically next door
at the Players Club. Still determined that their relationship
must continue until she herself terminated it, she sent him a
note. He replied that he was ready to call whenever she was
ready to receive him.[1] It was during this period that some of
Steffens' friends claimed they had to protect him from
Mary's relentless pursuit. Nothing could have been more ab-
surd. Steffens, "the gentle, little, steel man," always "very
kind and amused and patient,"[2] could more than take care
of himself.

True, he and Mary were often seen in the same circles. It was undoubtedly Steffens who introduced her to Mabel Dodge's celebrated salons at Number Twenty-three Fifth Avenue. He would have enjoyed bringing these two extra-ordinary women together.

On the surface it might seem that Mary would have found little in common with the rich young matron, Mrs. Dodge. Self-indulgent, spoiled, and somewhat shallow, Mabel was not noted for being either witty or well-informed. From their first encounter, however, Mary felt the subtle force of mystery and hidden fire that smoldered beneath the cool exterior of the woman's personality. Moreover, her story held a tinge of tragedy that could not help but capture Mary's imagination.

Born into an affluent setting with every advantage, Mabel had been widowed in her early twenties. Seeking to forget her grief, she had gone abroad with her three-year-old son. En route she met a wealthy architect, Edwin Dodge, and they were married in Paris. But marriage did not satisfy the seething inner drive that compelled her to seek ever-new avenues of expression. Purchasing a fifteenth-century villa outside of Florence, she focused her fiery emotions on trans-forming the Villa Curonia into a stunning showplace. For ten years it was a favorite rendezvous for the international set. Then the diversions of her pleasure palace began to pall, and she decided to return to the United States.[3]

The decoration of her apartment at 23 Fifth Avenue provided a temporary escape from ennui. She transformed the upper floor of an old brownstone into an opulent world of white. Gleaming white walls and woodwork formed a backdrop for the antique chairs and chaise lounges up-holstered in light gray-blues and pale yellows. A white bearskin rug lay in front of the white marble fireplace. White linen draperies curtained the tall windows. From the center of the living room ceiling hung an elaborately ornamented, white Venetian chandelier.[4] It was an appropriate setting for Mabel's "elusive but compelling personality," described as a combination of "Récamier, waif, Venus's fly-trap, and even sorceress."[5] Once the work was completed, though, she again became bored and restless.

The idea of having "Evenings," as she called them, originated with her friend Hutchins Hapgood, but it was Lincoln Steffens who suggested the organized form which made them famous. He told her that she had a talent for attracting and stimulating people. In her presence they felt enhanced. She should do something with her gift. Naturally, she was delighted. In the role of a catalyst for the creative process in others she would have an outlet for her pent-up energies, and so the weekly salons came into being.

An amazing variety of people attended them. They included socialists, journalists, trade unionists, anarchists, artists, clubwomen, suffragists, poets, psychoanalysts, and even an occasional murderer. Mabel received them in a flowing white dress, with a shawl of some vivid hue draped around her shoulders. Although not conspicuously beautiful, she had the grace of a Greek statue. Aloofly she extended her hand to each guest, smiling very briefly. For her, it was a wonderful new game.

There was an evening especially arranged for "dangerous characters." Among the participants were Big Bill Haywood, leader of the IWWs; Emma Goldman, with her lover Sasha Berkman, convicted slayer of millionaire Henry Frick; as well as the notorious anarchist Hippolyte Havel. Also present were Ida Rauh, Elizabeth Gurley Flynn, Max Eastman, John Collier, and Walter Lippmann.[6] Of course, Steffens was there, and so was Mary Austin, regal in prairie-colored satin.[7]

It was a memorable evening, although Haywood and Goldman were not in good form. As the radical side fumbled, Hippolyte's high, peevish voice rang out—"You talk like goddam bourgeois!" The next morning, Mary read newspaper headlines that gleefully proclaimed, "IWW Folk Are Guests Of Society Folk On Fifth Avenue."[8]

Courtesy of The Huntington Library, San Marino, California

Mary Austin between 1910 and 1914,
photographed in a New York studio

It was on occasions such as this that Mary first came to
know Mabel. They soon became close friends. There was
much in the younger woman's complex personality to which
Mary could respond. Undoubtedly Mabel's inclination towards mysticism was a factor. She had a penchant for the
occult, cultivating psychic phenomena and experiencing a
supernatural power which she termed "It." Besides, she
was an excellent listener[9] who enjoyed drawing people to
her and "flowing out" to them.[10] Before long, Mary found
herself confiding the anger and hurt she had suffered in
her affair with Steffens.[11] It was comforting to have a sympathetic ear. In addition, being with Mabel was always
a welcome diversion.

In the spring of 1914 Mary had undertaken a grueling workload. She was writing a series of articles for *Harper's Weekly*, delineating her iconoclastic ideas about love, marriage, and divorce. These were to be incorporated in a book entitled *Love and the Soul Maker*,[12] scheduled for fall publication by D. Appleton and Company. At the same time she was under contract to a British publisher, A. and C. Black, to produce a book of descriptive essays about California, also to be published in the autumn.[13] Though written under pressure, *California, the Land of the Sun* included some of Mary's most lyrical prose. Joyous passages reflected her love of the land and a sensitive appreciation of its ecology. For the book she was paid in a lump sum, which provided money to finance a summer sojourn in Carmel.

She had received a letter from Doctor MacDougal, now a trustee of the Forest Theater, with an offer to produce *The Arrow Maker* in July strictly according to her specifications. She was to have undisturbed use of the theater for rehearsals and a three-week run of performances. "It will be a great pleasure," he wrote, "to be useful in any phase of the matter."[14] Delighted that at last the play was to be put on properly, Mary accepted.

The first week in June she was back in her cottage, finding that the heavy winter rains and the incursion of a neighbor's cows had caused much damage to her garden.[15] The therapy of caring for her plants and taking long walks on the beach and in the surrounding woods soon restored her depleted energy. Eagerly she plunged into a vigorous round of rehearsals for the play.

The Sterlings had departed permanently from Carmel. Unable to tolerate George's philandering, Carrie had obtained a divorce. She was living in San Francisco, and he had gone to New York in search of greener pastures.[16] The mercurial Jimmy Hopper now occupied the Sterling bungalow and had become aggressively active in affairs of the Forest Theater. He did his best to challenge Mary's control of *The Arrow Maker,* but she had her way with the production. The results were impressive, and sufficient revenue was garnered to establish a fund for future projects of the Western Drama Society.[17]

Mary had little chance to rest on her laurels. Before leaving New York, she had approached Harper, her former publisher, about two books which had long been at the back of her mind. One was a novel based on her experiences in the San Joaquin and Owens valleys, and the other was a biographical study of Christ, stemming from her studies at the Vatican. She had barely begun the novel when she received a letter from Harper, inquiring about her progress on it.[18] In addition, she had been asked to handle East Coast publicity for the forthcoming San Francisco Panama-Pacific Exposition.[19] It was time to get back into harness. However, an event of great personal importance delayed her departure.

The summons to appear before the state superior court in San Bernardino, California, came late in October. Wallace had instituted proceedings for divorce.[20] He charged willful desertion and abandonment without cause, beginning during October 1907 and continuing until the present. At last, he had consented to free her.

It was what she had wanted. Still, she had mixed feelings. Some sixteen years later she would write in her autobiography, "We remained friends, but we were neither of us very happy; I am stricken still to recall the impulses which held us together and the lack of coordination which drove us apart."[21]

A property settlement was agreed upon, giving Mary the real estate she herself had purchased, exclusive title to all proceeds from her writings, and the right to one hundred shares of stock in the American Trona Corporation, Wallace's employer. Wallace retained all other properties. A life insurance policy for $2000, in which Mary had been named beneficiary, was reassigned to their daughter, Ruth.[22]

Reminiscing about her matrimonial experience, Mary later wrote, "On the whole, what I regret is not the lack of a satisfying marriage, but the loss out of my life of the traditional protection, the certification of ladyhood.... The experience of being competent to myself has been immensely worth while to me. It gives clarity and poise. But without the experience of being taken care of.... I feel always a little at a loss."[23]

Returning to New York, Mary resolutely went about the business of taking care of herself. For a brief time her mind was occupied by activities connected with the European war, which had begun the prior summer and threatened to engulf half the world. A prime concern was food conservation, and she became involved in setting up community kitchens where leftover produce could be canned instead of discarded.[24] Then Harper offered her a contract for a Life of Christ, with the stipulation that it be delivered by early spring,[25] and all of her efforts had to be diverted to the book.

It would have been an impossible undertaking if she had not already completed her research and developed a detailed outline.[26] Convinced that the incandescent personality of Jesus had been lost in a maze of ritual and theology, her objective was a portrayal of him as he had actually lived. The work proved exhausting. Sometimes she became so engrossed in the emotional content of her material that she ran out into the night, "her hair loose, her expression one of tortured pain, crying the words Jesus uttered in his passion of suffering."[27] Yet in little more than two months she had finished the manuscript of *The Man Jesus.*[28]

There was considerable criticism of Mary's treatment of the subject, and the book was not well received. There were also those who sought to reassure her. Jack London wrote, "...the majority of people who inhabit the planet Earth are bone-heads.... I never bother my head when my own books miss fire.... Just be content with being called the 'greatest American stylist'.... The world feeds you, the world feeds me, but the world knows damn little of either of us."[29]

Despite such comforting words, Mary was disheartened. She was only too aware that her financial situation was worsening. Most of her earlier books were out of print, and the magazine market had tightened. In an attempt to replenish her funds, she decided to reopen negotiations with Houghton Mifflin.[30]

Eight years had elapsed since her relations with the firm had been severed, and she still felt that they had treated her shabbily. Nevertheless, if she could interest them in another volume of Indian tales like *The Basket Woman,* it would be something she could produce quickly and for which she had ample material. In the meantime she might persuade them to reissue *The Arrow Maker.*

After a cautious correspondence Houghton Mifflin agreed to bring out an inexpensive edition of the play and expressed enthusiasm for a book centering on the Hopi or Pueblo Indians.[31] Their response was gratifying, but suddently Mary's spirit rebelled against the stifling regime that kept her chained to her desk. She felt the need to broaden her experience, to sample the city's life at many levels, if she was to write the kind of fiction to which she aspired. New York was a laboratory where she could learn about the human condition through direct participation.

Disguising her identity, she rented rooms in the poorer sections of the city and took odd jobs. She worked as a typist and in a factory that manufactured artificial flowers. For a while she peddled shoelaces and pencils, then took employment in a shop that specialized in wigs for mannequins. Seeking to be on familiar terms with her associates, she encouraged the attentions of a railroad engineer and almost became engaged to a cement worker from Chicago. To escape the latter entanglement, she fabricated a newspaper job with an out-of-town assignment.[32]

Shortly thereafter, she did in truth leave for Carmel.[33] En route she stopped in San Francisco to report excellent progress in her publicity campaign for the Panama-Pacific Exposition.[34] While there, she also supervised a highly successful production of her play *Fire*[35] and undoubtedly saw MacDougal, who was on several committees relating to scientific exhibits at the exposition.[36] Then, following a respite in

her seacoast haven, she was back in New York, still ambiva-
lent about the most profitable direction to pursue in her
work.

In a diffuse letter to Houghton Mifflin she confided her
confusion and ventilated some of her old grievances. To test
the security of any future relationship, she asked if they
would be willing to reissue *A Woman of Genius* and *The Lovely
Lady,* both of which were out of print. With complete candor
she also articulated her uncertainty about whether her future
work would be remunerative.

> ...I must frankly say that I can't speak with much
> security. I shall go on producing a book or a play every
> year and certainly I am willing you should pick the win-
> ner if you think you can.
> I shall give most of my time to fiction and drama,
> and there is no question in my mind that I am to succeed
> with drama on a very high level. As to fiction, I am artist
> enough to know that the only good fiction is pure crea-
> tion, and that problems except as they are eternal prob-
> lems of living, have no place in it, but I do not know if I
> am artist enough to resist the pressure of current
> thought....
> ...the truth is that my personal devil is the desire
> to be 'in' things and it was actually more fun to worry an
> International Exposition into letting me try an unprece-
> dented experiment than it was to write the play by which
> it was tried. You must draw what conclusions you can
> from my being able to do both.[37]

When she received an encouraging reply, her response was
infused with a characteristic combination of insecurity and
braggadocio.

> Pleased to find you still interested in my work, but once
> for all let us agree that the chances of your making
> money out of it are small.
> I don't know why because I get quite smashing
> reviews and there is not an English critic and few Eng-

lish writers who have not agreed in print that my work is easily the most distinguished in America. Add to that that I am one of the...most interviewed women in America, and say if you can why I am one of the poorest paid....[38]

A brisk correspondence ensued in which editor Ferris Greenslet tactfully tried to determine precisely what Mary was prepared to produce. She remained evasive, partly because she was bargaining for the reissue of her earlier books, but also in an effort to obtain an affirmation of faith in her work. She knew she was playing a tricky game, and she was enjoying it. Finally a meeting with Mr. Greenslet was arranged. It was a fiasco.

A few days later, she received a letter summarizing the results of the encounter. He had decided against purchasing the plates for *The Lovely Lady* and *A Woman of Genius.* Bluntly he stated his reasons.

> ...Apparently the chief end to be gained would be the privilege of standing over you with a lash, as you phrase it, to persuade you to finish a novel from which you might or might not be diverted to write a play, conduct a propaganda or what not. If there were a new book actually at hand, finished and ready for the press, the situation would be of a different quality, but as it is with so many important affairs pulling you in so many different ways we hesitate to assume the responsibility.[39]

Mary was disappointed but not overly upset. Anticipating Greenslet's decision, she had already purchased the plates herself and stashed them away.[40] When the novel she had in progress was completed, she would resume her campaign. Meanwhile, a great diversity of activities claimed her attention.

She was working on a children's play, to be entitled "The Man Who Didn't Believe in Christmas," and she had become involved in the little theater movement.[41] Some young people who called themselves the Washington Square Players[42] and had invited her to join. In addition, she was the center of a stimulating round of social events.

When the Herbert Hoovers and the William Allen Whites visited New York, she arranged a dinner party at the National Arts Club. Of it, White wrote her—"What a wonderful evening it was! We can only offer you in return the peaceful vale of Emporia. Come and visit us and let us know you and love you better."[43] Next, Doctor MacDougal arrived on the scene, accompanied by several other Carmelites, and she was again caught up in a whirl of festivities.[44] When she was asked to be a member of Henry Ford's six-week Peace Pilgrimage to Europe, she was flattered but declined.[45] How could she spare the time?

By the middle of March, however, Mary's euphoria had evaporated. Disenchanted with city life, she once again yearned to get away from New York. In a letter to a friend in Carmel, she confided her dejection.

> I wonder if you can appreciate how far it seems to Carmel this blustery March day, with snow and ice underfoot and sleet falling. I am sick for the color of the sea and the smell of wild lilac!...
>
> I am deep in a novel myself, one I began two years ago. I can't get wildly interested in it...but it seems to be flowing smoothly enough, and should be completed in about three months. I have written a new play and have another shaping, but I never like my plays well enough to push the marketing of them as they should be pushed....
>
> I wish that I could drop in on you for tea one of these days, then maybe the sources of inspiration would unseal themselves....I have been bone dry for long and long....even when I write it seems to pass under my hands without touching my soul, and the taste of literary life has gone flat and stale. I wish I could dig in a garden or build a house or any common, practical thing.[46]

Early in June her novel was finished. Entitled *The Ford*, it was a strongly plotted story based upon her personal experience of the water-rights controversy in the Owens Valley. Reopening negotiations with Houghton Mifflin, she demanded that a revised edition of *Woman of Genius* be brought out at the same time as the new novel was published. When they countered with an offer to publish *The Ford* the following spring and *Woman of Genius* in the fall, she capitulated, satisfied that she had won her point.[47]

By this time, ideas for several additional novels were brewing in her mind. *The Ford* would be the first of a trilogy. Next in the series would be a book called *Starry Adventure,* then one entitled *The Orchard*. A novel with a Mexican setting had also occurred to her, and for a time she toyed with the notion of taking a trip to that country.[48]

She was deeply involved with the controversy raging over Carranza's seizure of the government and the border raids led by Pancho Villa. After some lecture engagements in which she forcefully argued in favor of the revolutionaries, she was asked to go on "a vaudeville circuit," with a weekly stipend of $750, to present her views.[49] The proposal appealed to her as a lark, but, concerned that the venture might jeopardize her status as a writer, she refused. Besides, she was fully occupied and having a wonderful time.

That fall she attended a gigantic suffrage meeting in Atlantic City, where President Wilson spoke to a militant assemblage of women bent on winning the right to vote. There she met an interesting delegate from New Mexico, Ina Sizer Cassidy, with whom she experienced an instant affinity. Her husband, Gerald Cassidy, was an artist noted for his paintings of Indian cliff dwellings, and Mary was eager to meet him. Before the convention was over, she had invited the Cassidys to be her guests at the National Arts Club, and a close and significant friendship had been initiated.[50]

The year 1916 ended in a blaze of excitement. Mary's new play opened with good notices, and Doctor MacDougal's daughter, Alice, had a pantomime part in it. Now in her early twenties, Alice had ambitions to become a playwright. Mary was very fond of the girl, as indeed she was of MacDougal. Of course he appeared for the launching of the play, on December 26, and stayed for a gay round of holiday festivities.

At forty-eight, Mary was happier than she had been in years. She even had two offers to go on the stage. In a gala mood she purchased several new outfits. To a friend she wrote, "Truly the world is younger every way than it used to be, and I have more beans than I had at twenty.[51]

13

The Lure of the Southwest

DANIEL TREMBLY MACDOUGAL
AND MABEL DODGE LUHAN

ON APRIL 6, 1917, the United States entered the war in Europe. Galvanized by President Wilson's stirring words, "the world must be made safe for democracy," the nation rose to support a war it was led to believe would bring lasting peace. Mary was dubious, and in a letter to H. G. Wells she articulated her distrust of "fighting as a means of getting something done."[1] Still, she gave wholeheartedly of her energies to that part of the war effort concerned with food conservation.

Her old friend Herbert Hoover, who for several years had been head of the Commission for Relief in Belgium, was now director of the United States Food Administration. Meeting with Hoover in Washington, Mary offered her services in a program to educate women in the preservation of essential supplies. From the start, many of her ideas were too radical for his taste, but he recognized her competence as "general advisor on psychological propaganda"[2] and authorized her to use her talents in making speeches throughout the country.

While in the midst of a publicity campaign, Mary received word that her brother Jim had died of a heart attack.

[179]

It was not a surprise, as he had been seriously ill for over a year. Her immediate concern was for the welfare of her niece. Letters from Mary's younger brother, George, now married and a neurologist practicing in Los Angeles, did not reassure her. He wrote that the poor child was trying to be brave and comfort her stepmother, but she could be heard sobbing in the privacy of her room. Nevertheless, he thought it best that she remain with Georgia, as that had been Jim's express wish. He himself was the child's guardian and would look after her financial interests, involving about eight thousand dollars in life insurance benefits.[3]

Mary's heart went out to her namesake. Memories of the desolation brought by the death of her own father swept over her. Furthermore, she felt strongly that Georgia, an uneducated woman, was not the proper person to guide a sensitive and gifted girl on the verge of adolescence. All too vividly Mary recalled the lack of understanding she herself had experienced in her youth.[4] She wanted to rush to California and take charge of the situation, but she was inextricably committed to a series of speaking engagements. In addition, Houghton Mifflin was pressuring her to complete a new book of Indian tales for young people, entitled *The Trail Book*.[5]

During the first week in September she took a few days of respite in a mountain retreat located in Woodstock, New York. In a letter to a friend with whom she shared an interest in psychic phenomena she wrote, "I gave myself leave to go away into the mountains and mourn for my brother and release my soul."[6] She also wrote of an extraordinary vision concerning the progress of the war and the part that Russia would play in the outcome of events.[7] Clearly, she was in a disturbed state of mind. Then, shortly after her birthday, letters from both George and her niece, Mary, made her all the more anxious to intercede on behalf of the girl's future.

The child was obviously grieving for her father, while at the same time she was trying hard to measure up to the standard of being "a regular little woman." Moreover, Georgia had interrupted Mary's education at the Hollywood School for Girls and had enrolled her in the public school system. It was evidence that she neither appreciated the girl's creative potential nor understood the importance of giving her the best kind of preparation. Yet George counseled caution. Nothing must be said to imply criticism of Georgia's competence, as she was very defensive on the subject.[8]

Toward the end of September a lecture engagement took Mary to San Francisco,[9] and she welcomed the opportunity to go from there to Los Angeles, where she could evaluate her niece's situation firsthand. On the scene she became embroiled in a bitter quarrel. Most likely it was Mary's peremptory manner which aroused family resistance. She later claimed that her brother threatened to use "all his legal rights" to prevent her "interference."[10] Nevertheless, they must have arrived at a temporary truce, as the letters he wrote following her visit were filled with warmth and affection. In any event, there was nothing she could do except resolve to keep a close watch on future developments.

Upon her return to New York, problems connected with her work aggravated her unhappy frame of mind. Publicity for *The Trail Book* described the volume as "a kind of American Jungle Book," and she took umbrage at the implication that it was merely an imitation of Kipling.[11] Financial worries also contributed to her irascibility. The revised edition of *A Woman of Genius,* published in November, "ran into one of the worst months in the history of the book business."[12] To bring in some quick cash, she signed a contract with the Y.M.C.A. to write a 20,000-word pamphlet entitled *The Young Woman Citizen,* which she termed "a sort of valedictory to my career as a feminist."[13] In addition, she was working on a new novel, called *No. 26 Jayne Street,* set in Greenwich Village. Though she referred to the book as "a war novel from the American woman's point of view,"[14] the plot centered on a character patterned after Lincoln Steffens.[15] Still unforgiving of his behavior toward her, she intended it as a way of unmasking his duplicity.

Meanwhile, letters from Los Angeles continued to be disturbing. George had enlisted in the Medical Reserve and expected to be called into foreign service within a matter of months.[16] Distrustful of what Georgia might do in his absence, Mary felt that she must see him again before he left. The education of her niece had become an obsession, but motivation for a trip west came from other sources as well.

Ever since Alice MacDougal had come to live in New York, Doctor MacDougal's friendship with Mary had assumed a deeper dimension. Both his letters and visits had become more frequent. Now he was urging Mary to come to Tucson, with the inducement that she would discover a wealth of fresh material for her writing.

> Do please make every effort to get here by the middle of April...we could show you desert people and villages as far away as a hundred miles without any difficulty. Life at that time of the year would be very interesting and there would be enough taste of the desert weather to help your impressions without it being unbearably hot. Now don't be selfish about the matter, but put it on your schedule...and I say with the utmost confidence that it will be a pleasure for us to show you things that will amply repay you for your time.[17]

Mary was eager to accept his invitation. Moreover, the idea for an extended stay in the Southwest had long been taking shape in her mind. Ina Cassidy, with whom she maintained a lively correspondence, had suggested that Mary visit Santa Fe and had provided letters of introduction to several prominent people there.[18] Among them was Doctor Edgar Lee Hewett, director of the School of American Research, an organization established to conserve the scientific resources of the Southwest and to promote archaeological and ethnological studies. At the same time, Mary's friend Frederick Webb Hodge, whom she had first met at the Lummis house, was in New Mexico on a project for the Heye Foundation. In reply to her inquiries about research opportunities, he had encouraged her to come out and talk with Hewett.[19]

Access to materials at the School of American Research would offer tremendous possibilities. In addition, Mary had a standing invitation to stay with Mabel Dodge, now married to the artist Maurice Sterne and living in Taos.[20] This was a secluded spot, some seventy miles north of Santa Fe, where Mary would have the chance to finish her novel. Every aspect of the situation was enticing. First, however, she was determined to cope with the problem of her niece.

In the middle of May, Mary left for Los Angeles, where she stayed for several months. The visit did nothing to dispel her family's animosity. Both sisters-in-law were united against her, and she received no support from George. Finally, in August, she took her niece to Carmel,[21] hoping to stimulate her interests and foster a closer relationship. To her dismay, she discovered that the child had been prejudiced against her.

There was no indication of affection or even respect in her attitude. In fact, she spoke disparagingly of her aunt's work and generally displayed a supercilious attitude toward her. Several of Mary's friends were shocked, especially Mac-Dougal, who happened also to be in Carmel at the time. He asked permission to have a serious talk with the girl, and his effort did produce some improvement.[22] The situation remained strained, though, and it was almost a relief to Mary when her niece departed. Still, she felt strongly that something must be done about the child, now going on fifteen and especially vulnerable to adverse influences.

Then, without warning, word came that Mary's own daughter was dead.[23] It was deeply distressing news. All the pain she had experienced at the time of Ruth's commitment welled up in an agonizing flood of memory. At least she was thankful to be told that death had come easily and quickly. In fact, the cause had been acute spasmodic asthma, with contributing marasmus—a wasting away of the body associated with malnutrition.[24]

Throughout the fourteen years of Ruth's confinement, Mary had never ceased to be concerned about the girl's well-being. Though she had been unable to bear the torment of visiting her daughter, she had bent every effort to ensure her security. Always there had been the dread that the child would outlive those who loved her and be left without means of support. Now, at twenty-six, she was gone. The anguish was over, but as in the aftermath of an amputation, the nerves still quivered with pain.

In a poignant letter to Charles Lummis, Mary confided the depth of her feeling. "I meant to come...and talk with you, for after all, her friendship with Amado was the only thing that gave me any assurance that her life did not go out here like an unfruitful flower." She then recapitulated the incident of Ruth's seeing and talking with Amado on the night he had died. "We do not know what these things mean, but to me it has always meant the faith that back of her poor, imperfect body my child's soul waited its deliverance, and I am glad she will find one child who loved her in that country where they have both gone."[25]

After making the sad journey to Santa Clara, where she arranged for cremation of her daughter's remains, Mary was at last free to go to Santa Fe. As she relaxed in the train, traversing vast, open stretches of desert, gradually her spirits lifted. In this land of limitless space and sky, a well-remembered Presence beckoned. She felt that she had come home again.

Santa Fe stood at 7000 feet on the western flank of the Sangre de Cristo Mountains, named for the Blood of Christ because of the blazing color in which they reflected the sunset. Some sixty miles to the south, across rolling hills stippled in piñon and juniper, the Sandia Mountains soared in a giant arc. To the northwest, a luminous landscape of rosy pink swept beyond great, broken barrancas to the towering wall of the Jemez Mountains. The air was alive with a light so clear that prehistoric Indians had called the place "the dancing ground of the sun." Mary could not help but be enchanted.

Immediately after her arrival she located the School of American Research. It was housed in the Palace of the Governors, a low adobe building which occupied one whole length of a plaza. Constructed in 1610, it had been the official residence of governors under three regimes. The rest of the square was lined with a motley assortment of shops and cafes. In the center huge cottonwood trees showered their golden leaves on the hard-packed, earthen paths of a small park.

The scene was enlivened by Mexicans attired in brightly colored serapes and Indians with brilliant headbands folded across the bangs of their glossy, black hair. Some walked beside burros pulling picturesque carts piled high with piñon wood, while Anglos in broadbrimmed hats lounged outside the shops, their horses hitched to a rail along the raised sidewalk. Time seemed to stand still in this ancient town, where little had changed through the centuries.

Entering the deep-walled rooms of the Palace, Mary was impressed by the fine displays of Spanish and Indian artifacts. Here she would find a wealth of material exceeding her most optimistic expectations. Doctor Hewett welcomed her warmly, and she was given a place in the offices of the School where she could work with complete freedom. Elated, she wrote Houghton Mifflin on November 11, "I have just come in from dancing in the street in the Plaza"—to celebrate the armistice that ended the war—"and am now sitting in almost the oldest building....The school here has put every facility at my command and the field is so rich that I lie awake nights fearing somebody may take it away from me."[26]

Under the auspices of Ina Cassidy, Mary immediately became involved in community affairs. An article in *El Palacio,* official organ of the School of American Research and Museum of New Mexico, gave a laudatory account of her accomplishments,[27] and by the beginning of December she was being lionized. Enjoying the approbation, Mary launched a campaign to expand the town's cultural activities. First she held a series of teas in the newly constructed museum, situated just west of the Palace, at which she expounded her ideas.[28] It was said that her speeches "sparkled

with wit and humor, with eloquence and occasional pathos,"
moving her audiences to both tears and laughter. Soon she
had organized a community theater, offering her services as
director and general advisor.[29] Next she let it be known that
she was willing to provide consultation to local writers and to
give a course of lectures on literary craftsmanship.[30] Inevitably she dissipated her energies, and her own work suffered.
In addition, she continued to fret about Mary Hunter.

Released from financial responsibility for her daughter,
Mary was obsessed by the notion that she should adopt her
niece.[31] With the war over, George would soon be back from
France, and the time was ripe for her to act. To avoid the
unpleasantness of another personal encounter with her in-
laws, she engaged an attorney to handle the matter, though
she could ill afford the expenditure.

Money was still a problem. The School of American
Research had named her an Associate in Native American
Literature, but the appointment was without remunera-
tion.[32] Proceeds from *The Young Woman Citizen* had been
slight, and *The Trail Book* was selling poorly. Mary was dicker-
ing with Henry Holt about a book on psychic research[33] and
trying to persuade Houghton Mifflin to reissue *Love and the
Soul Maker*.[34] Meanwhile, she had obtained a commitment
from Horace Liveright to publish an American edition of
Outland. Alice MacDougal, now an editorial assistant on
Liveright's staff, might well have been instrumental in accomplishing this arrangement.

From Doctor MacDougal himself there was a steady
flow of letters exhorting Mary to come to Tucson.[35] At this
point, even the prospect of a visit with him held no appeal.
Physically and emotionally exhausted, she yearned only for
rest. Events of the past year had taken their toll. She was in
fact on the verge of complete nervous collapse,[36] and only
her faith in an ultimate reality beyond the petty intrigues of
her daily existence preserved her equilibrium. She was finding it increasingly difficult to free herself from the turbu-
lence of her emotions.

During this period she was corresponding with an acquaintance to whom she had promised an explication of her religious experiences. Her letters reflected both her conflict and her continuing struggle to reaffirm the essence of her beliefs. At one point she wrote, "...I can reach God almost at will. But I have special methods of reaching him on special occasions. When with him I am penetrated with a sense of well being, often of spiritual exaltation, not at all different from the feeling associated with any Beloved person...."[37] She also articulated the practicality of her concept of prayer. "I personally never undertake anything important without praying, and waiting for the inward voice....I should stop praying if it did not bring very practical results."[38]

In another letter she expressed the expedient as well as the transcendent aspects of her faith.

> A woman whose love life had been as unhappy as mine, who had no religion, would have gone mad or bad or committed suicide. I have been very near the last many times. But my religion has kept me occupied, has furnished me with the indispensable High States so that I have not had to drop back into my unhappy personal life too often....
>
> Once you accept God as a reality in life, a near, friendly reality, more powerful than your father, wiser than your friends, more understanding than your brother, more competent to produce exalted states than a lover, it seems inevitable that you turn to him in the failure of any of the lesser relations.[39]

Early in March, Mary fled to Taos,[40] hoping to find the refuge she needed to restore her peace of mind. The trip in a hired car over a narrow road full of frozen ruts took all day. On the right, mountains rose in huge, tumbled blocks, their peaks gleaming with snow. Occasionally a dip in the hills revealed low adobe houses that looked as if they had grown out of the earth. Bright geraniums shone in their small-paned windows, and the pale blue smoke from their squat

Mabel Dodge Luhan in Taos

chimneys perfumed the air with the scent of burning piñon wood.

By noon the car had entered a canyon where the Río Grande ran swift and green between dark lava slopes. The road mounted steadily, a slender ledge cut out of the side of the mountains, and at last emerged onto the high tableland of Taos Valley. Ahead, the Sangre de Cristo Mountains curved in a great arm, glowing with an unearthly radiance in the horizontal light of the setting sun, and in the foreground stood the massive, bow-shaped mountain from which the town took its name.

Mabel lived on the edge of Taos, immediately adjacent to the Indian Pueblo lands. She had replaced her husband with an Indian lover, Tony Luhan, and built a large, sprawling house in the midst of sloping fields and old orchards. Once again her talent for decoration had been given expression, this time in an exotic mixture of French, Italian, and Indian pieces.[41] She was delighted to have Mary as her guest and immediately began to give her sage advice about her problems.

Mary was going through a metamorphosis, she declared, a kind of rebirth. The emotional turmoil she suffered was only a prelude to the joy of full self-realization. She would do well to follow Mabel's example and settle in Taos.[42] Even an Indian lover might be worth a try. Tony had opened a whole new life for Mabel: he was unlike any man she had ever known. With him she felt not only protected, but tender and compassionate as well. He "had somehow touched her innermost heart, where nobody had ever before been permitted to go."[43]

In the weeks that followed, Mary came to know and appreciate Tony. He was a man of great dignity and presence.[44] His broad face, with deepset eyes, was imperturbably

Courtesy of the Museum of New Mexico, negative number 99879

Tony Luhan in Taos,
photographed by Witter Bynner

calm and kind, yet there was a childlike innocence in his behavior that could be most beguiling. Mary was concerned about his liaison with Mabel, surmising that it might cost him an estrangement from his tribe. He had a handsome wife who lived close by in the Pueblo, and opposition to the affair ran high in the Indian community as well as in the town of Taos.[45] Tony and Mabel were impervious to the criticism leveled against them.

Shortly after Easter, Mary left her haven. The rest and relative solitude amid beautiful surroundings had helped, but she was still in a disturbed state of mind. Mabel promised that she and Tony would work daily with prayers and incantations to bring Mary her heart's desire. With a touch of irony, Mary suggested that they concentrate on money, her most pressing need.[46]

Back in Santa Fe, she once again plunged into community activities, which took much of her time but gave little satisfaction. Her initial enthusiasm had waned. Quarreling with her colleagues in the theater group she had started, she became increasingly disenchanted.[47] Moreover, the battle over her niece continued to gall her.

The attorney she had hired was unable to effect a settlement. George had returned from overseas, but he was adamant in refusing to give Mary custody of the girl. Still hoping to win her niece's affection, Mary showered her with gifts and tried to interest her in spending the summer in Santa Fe. All her attempts were rebuffed. The politely worded letters from Mary Hunter, which came at maddeningly infrequent intervals, clearly indicated that she held her aunt at arm's length.[48] Beside herself with frustration, Mary struck out in a stinging, six-page letter to her attorney, recounting the situation as she saw it. The concluding paragraphs sounded an ultimatum.

She was offering her niece "the best education, the best opportunity the country affords." Accordingly, her brother must take responsibility for denying her these advantages.

"If he chooses inexpert education and the limited social and cultural outlook of her stepmother, he must...be prepared to accept the full consequences of having Mary blame him when she is old enough to understand what she has missed."[49]

The fact that her niece was now attending an excellent private school and seemingly quite content did not quench Mary's anger. She simply could not bear to be crossed. Seething with hostility, she found it almost impossible to keep open the channels of her spiritual awareness.

Letters from Mabel provided some solace. She insisted that Mary's torment presaged a tremendous improvement in every aspect of her life. "Always before a great joy is attained," she wrote, "the old conditions have to break up amidst confusion of despair—loss—and often temporary loss of faith. What you already have seems torn from you— every path seems to close around you—things overwhelm you—you feel you are lost. But at this worst time *hang on*! It always precedes the happy change."[50]

It was an apt description of what Mary was experiencing. Fortunately, at this point, she received an assignment that helped to occupy her mind. MacDougal had arranged for her to undertake a research project for the Carnegie Institution. It involved a survey of conditions in the Pueblos of northern New Mexico[51] and might lead to a similar study in Arizona. He was bending every effort to bring about her long-delayed visit to Tucson.[52]

During the summer, Mary made her headquarters in Taos.[53] It was an ideal location from which to conduct a large segment of her work, and the seclusion of Mabel's home offered an opportunity to finish her novel. Completion of *No. 26 Jayne Street* had become a financial necessity. The final chapters proved emotionally exhausting[54] but also brought catharsis. Mabel said that "Steff fairly leaped about in the pages."[55] At last Mary had revenged herself on Steffens for his inconstancy.

Meanwhile, MacDougal's endeavors had borne fruit. Mary was offered a series of speaking engagements in Tucson, beginning with four lectures during Thanksgiving week.[56] She was delighted at the prospect. There was a chance that "the happy change" predicted by Mabel was about to happen.

High point of her month's stay in Arizona was a trip with MacDougal through a portion of the Papaguería desert country. Here, among remote Indian villages, she discovered the dramatic setting and material for a dozen articles and stories. With a great surge of excitement, she realized the potential for a quality of work she had never hoped to do again.[57] Before she left for New York, she had resolved to write a series of sketches, similar to *The Land of Little Rain,* which she would call *The Land of Journeys' Ending.*[58] MacDougal agreed to help her with the research.

In the weeks that she had spent in his company, her feelings for MacDougal had intensified. His strong personality and authoritative manner gave her a sense of security, while his wide-ranging interests and satirical wit appealed to her intellect. Certainly he gave every indication of holding her in high regard, and this esteem flattered her ego. Only the fact that he was married inhibited the flowering of their relationship; however, there seemed to be little rapport between him and his retiring wife.[59] En route to the East on Christmas Eve,[60] Mary might well have mused over Mabel's prophecies. Perhaps, after all the wasted years, she would indeed receive her heart's desire.

14

Literary Conquest of London and New York

NEW YORK IN JANUARY was bitter cold. Blizzards laden with sleet and snow pelted the grimy streets and soot-stained buildings. Immediately after arriving in the city, Mary came down with influenza, complicated by an adverse reaction to the change in altitude. Temporarily quartered in a room at the National Arts Club, where she scarcely had space to unpack one trunk, she also succumbed to a numbing depression.[1] Happily, correspondence with MacDougal kept memories of the Southwest vividly alive and brought heart-warming reassurance of his continued interest. He wrote, "...we shall now be in the mood of always expecting you here when you can come."[2]

She replied, "I am finding ready sale for my southwestern material. Indeed I hadn't expected to put it on the market so soon, as I hoped to visit that country again before writing about it....Now that I have need of them, I realize how many more things I might have learned out there." Then she proceeded to ask him a number of exacting questions concerning details of the trip they had taken together. There was no hesitancy in her assumption that he would be willing to give time and attention to her needs. In conclusion she wrote, "By the way, when shall I see you again?"[3]

Her problem of lodging was partially solved when she moved into a three-room apartment on Grove Street in Greenwich Village. The accommodations left much to be desired, lacking light and heat, and the rent was $100 per month,[4] but at least she had a place to work. There was a continuing demand for entertaining short stories, and the *Ladies Home Journal* paid $700 for a single sketch about New Mexico. In addition, she was enjoying a considerable success with political articles[5] published in *The Nation*.

Still absorbed in the Mexican controversy, she wrote a piece entitled, "Wanted: A New Method in Mexico."[6] It constituted a pungent attack on government policy: "we have become bitterly involved with our sister republic over a sordid question of oil wells," she declared.

> It is true we have shambled into this pocket foremost position largely because of the propaganda of what are known as "the interests"....The result is an active propaganda, financed by those interests, to have the United States forcibly remake the economic system of Mexico as nearly as possible like the one under which "the interests" have thriven so well in England and America....
>
> There is an equally mistaken and probably sincere idea...that the majority of the Mexican people really want political and industrial conditions like ours and won't be happy until we go in and cram them down their throats....

In another article for *The Nation* Mary plunged into the dispute over the relative merits of Hoover and Hiram Johnson as Republican candidate for president in the upcoming election. Senator Johnson, a former governor of California with a reputation for aggressive reforms, was the choice of the progressives. Hoover's support came from the more conservative elements of the party, who admired his administrative achievements and impeccable ethics. However, his friends were aware that he lacked the skills of a politician, the all-important ability to appeal to the crowd. Mary's assessment of the two men was both astute and subtle. Without denigrating Johnson's accomplishments or obscuring Hoover's weaknesses, she managed to convey the impression that the nation would be more secure with Hoover at the helm.[7] In June 1920 the Republican convention settled the issue by nominating a compromise candidate, Warren Harding.

Meanwhile, Mary had been looking forward to a visit from MacDougal which did not materialize. He had been forced to cut short his trip to the East Coast because of a personal tragedy—the death of his daughter, Alice. Against his wishes, she had married a quixotic, albeit brilliant, young Greenwich Village writer named Harold Stearns. Bohemian in his lifestyle, he was a ne'er-do-well whom Van Wyck Brooks described as a kind of "literary bum."[8] Disillusioned in her marriage, Alice had returned to her parents' home in Tucson, where she died in childbirth.[9] A battle was brewing about custody of the child, Philip, and MacDougal asked Mary to talk with Stearns. Perhaps she could manage to give him some advice "without his realizing that it is advice."[10]

Although she grieved with MacDougal over Alice's death, Mary was pleased to have him consider her in this capacity. Even more gratifying was the pertinacious note in each of his letters, urging her to return to Arizona for a more extended tour. He made it a point to keep abreast of her work, complimenting her on every new piece of published material, but he was insistent that her most fertile field of endeavor lay in the West. She agreed wholeheartedly and longed to yield to his persuasion.

While working over a new edition of *Land of Little Rain*, she suddenly saw it from a fresh perspective. To MacDougal she wrote,

> Reading it after all these years.... I see now that where I came wholly into the presence of the Land, there was a third thing came into being, the sum of what passed between me and the Land which has not, perhaps never could, come into being with anybody else.

Now I see what you mean by your insistence that I should come to the Southwest until the same transaction takes place between my spirit and the spirit of the Land....

And I know that I shall die unsatisfied if that does not happen. I have been enough in the Southwest to understand that what would come to me there would be immensely more radiant and splendid than what came in California. I long for it with all my soul, as if it were something I was dedicated to before I was born, and can not fulfill myself without having....

It doesn't take long to know a land of which I already know so much. And I can take from you, I can use your experience exactly as freely as I use my own—how few people there are of whom we can say that![11]

Unconsciously her image of the land had begun to merge with her feelings for MacDougal. Both drew her like a magnet. However, her financial situation did not permit a prolonged period away from New York, and, furthermore, she was reluctant to leave the scene where she was enjoying so much ego satisfaction.

In a letter to Ina Cassidy, she wrote,

...I seem to have struck a vein of popularity with the sort of thing that I have been doing for the Nation and some other periodicals. I sell all I write and am always 2 or 3 commissions ahead...and though there is not much money in this sort of thing, there is the tremendous fun of knowing that I am stirring up something nearly like excitement in Intellectual circles in New York which is in the nature of achievement."[12]

As the year 1920 drew to a close, Mary's activities became increasingly diffuse. She wrote a detective story, which she was unwilling to publish under her own name,[13] and began a sequel to *No. 26 Jayne Street.* To Ferris Greenslet, at Houghton Mifflin, she explained that she might spend her next four years in Washington, depending upon whether newly elected President Harding appointed Hoover as his Secretary of Commerce. In that event, she would be too busy with affairs at the capital to produce any more novels for some time. "It is very difficult for me to make up my mind about these things," she wrote wryly, "I loathe this Siamese twin life that I lead, and I wish one of the twins would die."[14]

There was no dearth of excitement in Mary's life. She had made several new friends, including Fannie Hurst and Willa Cather. Moreover, her new apartment on Barrow Street was in the same building as that of Hendrik Willem Van Loon. She spent a good deal of time with the voluble Dutchman. Often they went over to the Mad Hatter, a favorite gathering place for Village intelligentsia, and were joined by Sinclair Lewis.[15] The tall, red-haired writer was then in his mid-thirties and about to publish *Main Street*. His wit and talent for mimicry[16] contributed much to the level of "good talk" that Mary savored.

Still, despite all these stimulating activities, Mary was restive. For some time she had entertained the idea of taking another trip abroad to shore up her reputation. Her contacts with Wells and Conrad had been highly significant in giving her prominence in the public eye.[17] Now, with *No. 26 Jayne Street* a financial failure,[18] she felt the need to build her fences, as she put it.[19] When a young woman acquaintance, a reporter associated with several newspapers, suggested that they do a series of articles on British literary celebrities,[20] Mary jumped at the chance. Delaying only long enough to see MacDougal during his semi-annual visit to New York,[21] she sailed for London on April 19, 1921.[22]

There she immediately became involved with a group of fascinating people. The novelist May Sinclair granted her several interviews for an article in the *Ladies Home Journal*,[23] and the two women quickly found mutual ground in their belief that there existed a kind of "racial memory," or storehouse of human experience, on which the creative writer could draw.[24] Mary was invited to stay with Miss Sinclair at her retreat in Stow-on-Wold, where they wrote in the mornings and spent the afternoons sharing confidences, particularly about techniques of prayer. Through Miss Sinclair, Mary met the celebrated mystic Evelyn Underhill, with whom she took delight in comparing notes about religious experience.[25] Undoubtedly she was enjoying herself enormously. But nothing quite compared with the thrill of being asked to lecture at the Fabian Summer School. Triumphantly she wrote to Houghton Mifflin that she was having "no difficulty getting...accepted everywhere on a footing with the highest reputations."[26]

Only a few Americans, and a lone Irishman who had come to plead the cause of the revolutionists, were in attendance that summer at the Fabian School.[27] The Webbs were in obvious control of the proceedings, especially the stately Beatrice. Then in her early sixties, Mrs. Webb was strikingly handsome, with snow-white hair and dark, glowing eyes lit by a keen intelligence.[28] In contrast, Sidney Webb was unprepossessing. Small, bearded, and solemn, his thick-lensed pince-nez gave him the air of a fussy civil servant. Nevertheless, he was the indispensable complement to his wife. Together they exemplified what a married couple could achieve by working in perfect intellectual accord. Pillars of the Fabian Society, they had devoted their lives to a form of evolutionary socialism in which the evils of society were to be remedied by improved governmental administration. Their aims were utilitarian, their principles of the highest moral caliber.[29]

One morning Beatrice Webb told the assembled Fabians that prayer was an essential element in the success of any sociological improvement. Afterward Mary walked with her in the garden and had the opportunity for a long, private talk. They agreed that all experiences, whether of the heart or the intellect, must be rooted in spiritual values if they are to be rewarding.[30]

The five lectures which Mary herself gave were well received. They ranged in subject matter from the community theater to her concept of "The American Rhythm," in which she expounded her theory that the so-called "new" American free verse was grounded in the ancient rhythmic measures of the American Indian.[31] George Bernard Shaw, who appeared for the last two weeks of the sessions, heard Mary speak and responded enthusiastically, suggesting that she enlarge her ideas on rhythm into a book.[32] Following this encounter, a friendship developed between them that was the crowning event of Mary's summer. Completely captivated by Shaw's charm, she sought his company on numerous occasions and was gratified that "he let himself go" with her in informal, free-wheeling talk.[33]

Referring to the interlude in an article, Mary described Shaw as "quite the tallest man in any company, straight as a pine.... The fox-colored hair and beard have gone moon-white around the Indian summer glow of his face, reflecting the autumnal mellowness of his mind. There is an extraordinarily clean-blown look about Shaw at sixty-five, such a windy, star-bright look as one surprises at the edge of October evenings...."

In that same article, entitled "My Fabian Summer," she told about some of the more frivolous activities that occupied extracurricular hours. "Between the lectures there were long walks in lovely Surrey byways, much tennis, folk dancing in the gymnasium, and jazz in the evening. Every Friday night there was a revue in which the Fabians wholeheartedly burlesqued one another to their own great delight...." For one of these, the Americans put on a skit, written by Mary, that caricatured the Court of Domestic Relations, "and the happy Fabians rocked with laughter."[34]

After the summer school was over, Mary went to Canterbury to see Joseph Conrad, whom she remembered affectionately from her visit in 1910. He was in poor health and dejected. All summer he had been grappling with his Napoleonic novel, *Suspense*. Shut up for hours at a time in what he termed his "torture chamber," he could produce only a few pages a day. In addition, he was plagued by financial problems.[35] Mary offered to help him. If he would give her some "personal and intimate" material on which to base an article, it would provide the publicity he needed.

Then she could promote the sale of one of his novels as a serial to an American magazine. He agreed, and later she was able to keep her promise.[36]

Meanwhile, she stayed on in Canterbury for several days to explore the historic area. One afternoon as she was coming out of the cathedral close, she heard someone call out, "Hello, Mary, what in hell are you doing here!" To her surprise, it was Sinclair Lewis. With him was his publisher, Donald Brace, and immediately they began to boast about how well *Main Street* was selling.[37] No fewer than 300,000 copies thus far. It was clearly a case of one-upmanship, and Mary rose to the challenge. Casually she asked if they would like to go with her to have tea with Bernard Shaw. She knew he was staying at Herne Bay, and she was confident that she needed no invitation. Lewis was duly impressed and eager to meet the famous dramatist.

Shaw received them warmly. In top form, he instantly took over the conversation—"looking not unlike some ancient pagan deity consenting to be pleased with mortals."[38] For once, Lewis, who had met his master, kept relatively quiet, but Mary was cast into the limelight when Shaw referred to her lecture on rhythm and urged her to expand and publish the material. Naturally, Mr. Brace asked to see the book as soon as it was finished.[39] Mary gloated over her triumph.

Returning to London, she spent the last weeks of her stay making additional contacts with literary celebrities, aware that her acceptance in these circles would bolster her bargaining power at home. Only once did she see H. G. Wells. He was on the last lap of *The Outline of History* and very tired. Speaking of the practical difficulties he had encountered, he wished he could have an American secretary. "You really have them," he declared, "but here, if I get a young man he climbs on me, and a young woman insists on being seduced." Mary bit back the comment that a more professional approach on his part, at least toward the women, might save him unnecessary embarrassment.[40]

By early November, Mary was back in New York. She soon found that she had been right about the salutary effect of her sojourn in England. Magazine editors were clamoring for articles,[41] and a huge testimonial dinner at the National Arts Club was being planned in her honor. Even more pleasurable than any aspect of professional acclaim, though, was a visit from MacDougal in December.

There can be little doubt that the time they spent together marked a turning point in their relationship. Following this interlude, MacDougal's letters arrived almost daily. They were filled with evidence of his interest and affectionate concern. He wrote, "The perspective becomes clearer hour by hour and the matters in which we are mutually and deeply interested loom up far above anything else of the last two months."[42] Also, he urged her to establish a residence in the Carmel Highlands, a new community south of Carmel, where he was building a house.[43]

Mary reciprocated warmly. With girlish glee, she shared her delight in the progress of plans for her testimonial dinner. "People are writing in and demanding opportunity to 'pay tribute,' and editors omitted from the guest of honor list are 'feeling deeply hurt'." She refused his request for a draft of her speech. "Making a speech of that kind is very much like love making," she commented flirtatiously. "It has to be shaped and informed by what is coming from the recipient. I shall have to assume that your experience in love making includes the possibility of things happening all at once and quite differently from what might have been anticipated."[44]

The interplay of veiled hints in their correspondence must have been titillating for Mary. Suddenly, however, she plunged into a deeper level of communication. In a burst of candor, she wrote,

> For a long time—more than a year—I have been dissatisfied with the letters I have been writing you. You are the one correspondent I have left, with whom I try to keep up a regular exchange of personal expression.

But for some time my letters have not expressed me. I am sure that anyone who happened to read them would find me hard, and wholly engrossed in rather grinding intellectual interests....

But this life of literary antics which I am leading isn't my real life, and this shell of hardness is only a shell—so far. And I should like very much to be able to write to you out of my real life....I feel that it is immensely important to me to have some one to whom I can express that rich life of emotional and spiritual experience which is still going on in me, now more than ever....

But I don't know how to begin. There is that book on rhythm I am writing. I don't really care about all this scientific confirmation. I am going through the paces of that merely out of consideration for the number of people who won't be able to discover what I am talking about unless I drag them over the rocky road of laboratory experiment....But I got to that place on wings of pure delight.

...Let me loose in the desert with the necessity for discovering truth about any creative process of the human mind, and I can pick up the thread from the movement of quail, from the shards of a broken bottle in the grass, from anything of beauty which comes my way....

And what I am really interested in isn't the theory of rhythm, but being able to experience rhythm in all its varieties. I like to dive into a rhythmic stream like a fish into the gulf current and go where it takes me. I like to be a sun swinging through space....Best of all I like to flash into the life rhythm of some other human being, and find myself suddenly knowing all about what it was, is now and will be. Then I like to repeat some of these experiences by writing books or poems about them.

Just now I am trying to write to you about them. So don't be alarmed if you get a great many 'queer' letters....

Desperately M. A.[45]

Undoubtedly, Mary felt stifled by the magazine work she was forced to do in order to earn a living. She described it as a "thin, glittering kind of intellectual essay"[46] and feared that she was in danger of losing her creative powers. Yet she had chosen to pursue material success as a primary goal, and she basked in the adulation of her peers.

On January 8, 1922, she swept into the National Arts Club, splendidly attired, "to take the center of the stage" at the event given in her honor. Her gown was fashioned of an iridescent fabric, "the rose of an Arizona sunset," and she carried both a black plumed fan and a bouquet of roses. "This with a Spanish comb and appropriate touches of black and silver," in her own words, gave her attire "the effect of having been made in a candy shop."[47] To add to the impact of her entrance, she had chosen as her escort the young Indian painter Overton Colbert.[48] He came dressed in embroidered buckskin and a magnificent headdress of black, white, and flamingo feathers that brought gasps from the reception committee.

In the banquet hall the city's most esteemed editors and publishers were assembled to pay homage. Glenn Frank, editor of *Century* magazine, acted as master of ceremonies. He read numerous telegrams from prominent personages, including H. G. Wells, Joseph Conrad, and May Sinclair. Next the speeches got under way. Henry Holt, Carl Van Doren, Henry Seidel Canby, John Farrar, and several other notables lauded the achievements of Mary Austin. Then she rose to speak, giving an address on "American Literature as an Expression of the American Experience." After the applause had subsided, there were impromptu expressions of praise from guests who had not had a part in the official program. Some of the remarks were amusing, like those of a young chap from the *New Republic*, who said that Mrs. Austin had taken "the horror off of middle aged femininity."[49]

At last the party was over. The very next day, Mary wrote to MacDougal, describing the happening in copious detail. "It was in a sense an admission of the complete subjugation of New York," she wrote. In the end, though, she wondered if anyone present had any intimate acquaintance with her books. "What's the use of being praised as a good mother by people who can't even remember the names of your children. However, let's hope that I will be read a little more, if only for curiosity."[50]

The rest of the winter was taken over by grueling work. Mary was struggling to finish *The American Rhythm* and also involved in a demanding lecture schedule. The weather was abominable, cold with sleety snow, and each day left her exhausted.[51] Only the steady stream of letters from MacDougal kept her in a happy frame of mind.

He wrote that he prized her letters, understood the direction in which she was flying, and wanted to share in all her adventures.[52] He was trying to arrange for her to give the commencement address at the University of Arizona, with an honorarium sufficient to pay her fare to Tucson.[53] "You may be sure," he said, "I'll leave nothing undone to bring you here...."[54]

In turn, she kept her promise to communicate thoughts too personal for anyone but him. In an ecstatic mood she wrote, "I have come upon the secret of rhythm....I have looked over the edge of things and seen...that rhythm is our mode of progression through the space-time dimension... and I am asking you to hold on to me, fast and hard, so that the idea doesn't fly away with me...."[55]

For Valentine's Day he sent her several gifts, including a wampum necklace, some cactus sweetmeats, and an amulet symbolizing the god of happiness.[56] He also provided her with money for flowers and other small purchases that she might fancy.[57] Then, in April, he was again in New York.[58] With the eagerness of two adolescents, they planned for Mary's trip west. They even collaborated on a couple of desert film scenarios which they hoped to produce together.[59] Meanwhile, she had asked her agent to arrange a lecture tour that would contribute toward paying her expenses.[60]

Money continued to be the main obstacle. She did obtain five speaking engagements at the University of California at Berkeley for July, as well as others in San Diego and La Jolla, but she needed funds in excess of what these would supply. The prospect of being selected to give the commencement address in Tucson did not materialize. Moreover, the lease on her apartment was expiring, and the new one she had located required an advance payment in rent of $500. Keeping her "finger on the push button to the Cosmic Consciousness," as she put it in a letter to MacDougal, she asked for his help in disposing of her Carmel property at a good price.[61] Then she turned her attention to making the rounds of magazine editors.

It was late in the season for getting commissions, as most of the periodicals had filled their quotas, but finally she found a young editor at *McCall's* magazine who gave her approval to go ahead on three stories based on authentic Indian material. Payment was set at $750 apiece, and she was confident she could produce one story immediately.

Jubilantly she wrote to MacDougal, "At last I feel free to plan definitely about my summer trip, having brought my affairs to that point at which I can see my path clear for four or five months." She asked him to engage a cottage at the Carmel Highlands Inn for a fortnight and hoped he could find a place for her to stay in one of the redwood canyons down the coast afterward.

In conclusion, she poured out her pent-up longing. "I can't tell you what it means to me to think of being at Carmel again. Do get a lot of work done so you can go about with me and rejoice occasionally. In three weeks I start. I can think of little else, how the pine needles felt under foot, how the sage smells and the sea sounds and the color of the bay......and a thousand other delights."[62]

15

The Promise of Fulfillment

THE CARMEL INTERLUDE in the summer of 1922 brought Mary more happiness than she had ever known. Finally, at fifty-four, she glimpsed the promise of a fulfillment long denied her. Her feelings for Sterling and Steffens had been but pale precursors of the emotional and intellectual riches she experienced in her relationship with MacDougal. In the poem entitled "Love Coming Late" she expressed something of what this attainment must have meant to her.

> Love came to me late
>   having sent on before him
>   all his great company.
> Young love with his perfumed torch
>   beguiling the senses;
> Passion, whose feet when I kissed them
>   blackened my mouth;
>   Duty that galled me worst
>   where the hurt was sorest.
> Then with a sound of wings
>   down-edged for silence,
> With a stir as of evening primroses blowing
>   wide apart among orchard grasses

Secret, contained and aware
    great Love came walking.
Came and sat down at the loom
    where I stooped overwearied,
Swift were his hands and light on the shuttle;
And suddenly, as he wrought,
    duty and passion and youth
    came back and served him![1]

There is little doubt that Mary and MacDougal were together much of the time that summer. Not only did she stay at the Highlands Inn, less than a mile from his house, but he arranged for her to spend several days at a remote camp in the Palo Colorado Canyon, some seven miles farther down the coast. From there they took trips inland to his "private preserve," where he owned forty acres of virgin wilderness.[2] Mary was entranced by the serenity and unspoiled beauty of the place. She thought it would be the perfect setting for a rural retreat.[3] Meanwhile, she stretched her finances to make a down payment on property in the Carmel Highlands.[4] If her hopes materialized, she and MacDougal would be neighbors.

That Mary was enamored of MacDougal is not difficult to understand. He was a very attractive man. Despite his dictatorial manner, he possessed great charm, and at fifty-seven he was in his prime. Stocky in build, with auburn hair and a full beard,[5] he was described as a "real Scotsman." Mary let it be known that she thought "a handsome Scot" was "the handsomest of men."[6]

The basis for MacDougal's interest in Mary is more obscure. One reason may have been that she was different from other women he had known. Undoubtedly her intellect and accomplishments intrigued him. Moreover, they shared a mutual passion for the outdoors, and she was eager to play a part in his activities. Very likely he also found her forthrightness, even her earthiness, an attraction. He enjoyed being with lusty, dynamic people,[7] and he perceived Mary as one who more than met these standards.

*Daniel Trembly MacDougal
in Carmel*

MacDougal's marriage of twenty-nine years had been unfortunate from the start. Impatient of any weakness, he had soon discovered that his wife could not keep pace with his demands. Sensitive and never in robust health, she was a retiring person who eventually became a recluse. Friends of the couple commented that she was "revolted by sex"[8] and that MacDougal could be expected "to be pursuing someone on the outside."[9] Nevertheless he kept his "Bohemian streak" well hidden.

In September, when their holiday was over, he arranged for Mary to join him in Santa Fe. As program chairman for a meeting of the American Association for the Advancement of Science, he invited her to be one of the speakers.[10] There was no question about her ready acceptance, even though it meant forgoing the opportunity to travel east with her niece.[11]

That fall, Mary Hunter was entering her freshman year at Wellesley College, on the outskirts of Boston. The prospect of having the girl nearby pleased Mary enormously. Insisting on a rendezvous in New York, she took delight in showing her niece the city and even bought her some new clothes. To MacDougal she wrote that Mary Hunter was extremely pretty, as well as modest and charming, "not in the least flapperish." "We are going to have a wonderful time together," she continued, "but also she is going to cost me a lot of money. I am never going to have the strength of mind to condemn her to ugliness and discomfort as I was at her age."[12]

After her niece's departure Mary settled down to work. Her apartment on East 19th Street was cramped for space, and it was difficult to adjust to the noise of the city. She was disturbed by sounds from the floor above, and the people who lived below complained about her typewriter. Nevertheless, she managed to keep a regular writing schedule of three to four hours a day.[13]

Letters from MacDougal were a constant reminder of the beautiful country in which they had shared so much joy. He wrote about his acreage south of Carmel, where she might build the retreat they had discussed,[14] and he was keenly anticipating his next visit to New York. She must have Thanksgiving dinner with him. If Mary Hunter happened to be in town, he wanted to take them both to a matinee at the Hippodrome.[15] His stay in the East would extend over about six weeks, so there would be ample time for them to be alone together.[16]

Meanwhile, Mary was determined to make their dream of a book about the Southwest into a reality. It was to be a joint venture, conceived in love of the land and brought to fruition through the coalescing of her perceptions with those of MacDougal. She approached Glenn Frank at Century Company, presenting the idea of a book about Arizona and New Mexico similar to *The Land of Little Rain*. When he responded with lively interest, she immediately communicated the results of the interview to MacDougal. Then, she asked that he set aside some pages in his notebook to record anything that might be helpful to her. "This book," she wrote, "must be in a sense, a monument to our common delight in the Southwest."[17]

Undoubtedly her enthusiasm for the project was heightened by the fact that it would make possible another sojourn with MacDougal. During his stay in New York they planned the itinerary for a trip which would provide her with firsthand research material, and he offered to act as guide on the first leg of the tour. He insisted that she be in Tucson not later than the first of April, when the palo verde came into bloom in the outlying desert country.

To solve the problem of transportation on the projected 2,000-mile motor trek, Mary asked her friends the Cassidys, in Santa Fe, to drive her. Specifying the places she wanted to see, she suggested that they work out the details of the route. In return for their help, she suggested the possibility that Ina Cassidy could write a series of travel articles stemming from the trip and that Gerald Cassidy might have the opportunity to illustrate her own book.[18]

When the Cassidys agreed[19] and Century gave Mary an exceedingly favorable contract, including a $1,000 advance,[20] there seemed to be no impediment to her plans. As the date for leaving New York approached, however, she became increasingly anxious and harried. Bitterly resentful of the type of work that consumed her energy, she vented her feelings to MacDougal. "I am writing and writing the same kind of hack work I have been doing for the past three years, liking it less every day, and not yet seeing any way out of it."

Worst of all, insecurity had begun to plague her. To MacDougal she confided, "I am trying not to think of the New Mexican book at all, lest I grow afraid of it....I am counting on the magic of the southwest to get hold of me after I submit myself to it. Otherwise the book will amount to very little. Don't expect a great deal of me personally, and for Heaven's sake don't be too cheerful over it!"[21]

Meanwhile, despite a heavy workload, Mary was unable to resist an appeal from Mabel Sterne, urging that she participate in an organized project against the Bursum bill, then pending in Congress.[22] The legislation would deprive the Pueblo Indians of land and water rights crucial to their survival. Rallying to the cause, Mary journeyed to Washington, where she gave an eloquent address before the National Popular Government League.[23]

"These Pueblos," she declared, "are the last that is left to us of the beauty and strangeness of primitive life, the last that is left to the whole world. The Puebleños possess a secret which our more complex civilization has lost, a secret without which we shall never achieve the ideal democracy." Not only was the proposed measure a dishonorable violation of treaty obligations, she asserted, but it would result in destruction of a priceless heritage.

Mary's impassioned plea elicited a strong response. Also present at the meeting was a delegation of Indians from New Mexico, for whom Mabel had arranged transportation. She asked that Mary take them under her wing and set up meetings in New York, where sentiment could be aroused in their support.[24] Enthusiastically Mary complied, organizing several occasions at which they were heard.[25] Finally the bill was defeated, but, when the campaign came to an end, she was physically and emotionally depleted.[26]

On the verge of nervous collapse, she wrote to Mac-Dougal that after her trip west she would have to get away—

> I don't know where, except that I am not going to come into contact with people I know, or people who will expect things from me, for months, maybe years....
>
> Please, please, do not make it more difficult for me even to the extent of saying that you hope or expect that things will be different....
>
> ...just now I wish the world would stop turning on its axis. It irritates me to find the sun getting up every morning.[27]

Shortly before Mary's departure *The American Rhythm* was published, and several letters of commendation lightened

Daniel T. MacDougal and Mary Austin with MacDougal's
device for measuring tree growth, in Tucson, 1923

her spirits. One from Frances Perkins, already a prominent figure in the field of labor relations, brought the highest approbation. Of the book she wrote, "It is by all odds the most stupendous and moving thing I have read in years.... Bless you for being alive and doing it."[28] Such praise was proof to Mary that she had not entirely lost her creative powers.

With renewed hope she set out for Santa Fe, and on the first day of April she was at the home of the Cassidys. Lounging in front of a fragrant piñon wood fire, she talked with Ina and Gerald about what she hoped to accomplish through the trip. "I'm going after a mood," she said. "I want to find the old mood of *The Land of Little Rain*." Then she added wistfully, "I want to lose my sophistication."[29]

Five days later they met MacDougal in Tucson. He was a genial host, greeting them exuberantly. Through his connection with the Carnegie Institution's Desert Laboratory, he had arranged for the Cassidys to camp in one of the buildings and had secured accommodations for Mary at the home of a staff member. During dinner he regaled them with plans for their three-day pilgrimage through the Papaguería. "None but famous people make this trip with me," he boasted. "If they are not famous before they come, they are after making the trip."[30]

The first lap of the journey took them through thick ranks of stately saguaro to the crest of Robles Pass. There they saw spread before them a vast tapestry of desert flora, rimmed by mountains. Then, as they rode across the valley floor, Mary suddenly spied a palo verde tree, its swarm of golden flowers ensnared in delicate green foliage. With a triumphant cry, she ordered the car to stop and got out to pluck a branch. MacDougal gazed at her affectionately. "I hope now you may be happy," he said.[31]

Indeed, she was enjoying herself enormously. As the tour progressed, she took delight in lecturing the group about the history and culture of the prehistoric people whose land they were traversing. Somewhat amused, Ina Cassidy noted how much Mary reveled in the role of mentor and speculated as to whether her motive was generosity or just egotism.[32]

After Mary and the Cassidys parted company with MacDougal, the trip became more strenuous. First there was car trouble on the way to Phoenix.[33] Then there were four days of hard driving over rough roads to Zuni, in New Mexico, where they found themselves engulfed by a raging sandstorm. Unperturbed, Mary curled up in a blanket beside a sheltering adobe wall and "made medicine" for the wind to abate. Eventually they were able to proceed to Ramah, gateway to Inscription Rock, where the ranger-custodian provided lodging for the night.

The next morning, Mary made the arduous climb to the top of the massive sandstone bluff, named El Morro by the early Spaniards. The trail that scaled its forbidding bulk was a perilous ascent. Yet Mary was to give a lyrical interpretation of the experience in her book. Identifying with the spirit of this veritable island in time, she longed to be forever at one with it. Here, she prophesied, she would always haunt,

> and as the time-streams bend and swirl about the Rock, I shall see again all the times that I have loved, and know certainly all that now I guess at.... You, of a hundred years from now, if when you visit the Rock, you see the cupped silken wings of the argemone burst and float apart when there is no wind; or if, when all around is still, a sudden stir in the short-leaved pines, or fresh eagle feathers blown upon the shrine, that will be I, making known in such fashion as I may the land's undying quality.[34]

The trip ended with a visit to Acoma, the spectacular redrock mesa on which stood the ancient pueblo known as Sky City. Then Mary was back in Santa Fe, completely exhausted from the month's journey of almost 2,500 miles. Fortunately the Cassidys offered her the hospitality of their home, and she was able to rent space next door in which she could work. Mustering what energy she could, she immediately began writing the Papaguería chapter of the book. There was a pressing need to push ahead, as a letter from Century indicated that an early publication date was to be set.[35]

At the same time, MacDougal was expecting her to join him for a tour of the Grand Canyon. However, a physical examination disclosed that such an undertaking would be impossible for Mary for some time. She was suffering from acute high blood pressure, as well as a glandular imbalance which contributed to her discomfort.[36] It was a cruel disappointment. She missed the stimulus of MacDougal's company and yearned to consult him about the book. Though he continued to send material, she felt insecure without the reassurance of a personal encounter.[37] Then an opportunity for a rendezvous appeared which she could not resist.

A meeting of the League of the Southwest, an affiliate of the American Association for the Advancement of Science, was scheduled for June 7 in Santa Barbara. Topics for discussion included the still-endangered status of Indians in the Southwest, and she was asked to participate in the program.[38] Thrusting aside misgivings about her health, she accepted the invitation and suggested to MacDougal that they get together either before or after the convention.[39]

As it turned out, the trip did her more harm than good. The excitement of making speeches and giving interviews, in addition to the oppressive heat en route on the train, left her in a seriously weakened condition. Shortly after her return to Santa Fe, she escaped to Taos for a month's seclusion.[40]

Mabel was now married to Tony Luhan and blissfully happy.[41] She was delighted to have Mary stay with her and invited MacDougal also to be her guest,[42] but he seemed to have more important matters to claim his attention. Meanwhile, Mary's health worsened rapidly. The breakdown which she had been fighting finally overwhelmed her.[43] Then, an endemic intestinal disorder added to her misery, and she was hospitalized.[44]

In a letter to MacDougal she wrote,

I have been neglecting you more than was necessary perhaps, though I have been very ill.... There has been a rather serious physical derangement, but all the doctors are agreed in attributing that to the psychic compulsion that I have been putting on myself for the past four years. They are equally agreed that any hope of my attaining a tolerable physical equilibrium depends on my... never again putting on myself the strain of any kind of work that I do not naturally wish to do. At present I can see no way of accomplishing that and at the same time providing myself with a comfortable home and reasonably happy surroundings.

So if I don't feel able to keep up a cheerful, impersonal correspondence for the present you must bear with me, and refrain, as far as it is humanly possible

from assuming, as practically everybody does, that the
situation is one I can be cajoled or soothed or flattered
out of. How terribly alone we all are! Outside of you
and Mabel I don't know a soul who would treat this
crisis as anything more than a phantom of the literary
"temperament."[45]

Several letters from MacDougal brought evidence of his continuing devotion. He was distressed about her illness and
wanted very much to be of help. Was there not something he
could do "to furnish some basis for cheerfulness?" He would
try to accompany her on the trip back to New York or to
meet her anywhere she specified. Was there anything he
could send her? He also mentioned having been down to his
acreage south of Carmel—"it was as beautiful as a dream and
as it was a year ago." Obviously he had not forgotten their
idyllic interlude.[46]

By the end of August, Mary was sufficiently recovered
to leave Taos. Undoubtedly she was motivated to make the
effort by the impending visit to Santa Fe of her niece, who
would be accompanied by Agnes de Mille. The girls had been
close friends since the days when they had been enrolled in
the same private school in Hollywood.[47] Now on their way
east from Los Angeles, where Mary Hunter had been staying
with her family during the summer vacation, they planned a
stopover in New Mexico. It was an event that Mary Austin
could not afford to miss. She had developed a more-than-
casual acquaintance with Agnes's mother, who was married
to film producer William de Mille, and she was eager to
cultivate the contact. Most of all she wanted to introduce
Mary Hunter to Santa Fe.

A gala week ensued in which there were numerous
parties given in honor of the celebrated Mrs. Austin's niece
as well as the daughter of Hollywood's glamorous elite.[48]
Mary herself considered it a personal triumph, but in the end
the round of social festivities proved too much for her
strength. Following the girls' departure she was forced to
take a complete rest. Meanwhile, Century was prodding her

for finished manuscript, and she also faced a deadline on revisions of *The Man Jesus*, which Harper planned to reissue. Still, she did not give up hope of another rendezvous with MacDougal.

Finally, she felt able to set a date for meeting him at the Grand Canyon at the end of October. She wrote him accordingly.[49] Two weeks elapsed, and there was no reply. Suddenly a black depression overwhelmed her. She wrote him again, pouring out the anguish that darkened her days.

> ...All my life I have lived with the idea that I had gifts that would justify me in trying for success on a large scale; and I don't just mean the fruits of success. I could have put up with poverty and with the lack of public acclaim if I had been able to do the work that I felt that with only moderate good luck I might have done. And now I find myself at the time when I ought to be doing that work, a hack writer, sick and hurried and overworked....
>
> And the one thing I can't bear is that there doesn't seem to be anybody who cares enough about it to lift a finger in my behalf.... In order to be allowed to go on making a living, I have to pretend that this is the thing I want most to do. But I simply can't bear to pretend to you....
>
> If I am writing all this now, it is chiefly to say that I don't feel equal to seeing you unless you see it that way too. I simply couldn't bear to be cheered up. I want nothing less than absolute sincerity from my friends now. If I must take failure I will take it straight, and not sweetened with compliments and consolations.... If I have been, as most people think, a conceited pompous fool, then I must find it out.
>
> ...But I have supposed that some sort of truth is discoverable, and that I have discovered some of it. ...But I haven't at least discovered how to free myself from sickness and failure....[50]

His letter crossed Mary's in the mail. It brought word that his schedule would not permit him to meet her at the Grand

Canyon.[51] Somehow the rendezvous no longer seemed to matter. She wanted only to be left alone. Nevertheless, she clung to MacDougal as a lifeline in the midst of her despair. Once again she wrote him, laying bare the agony she suffered at having to strangle her creativity in order to earn her keep.

> ...Try to think of me as if you had heard that I had been widowed or robbed of an only child....If it were so simple that I could simply bury my creative impulse and adjust my life to living without it! But the real anguish of my situation is that the more it is repressed, the more the creative impulse torments me. Consider that the greatest effort of my life for twenty-five years has been to encourage and increase that impulse, and judge how difficult it is to crush it.
>
> Nor can I look forward to turning all my energies into intellectual effort. If I could do that, the creative impulse might eventually be sublimated and flow in that direction and I should find peace. But unfortunately there does not seem to be any room for me in the intellectual world. The American Rhythm...has been a total failure. I mean literally that.
>
> In six months it has not sold enough to pay for the correction of the proof and the copies I gave to my friends. And that means...that the publishers will in all probability let it go out of print as soon as the first edition is sold, and will decline to publish any more books by the author. It also means that the general sale of my books as I grow older, is not increasing, and that the possibility of my remaining among those who can get books published diminishes.
>
> ...My one hope now of keeping in the ring lies in keeping this from the public. If my publisher is telling this around New York, it will make a difference in the price I can get for my magazine articles....
>
> At any rate you can see that I won't be much good to you as a friend. Somehow or other I must manage to turn this corner....I am just holding myself together now by will power, just to get through day by day.

It is too bad that you should have all this poured into your ear, but after all it is the only thing anybody can do for me...listen while I hammer out some kind of salvation for myself. What I can't understand is what the gods I have served so faithfully all these years are doing, that they do not turn back the screws for a few months at least....

Why on earth, or why in heaven for that matter, should anybody make a mind like mine and then not use it. I wish I could come to the conclusion that there is no Maker. If I could only say to myself, and believe it, I am just a by-product of evolution and it doesn't matter what becomes of me individually—but I can't believe that. I believe that there is a power that would help if I could find out how to persuade it, and I can't find out....[52]

The foundations of her faith had been shaken. Not only had she failed in terms of material success, but she had lost touch with the Power in whose Presence she had experienced ultimate reality. For the first time, she had to accept the fact that her attempts to manipulate that Power, her pragmatic approach to mystical experience, simply had not worked. Confused and frightened, she could only rely upon her will power as an impoverished and isolated human being.

One thought remained. If she was ever to recapture that radiant state of at-oneness with pure Being that once had been home to her, she would have to separate herself from the turmoil and anxiety of life in New York. Before leaving Santa Fe, she purchased a small piece of property on which she resolved to build a permanent home.[53] But the inner conflict remained. The egoism and insecurity of Mary-by-herself kept her from reaching the spiritual strength and solace of the I-Mary from whom she had long been estranged.

Afterglow
1924-1934

16

Santa Fe

HOME TO HER HEARTLAND

FREQUENTLY DURING THE SPRING OF 1924 Mary had the feeling that she was living in a nightmare. A fall publication date had been set for *Land of Journeys' Ending,* and there were several chapters still to be written. Meanwhile, the editors at Century were badgering her to make corrections in finished copy. The book begun as a labor of love had become an intolerable burden. Worst of all was her physical condition. Tormented by the bacterial infection which she had contracted in New Mexico, she was too weak to work more than a couple of hours a day. Twice she was hospitalized for treatment, but even the specialists were unable to help her.[1]

Yet there were moments when her spirit soared. Walking through the congested streets of New York, she moved her feet in rhythm to words from the Navajo which she had adapted as a personal invocation.

> As I walk..as I walk..
> The universe..is walking with me..
> Beautifully..it walks before me....
> Beautifully..on every side....
> As I walk..I walk with beauty.[2]

[223]

This chant was one of the many techniques she had developed to transcend the preoccupations of everyday existence, thereby releasing the wellspring of creative energy that lay below the surface of the mind. For some time she had been incorporating these devices into a series of articles for the *Bookman*, called "Making the Most of Your Genius." Impetus for the material stemmed from her original encounter with William James, reinforced by years of experimentation with the concept of creativity as a function of the subconscious.

She believed that genius was the capacity to draw upon that vast stream of human experience, or "racial memory," which was part of the "deep-self." Inhibitions of environment, inertia, and psychic disorganization blocked the individual from realizing his potential for fruitful endeavor. To overcome these impediments, she suggested specific forms of meditation and prayer. Her ideas were soon to be published in the book entitled *Everyman's Genius,* for which she was under contract to Bobbs-Merrill.

Ironically, during one of the most difficult periods of her life, she was involved in writing about techniques that were failing her. Committed to complete three books before the end of the year, she struggled with a workload that seemed insurmountable. Harassed and chronically exhausted, she longed only for the day when she could move to Santa Fe. Even her feelings for MacDougal had changed. Their correspondence took on the aspect of a chore, and she stopped writing to him.[3] He was vexed at her neglect, and their relationship soon petered out.[4]

When *The Land of Journeys' Ending* finally came off the press, Mary could hardly bear to open the book, so vivid was her recollection of the ordeal it had been to produce it.[5] Despite the anguish she had endured, however, its singing prose was a testimony to the incandescent quality of her feeling for the land. Only once before, in *The Land of Little Rain,* had she reached such heights of lyrical expression. A letter from Mabel in Taos brought glowing praise. "Your book came and I devoured it and found it full of beauty. An evocation—something mesmeric about it."[6]

Mabel also invited Mary to spend Christmas with her at Finney Farm, a country house she maintained at Croton on the Hudson River in New York. The invitation was especially welcome, as it included Mary's niece. Now in her twentieth year, the girl was talented and attractive but had been suffering from a form of glandular imbalance which had given concern to the staff at Wellesley as well as to her aunt.[7] Mary felt that a change of scene would be beneficial to both of them. It more than met her expectations.

The handsome old farmhouse, meticulously renovated, overlooked delightful vistas of snow-mantled hills and rolling meadows. Inside all was bright and shining, the gleaming white walls and polished floors reflecting sunlight and the rosy glow of hickory fires.[8] Colorful Indian blankets covered the comfortable chairs and couches, and everywhere huge bunches of narcissus flooded the rooms with scent.

Mary relaxed in the gemütlich atmosphere and thoroughly enjoyed the other guests. Among them was Robert Edmond Jones, the innovative stage designer who was associate director of the Provincetown Theater with Eugene O'Neill. He was pleased to talk shop with Mary and took a special interest in her niece. Before the visit was over, he had invited the eager young woman to attend one of his rehearsals. She in turn was captivated by his warmth and sensitivity and later credited the encounter as being her initial motivation toward a career in the theater.[9]

After the brief holiday respite Mary concentrated on bringing her work to a conclusion. In February the revised edition of *The Man Jesus* was published, entitled *A Small Town Man,* and the manuscript of *Everyman's Genius* was completed. At last the time had come when she could make her move to New Mexico,[10] and the sale of her Carmel property had provided funds to accomplish it.[11] Only her precarious health was a deterrent, but she held fast to the hope that a different environment and release from pressure would heal her. Her confidence was bolstered by the fact that Mary Hunter had volunteered to spend most of the summer with her. She had chosen to do so in lieu of a trip to Europe with Agnes de Mille.[12] The girl's companionship and moral support would be a tremendous help in the many trying tasks that lay ahead.

Early in March 1925 Mary arrived in Santa Fe. After a short stay with the Cassidys, she rented temporary quarters near the site of her new home and engaged a builder. The location on Camino del Monte Sol was above the town with a splendid view of the mountains, from the Sangre de Cristo to the far, blue heights of the Jemez range. She specified a simple design for the house: a large, central living room with a small study adjacent to the bedroom, and a dining room-kitchen wing facing the patio.[13]

Mary's nearest neighbors were the Applegates, wonderful people for whom she felt an instant affinity. Frank Applegate was in his early forties, an easygoing, kind-hearted man blessed with a gift for friendship. As an expert ceramist he had soon become an authority on Indian pottery, then expanded his competence to other facets of Indian and Spanish colonial art, including the construction of houses that reflected the architectural traditions of the region. With him Mary had much in common, from their early backgrounds in the Midwest to his intense interest in perpetuating New Mexico's cultural heritage. She was also strongly attracted to his wife, Alta, an endearing person who somehow reminded Mary of her long-departed but still-beloved sister, Jennie.[14]

At the time Mary commenced building her house, Camino del Monte Sol was the focus of a budding artists' colony. A nucleus had been established around the residences of William Penhallow Henderson, Fremont Ellis, Joseph Bakos, and Will Shuster.[15] To Henderson, an architect as well as an artist, Mary entrusted construction of her house.[16] She already enjoyed a friendly working relationship with his wife, Alice Corbin, a well-known poet and associate editor of *Poetry* magazine.

The atmosphere of the Camino was exactly the kind of environment for which Mary had hoped. She also delighted in the town, "touched with the quaintness of an alien sort of life," as she put it, "walled gardens, flat roofed houses mostly of adobe, mellowed with time." There on the plaza could be seen the scions of old Spanish families, Indians brilliantly attired in blankets, black-shawled women on their way to the cathedral, and occasionally a musician strumming his guitar. One also encountered writers, artists, and scholars, whose talk sparkled with élan. Best of all commercialism was almost nonexistent. A holiday mood seemed to prevail, and, on a deeper level, a sense of rootage and wholeness that gave assurance of unity in all things. The singular quality of life in Santa Fe was that it afforded a release from the frustration and futility of striving for achievement.[17] This aspect Mary found very precious.

Unfortunately, her financial situation continued to be a goad, making it impossible for her to relax in her beneficent surroundings. The prior year her total earnings had been little more than $2,700[18], and revenue from the sale of *The Land of Journeys' Ending* thus far had been insufficient to cover the advance she had received.[19] Driven to seize any opportunity for additional cash, she accepted a lecture engagement in Los Angeles for the weekend of May 30. She was to speak before the Woman's University Club, and inadvertently her brother's wife, Geraldine, learned that she was to be in the city.

Since the bitter quarrel about Mary Hunter, the family had been estranged. Now George wrote a touching letter in which he humbly apologized for the past and pled for a reconciliation, so that his daughter, Denie, might have a chance to know her Aunt Mary. "No matter what you may think of me...can't you forget it and...take up our relations again at least with the outward semblance of good will. We are neither of us as young as we used to be and someday one of us will be left with a great heartache...."[20]

The ensuing encounter took place without overt unpleasantness, but before long the battle would break out in renewed violence. Regrettably, it raged over a sensitive young woman held hostage in a situation beyond her control. Torn between obligations to the several members of her family, Mary Hunter divided her summer between Los Angeles and Santa Fe. There is no doubt that she was deeply concerned about her aunt's health and felt compelled to put aside personal considerations in deference to duty. There are also indications that her aunt did not hesitate to play upon the girl's emotions. In the end, she decided to give up college, despite the stern opposition of her Uncle George. When she heard that her aunt's condition had taken a turn for the worse, she flew to her side. For the time being, at least, it seemed unthinkable to leave her alone.[21]

For more than a month Mary Austin was ill with severe abdominal pain. The difficulty was thought to be related to her gall bladder, and there was the possibility that she might need surgery. Confined to her bed, she fretted about her inability to work. Meanwhile her house moved toward completion, thanks to Mary Hunter's assiduous efforts. By the middle of December, it was ready for occupancy.

In a moderately cheerful mood Mary wrote to Ina Cassidy, who was then in the East:

> I'm getting along fairly well myself. Doctor Foster comes in once a week to see me but gives me no medicine. I'm depending on those mental powers which I have used to such good advantage in my work. I don't feel certain yet that I shall entirely escape an operation; at least I shall escape having it until I am better prepared for it both physically and financially.
>
> We have moved into our new house and are delighted with it though there still remains much to be done before it is entirely comfortable. We haven't enough furniture and there is none to be bought in

> Santa Fe that matches with what we have.... We are hav-
> ing a very quiet Christmas as we have neither the time
> nor the strength for anything more....[22]

Mary's indomitable will kept her going through most of the
spring. In addition to resuming her writing, she became involved in several community activities. Among these was the
newly incorporated Indian Arts Fund, founded for the purpose of preserving and encouraging the arts of the Pueblo
Indians.[23] Of equal concern to her was protection of the
cherished ambience of Santa Fe, and when it was threatened
by the proposal that a Chautauqua summer colony be established at the edge of town, she jumped into the fray. Fierce
opposition to the project came from the art colony, while the
Chamber of Commerce gave it unqualified support. At a
mass meeting Mary delivered a forceful speech.

"The Chautauqua type colony never has helped any city
at which it has been located," she declared. Quoting from
personal experience, she alleged that it caused the construction of flimsy buildings, brought little money to the community, and temporarily raised the property values following
which there was inevitable deflation. In conclusion she added
a fine touch of irony: "I do not mean to say that Chautauquas
do not do fine work; my mother helped to establish one,
and it was of great service to many people of the kind who
seek culture en masse, rather than through individual
initiative."[24]

Before the meeting was over, the group had organized
into the Old Santa Fe Association, for the purpose of guid-
ing growth and development "in such a way as to sacrifice
as little as possible of the unique charm and distinction of
this city, born of age, tradition and environment...." The
controversy continued to rage, eventually receiving national
attention. Articles appeared in eastern newspapers and
periodicals. Mary herself wrote one for *The New Republic*.[25]
Finally the project died in the face of the intense hostility
it had aroused.[26]

In view of Mary's vigorous behavior, few of her fellow Santa Feans could have surmised that she was ill. By the end of May, though, she could no longer evade the fact that she needed surgery. Doctor Foster suggested that she go to the Missouri Baptist Hospital in St. Louis, where she could receive good care at a modest cost. Another reason for choosing a hospital in that area was that it would afford an opportunity to take Mary Hunter to the Menninger Clinic, in Topeka, Kansas, for a checkup.[27] She was still subject to physical and emotional disturbances, which local physicians had not been able to treat successfully. They agreed there was a glandular problem, compounded by psychic repression,[28] but did not seem to suspect that close association with her aunt could be a cause of her malaise.

In preparation for their departure Mary took steps to put her own affairs in order. She was not unaware that the abdominal operation she must undergo might reveal a critical condition. Both her home, which she called *Casa Querida*—The Beloved House, and the activities of the Indian Arts Fund were very close to her heart. At that time the organization had no permanent place to house its rapidly growing collection of artifacts. Despite her limited financial resources, she purchased the parcel of property to the north of her house and deeded it to the Fund for a museum site. In addition, she made provision in the event of her death for her house to be a center for the Fund's activities and designated the royalties from her books for its use.[29]

Results of the operation, performed on June 26, were far from satisfactory. Mary later alleged that "the physician in charge did not entirely understand the case."[30] In any event, she was unable to come home for a month and then spent several additional weeks in bed. Meanwhile, Mary Hunter had received a verdict from the Menninger Clinic that her health was sound.[31] This conclusion her aunt refused to accept.

Ill and irascible, Mary lashed out at her brother, George, charging him with responsibility for what she described as her niece's disability. Finally she exploded in a succession of scathing letters in which she accused him of conniving to turn Mary Hunter against her. At the same time, she decided to make an issue of some family papers and photographs which she claimed her sisters-in-law had stolen from her. Incoherent and vitriolic, her language revealed a state of mind bordering on psychosis.[32]

In public she maintained a rational demeanor, albeit increasingly egocentric. Driven by the need to command adulation, she continued to take a prominent part in community affairs, always insisting upon being the center of attention. But she was also unsparingly generous in giving time and effort to help others develop their creative potential.

She had organized a group of writers, called the Genius Club, who met regularly in her home for criticism of their manuscripts. One of its members was Frank Applegate, whom she interested in contributing several articles on the Southwest to national magazines.[33] With him she also became involved in a movement to arouse enthusiasm for the Spanish-colonial arts. Aware that tangible appreciation must be shown for the native crafts, or their quality would degenerate and eventually disappear, they launched their project with an exhibition in the plaza to which artists brought samples of their weaving, woodcarving, tin, and leather work. Competition for prizes, as well as the promise of sales, provided monetary incentives. Both Frank and Alta Applegate took active roles, but Mary assumed a major responsibility.[34]

Meanwhile, additional impetus had been given to the work of the Indian Arts Fund through affiliation with the newly incorporated Laboratory of Anthropology. The cooperative agreement included plans for a museum to house the Fund's collection and provide research facilities. A site had been selected, and there was promise of substantial financial support from John D. Rockefeller.[35] Thus Mary's dream of making her home the principal center of Indian Arts activities came to an end.[36]

During the early months of 1927 Mary cast about for ways to recoup the financial losses her illness had cost her. She succeeded in persuading Houghton Mifflin to bring out a new edition of *California, Land of the Sun,*[37] first published by Black of London in 1914, and was negotiating with them about a possible book on American aboriginal literature.[38] Most of her working hours were devoted to short articles which brought in quick cash, for she found it exceedingly difficult to concentrate for prolonged periods. In addition to her personal problems, word of George Sterling's suicide the prior November had been deeply disturbing to her.

Although she had been out of touch with Sterling for many years, the remembrance of their friendship was poignantly fresh in her mind. Her heart ached for the despair he must have known in his last days. Only by writing a tribute to his memory could she exorcise the pain. Lovingly she put into words her recollections of the incandescent personality who had streaked across her life, awakening her to new perspectives. Two articles[39] and a long poem[40] were the result. The poem's concluding stanza laid bare the intensity of what she felt.

> If ever I walk in Carmel woods, if ever on Lobos,
> I shall hear him shout in the morning surf
>   undulant, sapphire sparkled.
> I shall see him run with the warm noon wind
>   where the leopard bright herd grass wavers,
> When the winds of Sur go wing and wing to evening
>   blueness
> My friend shall come out as a star
>   and I shall know him.

In connection with preparation of the articles Mary had initiated correspondence with several persons closely associated with Sterling. Among them was Albert Bender, San Francisco philanthropist and patron of writers and artists, who had been a devoted friend of the poet. With characteristic generosity, Bender responded warmly to her letters, going so far as to send her a valuable first edition of *Testimony of the Suns* to replace a copy she had lost. Then, in April, Bender came to Santa Fe, bringing with him the twenty-five-year-old Ansel Adams.[41]

Though Ansel was just embarking on a professional career in photography, Bender recognized him to be possessed of a Promethean talent. Announcing that "the greatest writer in the West" should collaborate with its "greatest photographer,"[42] he arranged an interview. It was a fateful meeting for all three.

Ansel was somewhat discomfited by Mary's formidable manner,[43] and she was not overly impressed with his youthful exuberance.[44] Nevertheless, she agreed to a joint endeavor. The result would be the book entitled *Taos Pueblo*,[45] published three years later.

Mary was instantly attracted to Bender. A bachelor of sixty-one, he was a tiny man, rotund and jaunty, whose high spirits made everyone feel good.[46] He and Mary became friends at once, parting with promises to keep in touch. It was the beginning of a close and tender relationship.

That summer, Mary was in need of being cheered. Subject to recurring bouts of illness, she was oppressed by the threat of additional surgery. Seeking projects that could be accomplished quickly and with a minimum of effort, she dashed off two novelettes, entitled *Thinking White* and *Cactus Thorn*. Both were rejected by Houghton Mifflin.[47] Her mind was a beehive of ideas, but she seldom had the strength for a full day's work.

Frustrated and irritable, she began to find fault with Mary Hunter. Now teaching in a town some twenty-five miles north of Santa Fe, the young woman seldom spent even weekends at Casa Querida. Her seeming indifference became a cause for friction. Then, in July, an event occurred which temporarily united them in a common cause.

Agnes de Mille, accompanied by her mother, arrived in Santa Fe to give a dance concert. Little known at the time, Miss de Mille needed help to insure an audience sufficient to

Edward Weston portrait of Albert Bender,
philanthropist and patron of the arts

pay the expense of the performance. With the superb sales-
manship of Mary Hunter and the support of Mary Austin,
"who was by no means to be brushed aside,"[48] the necessary
number of tickets was sold, and the recital was a rousing
success. Afterward there was a picnic supper on a slope below
the Sangre de Cristo mountains. Some twenty years later,
Agnes de Mille described the occasion in her autobiography.

Mary Hunter seemed depressed and exhausted, but her
Aunt Mary was in fine form. Wrapped in an Indian blanket,
a high tortoise-shell comb perched in her hair, she presided
over the campfire, barbecuing pieces of meat on a sharpened
stick. "She spoke like a sibyl," Miss de Mille recalled. "But
there was prophecy in Aunt Mary's words and there was
revelation....

"'In every Indian ceremonial,' she said, 'there is the
moment when the priest says the word that makes the magic.

Up to that point, it has been ceremonial, after that it is potent. Your hands have that power.'" Fixing Miss de Mille with "the sharp steady look of a frontier woman," she continued,

"'Never let the God be absent from your stage. Say your prayers before you dance.... You must let the rhythm of the American earth come through what you do.'"

It was a memorable encounter for the dancer. Of it she wrote, "She was making magic between her and me. We both knew this. I have not forgotten anything she said to me."[49]

The de Milles' visit brightened Mary's outlook. In the weeks that followed, even her health seemed to improve. Then her morale received a tremendous boost when the governor of New Mexico appointed her a delegate to the Seven States Conference on water resources to be held in Denver.[50] At the meeting she took up cudgels for Arizona in its controversy with California over distribution of Colorado River waters, and she wrote a stinging article for *The Nation* condeming the proposed Boulder Dam project.[51]

Meanwhile, her friendship with Albert Bender had been deepening. In addition to engaging in a lively exchange of letters, he began sending her gifts: a lovely square of gull-grey silk, a card case, some Chinese ceramic bowls. She was profoundly moved. Writing to express her appreciation, she suddenly felt free to give him a glimpse of the anxiety that perodically enveloped her.

> ...I have had to face the certainty that the operation I underwent last summer will have to be done over again and I am now struggling with totally inadequate strength to earn the money to enable me to have another short session in hell.... I know that a hospital ought to be a helpful seeming place but to me it always presents itself as a sort of place I have to spend my time in for the next life if I don't behave myself in this.[52]

By the end of the year, she had decided that she should go East for medical consultation with specialists.[53] Several other considerations spurred her to make the trip. She realized the importance of having a face-to-face discussion with the editors at Houghton Mifflin, or as they put it, "a grand pow-wow on your future as a whole."[54] There was also the matter of her niece, who had departed to attend the University of Chicago and on whose situation she felt compelled to check. Finally, she had succeeded in arranging a speaking tour in several major cities, including Boston and New York,[55] from which she would garner much-needed funds, and she had the promise of a possible lecture arrangement with Yale University.[56]

On January 2, 1928, she left Santa Fe. The journey she undertook was to initiate a new and triumphant phase in her career. This time her faith in I-Mary would not fail her.

"A Little Space to Love the World Before I Leave It"

THE LECTURE TOUR was highly successful. Clad in a blue velvet gown with stout oxfords on her feet and a Spanish comb surmounting her huge coil of greying hair,[1] Mary may have appeared a bit ludicrous, but she held her audiences enthralled. The press described her as "a woman of tremendous power, wisdom, and charm."[2] Once again she reveled in the role of a celebrity. Even more exhilarating was the news she received from the physicians she consulted.

In a burst of euphoria she wrote Albert Bender,

> You will rejoice with me that the doctors here think I may delay an operation and perhaps avoid it entirely by infra-red ray treatment.... This is a great relief for though it will probably be as expensive as surgery—I have to buy an infra-red machine—it will take nothing else out of me and I can probably go on working just the same. But think of the simplicity of it. A tiny invisible ray searches out my vitals, destroying what is evil and stimulating what is good! And there are people who do not believe in miracles.[3]

Mary's "miracle" stood her in good stead for the rest of the year. She was in excellent spirits, optimistic about her health, and furiously busy.[4] The conference with Houghton Mifflin had resulted in three projected books. Both her proposal for a novel set in New Mexico and her plans for an autobiography had been accepted with enthusiasm. In addition, they were to publish a volume of poetry, entitled *The Children Sing in the Far West,*[5] made up mostly of verse she had written in her early days of teaching in California.

Upon her return from the East, she spent a stimulating week in the San Francisco Bay area, visiting with Bender and lecturing at Mills College as well as the University of California. Then, back at Casa Querida, she settled down to work, giving priority to the novel. Entitled *Starry Adventure,* the book afforded an opportunity for her to reiterate much of the philosophy she had forged in sixty years of living. Richly tapestried with the colorful background of New Mexico, its theme was the quest for personal fulfillment. It was a rewarding and enjoyable task. Despite the depth of her involvement, though, another writing project repeatedly took over her mind.

During the period when she had been recovering from surgery, her thoughts had often centered on death. Now that the episode was over, she wanted to share her thinking with those who might be vulnerable to the fear of dying. Entering into a contract with *Forum* magazine, she wrote a series of articles entitled "Experiences Facing Death,"[6] in which she reviewed the whole sweep of her spiritual odyssey from early childhood to the present. The result was a radiant reaffirmation of her faith that personal consciousness persists beyond death.

This belief was not an intellectual conclusion, she wrote, but an "innate conviction that something in me does not die when I let go my hold on physical reality."[7] For her the conviction was rooted in that never-to-be-forgotten ontological experience, at the age of six, when she first became aware of the presence of God. She was careful to define her meaning: "...it must be understood that to me God *is* the experienceable quality in the universe. He is the Universal Consciousness out of which my own consciousness stems—never a person, only faintly descried in the inknowing core of perception as Being."[8]

She had come back to the awareness of I-Mary, the essential self that was part of all Being and Becoming, forever inseparable from the universe. Caught up in the restorative power of her writing, she plunged into a work schedule which she allowed nothing to interrupt. Even an invitation to attend the commencement exercises at Mills College, where she was to receive the honorary degree of Doctor of Letters, did not lure her.[9]

Soon the old devil of too many irons in the fire began to ride her. She was trying to interest the Book Club of California in a fantasy entitled *Lost Garden*,[10] while also negotiating with Bobbs-Merrill for book publication of her *Forum* articles. Two visits from Ansel Adams brought added impetus to their collaborative efforts,[11] and there was the need to push ahead on her novel. Meanwhile, she bombarded Houghton Mifflin with suggestions for additional publications. Ferris Greenslet wrote to chide her about the "variety and complexity" of her propositions, cautioning her to concentrate on the two books that most interested him—the novel and her autobiography.[12] At this point her attention had already turned to preparations for her second lecture tour in the East.

For the first three months of 1929, Mary spent most of her time at Yale University, lecturing on primitive drama and producing a Spanish play.[13] While in residence there, she suddenly received distressing news. Word came from Frank Applegate that El Santuario, the chapel at Chimayo, was in the process of being sold.

One of New Mexico's priceless treasures, the jewel-like church had for more than a century attracted pilgrims to its miraculous shrine. Built by an old Spanish family as a private chapel, it contained exquisite altar screens, paintings, and images of saints. An inner chamber housed a shrine in which there once had been a spring of healing water. Although the well was now dry, its soil was still believed to have curative powers. That this rare artistic creation, deeply imbued with spiritual values, should be dismantled by a curio dealer was intolerable to Mary.

She paced the grounds of the Yale campus, praying for a solution. Then the name of a man whom she scarcely knew came to her mind. She contacted him, and within two days he had located a donor who gave the $6,000 required for purchase of the property, with the proviso that he remain anonymous. Thus the venerable chapel was preserved and deeded for safekeeping.[14] It was an accomplishment in which Mary took great satisfaction.

Before returning to Santa Fe, she was forced to make a lengthy stopover in Carlinville, Illinois, her first visit to her birthplace in over forty years. She was there to assemble materials for the opening sections of her autobiography. It was not a pleasant interlude, for there were many changes in the town as well as disturbing memories.[15] A contract with Houghton Mifflin, which gave her an advance of $2,500 to be paid in five installments, required that the manuscript be delivered not later than the end of the following year.[16] It was a tight deadline, and she was beginning to fear that the task would prove more difficult than she had anticipated.[17]

Early in April she was back at her desk. Ansel Adams and his bride, Virginia, were staying in a wing of her house at the time. They observed that Mary "worked within a shell of intense concentration. Even while making bread or weeding her garden," she could not be "spoken to or disturbed in any way, until she herself gave the signal for talk, laughter, and music to begin."[18]

Ansel also was hard at work. In addition to the Taos book, he was involved with Frank Applegate on a project to record the Spanish colonial arts of New Mexico. Text to accompany his photographs would be provided by both Frank and Mary.[19] She had approached Yale University as a possible publisher for the volume and was optimistic about the response.[20]

Ansel Adams portrait of Mary Austin, circa 1929

It was a happy period for Mary. Ansel's enthusiasm was irresistible, and she became especially fond of his lovely young wife, to whom she entrusted the job of sorting her own personal correspondence of a lifetime.[21] All too soon, however, lecture commitments in Los Angeles forced Mary to be away,[22] and when she returned, the felicitous atmosphere was dispelled. With the departure of the Adamses, work on the autobiography had to begin in earnest. Meanwhile, Bobbs-Merrill was pressuring her for the manuscript of *Experiences Facing Death*, she was preparing revisions for a reissue of *The American Rhythm,* and the Taos text was due on September 1. Once again tension had begun to build.

Fortunately, during this period Mary had as her secretary a young woman who was remarkably understanding and forgiving of her irritability. Forty years later, Kathryn

Frazer's reminiscences mirrored the affection and admiration she felt for her employer.

> Mary Austin's genius showed through not only in her work, but in her way of life....My first impression of Mary Austin was her seriousness and her dignity. Her home, however, was a reflection of another side of her personality. *La Casa Querida* was a warm, inviting place, with flowers blooming on window sills and Indian treasures everywhere.
>
> Most of the time the dictating was done in the living room, but sometimes she would dictate in the patio while watering the plants. The picture of her standing there, hose in hand, is something I shall never forget....At times Mary wore a plain, gray dress which she explained was a prison uniform someone had given her. It had a high, collarless neck and long sleeves. The waistline was fitted and beltless, and the long, gored skirt buttoned down the front. Her heavy, iron-gray hair hung down her back in a braid. Thinking back on the simplicity of that gray costume, her graceful hands holding the hose in her calm, dignified manner, I only wish Grant Wood could have painted her.

On the other hand, there were times when tranquility gave way to one of Mary's rages. "I'm sure her illness was the cause of her ill temper," Mrs. Frazer recalled sympathetically. "At any rate, I didn't feel that anything I had done should have caused such outbursts. Besides, by the next day they were forgotten."[23]

That summer Mary was hospitalized, and the possibility of additional surgery seemed imminent. Faced with another long period of inactivity, she hastened to complete work on *The American Rhythm* and *Lost Garden*. About the latter, she wrote Albert Bender, who was handling negotiations with the Book Club of California, that she would "like very much to get something out of the book because it seems I cannot keep off an operation much longer."[24]

His reply, telling her that the Club was not financially able to make her an offer, came as a harsh blow.[25] Then she received a follow-up letter, marked "confidential." The tender concern it expressed must have moved her deeply. Moreover, Bender had enclosed a sizeable check. He wrote,

> A woman of your rare calibre owes it to herself and to the world to take every precaution to ensure the protection of her health. An operation of the nature required to restore you to your maximum usefulness is difficult but by no means dangerous enough to anticipate unfavorable results. A skillful surgeon and a long rest, nine months or a year, will surely restore you to good health....I am allowing myself a great privilege to send you a gift of friendship in these trying days. I know you will understand without explanation how highly I value your friendship....I hope the good Lord will bless you and carry you safely through your present troubles. All good wishes and kind thoughts."[26]

Mary was strongly tempted to accept Bender's gift, but she was aware that her contractual commitments virtually precluded an operation unless an actual emergency arose. After pondering the problem for several weeks, she returned the check, conveying her profound gratitude and promising that she would ask for the money if she really needed it. She also told Bender that her physician was experimenting with a "serum" which seemed to be relieving her pain.[27]

Less than a month later she was forced to acknowledge that the money had indeed become a necessity. "Dear Friend," she wrote, "After all my fine gesture of independence, I find I must...accept your generosity....Last week I had another reverse, which the doctor attributes wholly to my failure to rest properly, and he gave me a terrible scolding." She explained that success of the serum treatment was dependent upon her having a week's rest after each medication.

So if you are still as generously inclined as before, I shall
have to accept at your hands the one week in four...
that Dr. Foster insists upon....

...I won't make the unnecessary gesture of accepting this as a loan. I should like to do so, and I hope it will
turn out that way, but I realize that it may not do so. You
will have to take that chance with me. But this I know,
that if I can keep on with even reasonable working
power for two years longer, I will have put several of my
dearest enterprises in such shape that they will be able to
go on without me....

Of course what is likely to happen to me, that no
sooner will all this be off my hands then I will see other
things to do. I suppose when I no longer have vision, my
time will come to go; but in fact, I should like a little
space in which to love the world before I leave it....[28]

For the most part Mary's hopes were realized. The ensuing
two years were happy, productive, and relatively free from
illness. Despite annual lecture tours on the East coast and a
rigorous writing schedule, she was able to give considerable
attention to community projects close to her heart. With
Frank Applegate, she persisted in the Spanish colonial arts
movement, assisting in the establishment of a shop where
artists could sell their work and purchase raw materials at
minimal cost.[29] She was also instrumental in developing a
program of bilingual instruction for Spanish-speaking children, as well as a training curriculum for Indians in their
native arts and crafts.[30] In addition, there were other diversions that added zest to her days.

In July of 1930 she went to Mexico to participate in
seminars sponsored by the Ministry of Education. There she
conducted discussions on Indian art and culture, with em-
phasis on the ancient drama of the dance. The experience
proved memorable. Never before had she been in a country
which affected her so profoundly. To Bender she wrote,
"I never came so close to that experience which is known as

the practice of the presence of God, nor found it easier to remain in that frame of mind."[31]

She was especially impressed by Diego Rivera, both the man and his work. His murals moved her to tears. In them she saw patterns of color and emotion, of compassion and community, that she had tried to express in *The American Rhythm*. So beneficial was the Mexican interlude that she returned feeling better able to work than she had in almost a decade.[32]

Her dedication to routine did not prevent her from taking part in community events, such as a benefit held for the New Mexico Association on Indian Affairs. Termed the "Poets' Roundup," it was a stimulating affair at which Santa Fe's finest verse writers presented selections of their work to an enthusiastic audience of more than two hundred people. Mary's contribution was from *The Children Sing in the Far West*.[33]

Then, early in September, a visit from Martha Graham provided an interval of personal excitement. The dancer was a great admirer of Mary's work and much interested in her theories of rhythm.[34] Moreover, the ritualistic elements of Spanish and Indian culture, especially the cult of the Penitentes, captured her imagination. Mary's knowledge of primitive dance drama brought the two women into close rapport. Out of Martha Graham's fascination with the exotic milieu of New Mexico came two of her finest choreographic creations: "Primitive Mysteries" and "Two Primitive Canticles."[35]

By the end of the year, Mary had several reasons to celebrate. She had completed *Starry Adventure* as well as the manuscript for *Experiences Facing Death,* and in December *Taos Pueblo* came off the press. It was a stunning book, which even at $75 a copy was soon sold out.[36] Naturally, she was delighted. Then her Christmas gifts from Albert Bender brought her the greatest joy of all. In addition to a beautiful length of Chinese brocade, he had sent her another sizeable check. The depth of her appreciation encompassed much more than the material value of his generosity.

Exuberantly, she wrote him,

> I don't know just how you have managed it, to have me so happy to accept from you presents I have refused from everybody else all my life, but I should think that when a lady reaches my age she should be allowed to have presents in spite of the Victorian conventions. It seems to me that it has been one of my major occupations, ever since I can remember, to get rid of the conventions in which I was brought up, and I have only come to realize in the last two or three years how much happier I might have been, and perhaps even more successful, if there had not been quite so many of them....
>
> I am taking the lovely piece of gray brocade to New York with me and I am going to have it made into a special dress to receive newspaper reporters in when I am on these hasty tours through the country and am always betwixt and between my full lecture regalia and my traveling dress. I am going to have something made that will express exactly what I want the reporters to get....
>
> As for the other gift, that will find its proper place in what I expect to do as soon as I return from the East. I am going to have my assembly room in my house finished and the house heated with gas....I have suffered a good deal from the fact that my Native maid can never be taught to take care of a coal fire, so that I am always either too hot or too cold. Now I am going to have an automatic gas heater....

Then, commenting on *Experiences Facing Death,* she confessed that she had not dedicated the book to him because he might not agree with the views it expressed. In the future she hoped to have a more appropriate book which would depict how she felt about life. "I should like to write a book like a Christmas tree with real stars on it and also a few little homely hearth side candles and quite a lot of bright tinsel. I am sure we don't use enough tinsel in life. In so many things we keep striving after real gold when tinsel would do just as well and could be so much more easily obtained.... Anyway, I am going to have all the tinsel and synthetic sparkle that I want hereafter."[37]

Mary left for her lecture tour on the East coast in an exceedingly happy frame of mind, but her high spirits were suddenly quenched when she received the shocking news that Frank Applegate was dead. With no warning signs of illness, he had suffered a fatal heart attack.[38] Deeply saddened by the loss of her friend, she returned to Santa Fe in March, determined to bring his unfinished literary projects to fruition.[39] First, however, she had to give priority to her autobiography, a task that she dreaded. The manuscript was long overdue, and the book not only bored but also depressed her. A problem with her eyesight further impeded her progress.[40]

During the rest of the year, she doggedly pursued her distasteful job, but she did not let it interfere with other activities that claimed her interest. Continuing to concern herself about the welfare of the Pueblo Indians, she took an aggressive role in fighting federal legislation which threatened the preservation of their cultural heritage.[41] She also served as president of the Spanish Colonial Arts Society and busied herself raising funds to purchase Frank Applegate's collection of *santos* (saints' images) for that organization.[42] In addition, she never failed to find time for her garden, always her favorite hobby.

By October, Houghton Mifflin was pleading for even "a few chapters" of the autobiography, so that it could proceed with plans for spring publication.[43] Meanwhile, Mary had impulsively begun a class in article-writing for local aspirants.[44] She was quite incapable of conserving her energies. Finally, a third of the manuscript was completed, and she felt that the most difficult part of the task was over.[45] Then, just as she seemed to be headed for the homestretch, a near-catastrophe occurred.

Alone in her house, one night early in December, she was overcome by fumes from the newly installed gas heater. It was many hours before her secretary arrived to find her unconscious.[46] Recovery from the accident was slow, and for a time Mary's friends were greatly concerned about her state of utter despondency and withdrawal.[47] Eventually she rallied her resources, however, and finished the book in February.

Immediately she began to worry about whether her publisher would like it. To Bender she confided, "I covered the Carmel chapters pretty thoroughly, but from that on the account is rather scrappy. I am still in doubt about those last chapters. My publisher may require me to do them over again."[48]

Her fears were soon confirmed. A letter from Ferris Greenslet brought a mixture of praise and criticism. "It is good reading and, in the best sense of the words, important and significant." However, he added,

> As it stands it is perhaps a little out of balance, the first half being...so much more detailed and intimate than the last half....As I understand it, you are willing to leave it to us to prune the first two books somewhat, while you yourself will re-write and perhaps elaborate the final book, which is the point where the reader feels, I believe, that the thing is being a little skimpy....If we could have the whole thing in hand around April 1, we would like it, so as to make early dummies for autumn publication.[49]

Once again Mary felt the weight of the albatross around her neck. But with the end of her ordeal in sight, she redoubled her efforts and pushed through the revisions. Then in March, despite frail health, she went east for a short lecture tour, mostly in the Chicago area.[50] Undoubtedly a visit with her niece, who had a good job in that city and seemed happily situated, gave Mary much comfort. Best of all was the relief of being free from the grueling task that for so long had sapped her vitality. During the ensuing months she was able to enjoy her garden and her friends, while working intermittently on a new novel[51] and a collection of previously published short stories.[52]

Elaborate plans were under way for launching the autobiography, entitled *Earth Horizon*. It had been adopted as a Literary Guild selection, giving Mary a half share in the $6,000 "honorarium" to be paid, and advance bookstore sales were most encouraging, considering the depressed condition of the market.[53] Late in October 1932 she left for New York to participate in the many gala events scheduled in her honor.

Soon after her arrival at the National Arts Club she received a startling letter from Ferris Greenslet. Staring at the words in disbelief, she read, "This morning bright and early we had a cable from H. G. Wells, stating that he considers himself 'grossly libeled' in *Earth Horizon*, asking what we mean to do about it and suggesting that the book be withdrawn from circulation."[54]

A second cable, received later in the day, had made it clear that a libel suit was indeed a possibility. The passage to which Wells objected had to do with his affair in 1909 with the young girl who had borne his illegitimate child. It was only cursorily mentioned in the book,[55] but he insisted that it was an error and must be deleted. Inasmuch as Wells might obtain an injunction prohibiting sale of the book, Houghton Mifflin requested that Mary immediately rewrite the paragraphs in question. Though nothing could be done about the Literary Guild edition or copies already in the bookstores, a prompt reissue was planned to fill anticipated reorders.[56]

Of course, Mary had to comply, but the nervous strain caused by the incident took its toll. While in Boston, she suffered a heart attack, diagnosed as involving "grave myocardial damage."[57] Still, she chose to regard the incident lightly. Back in Santa Fe at the end of November, she wrote to Bender, "I had just been overdoing a little. Now I am going to settle down quietly and finish the novel on New Mexico which I began six months ago."[58]

18

"I Am Unconvinced of Death"

On Sunday evening, December 5, 1932, forty guests were assembled in the home of Alta Applegate to celebrate publication of *Earth Horizon*. Handsome in a purple velvet evening gown, Mary held court.[1] Seated in a high-backed chair, she addressed the group, reminiscing about her experiences as a writer. In the dusk of the cavernous room, with firelight casting shadows on the white adobe walls, she had the look of a priestess presiding over a tribal council. Her voice, though calm and pleasant, held the timbre of authority.[2]

She spoke of the loneliness she had known and the sense of mission. Denying the oft-repeated allegation that she was egotistical, she said, "I have always felt that I was part of everything around me, that I belonged to it, and that it was moving somewhere with me. From the time I was thirteen, there has been nothing new in my life. What I should do later on was pretty clear to me then."[3] She recalled her early awareness that she would write imaginatively, not only of people but of nature, and that she would experience much of what is known as mystical.[4] Alluding to the pattern which she believed had shaped her life, she said, "I was the medium, the tool of forces I could not control."

The poet Witter Bynner, a close friend of Mary's, asked, "Didn't you want anyone to share your work with you?"

"Yes, I did," Mary replied. "But I never found anyone. There were two or three men with whom I was congenial....But when we went places they usually came home mad. Either I had more attention than they did, or I had to tell them to shut up and let me talk, and they came away mad."

A titter of amusement ran through the crowd. Then Mary continued. "I know that many people are disappointed that I didn't write more of my sex life, but all that was important to me I wrote about it. None of my affairs of the heart ever made any difference to me, to what I had to say." She laughed. "I'm writing a book now on the subject. The title may be *Love Is Not Enough*."[5]

Despite the brave front Mary presented that evening, she was not well.[6] During the following months she established a quiet routine, determined to take the best possible care of herself.[7] As the snows of winter gave way to the full sunlight of spring, the earth exhaled a delicate fragrance and every breath of air carried the promise of renewal. With the advent of April, wild plums frothed in fleecy white along the creek borders, and the cottonwoods began to show thin green flames. Then it was June, and Mary's garden was radiant with white and yellow roses, flowerbeds in full bloom, and hollyhocks that stood ten feet tall. Her happiest hours were spent there.

She was able to work only sporadically, having suffered a second heart seizure which put her to bed for several weeks. Still, she was optimistic about a complete recovery, confiding to Bender that she fully expected to live another twenty years.[8] For, notwithstanding her convictions about immortality, she was exceedingly reluctant to leave a world which continued to give her much pleasure.

In *Experiences Facing Death* she had written,

> It seems scarcely decent...to insist that one goes about the world with a singing bird inside and a leaping flame on either hand. But it is permissible to say that I like my friends, my work, and my house here on the

loma; and the thought that I should never again see the
wild plum blossoms storm the banks of Peña Blanca,
never hear the drums of the Keres calling up the He-
rain with its wing hollows filled with evening blueness,
smote me with an insupportable pang.[9]

It was not that she was "terrified at the idea of leaving life,
but only of leaving *this* life." She dreaded separation from
the natural beauty which for her had always been the gateway to spiritual sustenance. So with an indomitable will, she
clung to the familiar world of sensory reality.[10]

Unfortunately, financial problems continued to plague
her. The nation was still in the throes of the Great Depression, with book sales at a low ebb and most new publications
postponed indefinitely. Mary's collection of folk tales, entitled *One-Smoke Stories,* had been put forward to the following
year, and revenue from *Earth Horizon* had not entirely met
her expectations. Once again she was forced to renew her

Mary Austin's garden and patio at Casa Querida in Santa Fe

contract for a lecture series. This time it was to be confined to
the West Coast. In a way she looked forward to the trip,
hoping that it would include a visit with Bender.[11]

Meanwhile, she took pains to arrange her affairs so that
in the event of her death everything would be in order. A
new will was drafted in which she further clarified her intent
that the bulk of her estate be left in trust for the Indian Arts
Fund. She reiterated her wish that her home be used as
a meeting place and guest house for visitors involved in
activities of the Fund but did not make this suggestion a
requirement. The document also specified a cash bequest
to Mary Hunter, in addition to such personal effects as cloth-
ing and jewelry, and stipulated that manuscript material for
the book on Spanish colonial arts become the property of
Alta Applegate.[12]

Late in October, Mary left for California, keenly disappointed that her itinerary did not include any engagements
north of Los Angeles. She longed to see San Francisco once
more, as well as to have a heart-to-heart talk with her dear
friend Albert. Before her departure she wrote him, express-
ing those thoughts uppermost in her mind.

If anything should happen to her on the trip, her primary concern was that her body be sent back to New Mexico
for burial. For this request she depended upon him. "You
must not let them keep me in California under any circumstances. Everything else is arranged for, and I hope this
isn't a premonition, but my heart has not been behaving well
of late...."[13]

Proceeding to other matters that troubled her, she mentioned her regret at not having placed the Spanish arts book
on which she and Frank Applegate had collaborated with
Ansel Adams.

> I had arrangements made for publication...but unfor-
> tunately Yale University...broke their contract with me
> on account of hard times, and I haven't been able to
> make other satisfactory arrangements yet. I am hoping I
> will be spared to do that and my book on Indian Art....

> I wonder what this mystery of Time is, that so
> many of us seem to get through with it so fast? Sometime
> I want to talk with you about the mystery of foretelling. I
> have had so many experiences with it; knowing things
> absolutely before they get here for other people. I am
> sure the secret of it is something quite simple, if we
> could once get to know it.

Then she shifted to a comment on world problems.

> ...Maybe war is what we are drifting into because
> there is nothing else sufficiently exciting....I have a no-
> tion, you know, that one of the causes of war is a kind of
> pressure that is on the people to get across to the other
> shore of life possibility....At any rate I feel we'll have to
> know something more about what death means before
> we can understand our frantic urge to meet it in great
> numbers....
> I am afraid this sounds a pessimistic letter, but it
> isn't. It's really that I feel something within my own life
> pressing forward in me. Let us hope it is recovery of
> health and a new capacity for work. I feel the spirit of
> adventure moving in me, and I'm too ill to take advan-
> tage of it, so that my mind is on the possibility of its
> being the last adventure. Maybe I'm only getting well
> and don't know it.[14]

Mary's sojourn in California was brief but pleasant. She
stayed at the home of her old friend Frederick Webb
Hodge,[15] then director of the Southwest Museum, founded
by Charles Lummis before his death in 1928. Her lectures
were well attended, and the change in altitude proved beneficial to her health. Within a week after returning to Santa
Fe, however, she suffered another heart attack which in-
capacitated her for the rest of the year.[16] While she was still
confined to her bed with a nurse in attendance, she received
word that her brother, George, had been shot by one of his
psychiatric patients.

The patient, a woman with a heart ailment, had shot
him as he turned to leave her bedside. The bullet had en-

tered his abdomen, and a few days later he had died of the wound. There was some question about whether the patient could be held responsible for her act, as she denied knowing that she had fired the gun.[17]

The shock of George's death threw Mary into a paroxysm of grief and remorse. She deeply regretted the bitter quarrels that had estranged her from her brother. Most of all she mourned the missed opportunity of seeing him when she was last in Los Angeles. Though she blamed his wife for the rift in their relationship, she wrote her, offering support in any court action she might take to recover damages.[18]

By New Year's Day, Mary was up and about, feeling a great deal better. Dressed in a handsome Chinese housecoat,[19] one of Bender's many gifts, she received her friends the Cassidys. Cheerfully she informed them that the doctor had changed her treatment, and as a result she was improving.

"He thinks it's not my heart after all," she said. "I told him about the terrible vomiting spells I'd been having. So now he thinks he know the real cause of my trouble."

The Cassidys exchanged glances. Both had heard rumors that Mary's illness was stomach cancer, but apparently this was not the diagnosis she had been given.

"Of course," Mary continued brightly, "it all came about in the first place from my high blood pressure." Then she smiled and took a deep breath. "You know I have never been afraid of death. I've always thought of it as a great adventure. But lately I've resented the idea of dying. This is a wonderful world, life is wonderful, and there are so many things I want to do. Why should I have to die?"[20]

The treatment prescribed by Doctor Foster consisted of a liquid diet and subcutaneous injections[21] for pain. As Mary's strength returned, she was unable to tolerate continued inactivity. Resuming work on the Spanish arts books, she put it into shape for submission to a publisher. Then she turned her attention to writing some articles on her metaphysical beliefs, entitled "Can Prayer Be Answered?"

This work was a rewarding task. Reaching back to the principles she had learned from the Paiute Indians, she reviewed the practices she had evolved from a study of all the world's great religions.

In conclusion she wrote, "...I have never taken the whole measure of what I pray to. I do not know its one unchanging name. Whatever I, being sincerely moved by the need of it, pray to, it works....It is tied up with all our processes of being and becoming. But I don't know yet what it is."[22]

During the spring of 1934 Mary fluctuated between spells of severe illness and periods of relative comfort. Unfailingly optimistic, she agreed to a California lecture series scheduled for early December. To Bender she expressed her eager anticipation.

> ...I shall want to see Ansel, and see what can be arranged by way of illustrating the book on Spanish Arts....I have finished the manuscript, and am hoping I can do something about getting it published....I mean to try the University of California, or Stanford University....
>
> I am recovering my health somewhat so that I can go on with my work....Two articles on Prayer, which I sold to the Forum, are to appear in book form immediately....It is possible that under the circumstances, the book may have considerable sale. People are very much interested in getting their prayers answered just now.
>
> I am looking forward to having a few days visit with you when I get to San Francisco for lectures."[23]

The letter was dated May 28. It was the last one Bender would receive from Mary. Her condition worsened rapidly, and by the end of July her attorney felt it necessary to summon Mary Hunter from Chicago.

Considerable time had elapsed since the two women had seen each other, and Mary's niece was shocked at the appalling condition in which she found her aunt. Cerebral hemorrhages had affected the functioning of her mind, as well as her speech. Her business affairs were in a state of utter confusion, with neglected bills, misplaced royalty checks, and practically no cash in the bank. Appointment of a conservator seemed the only solution. Yet everyone was reluctant to take the step, as they feared Mary's wrath if she happened to recover.[24]

And quite suddenly and most unexpectedly, she did. On August 9, to the astonishment of the assembled company, Mary Austin appeared at the annual Poets' Roundup. Wearing a dark blue silk dress with a lace shawl thrown over her shoulders, she walked out onto the terrace of the private residence where the affair was being held. The familiar high comb was set in the great coil of hair, and, despite the pallor of her face, her gaze was direct and compelling. Introduced as "for years the boss of the crowd," she read several poems from *The Children Sing in the Far West.* Her voice was firm and resonant. Once she swayed a little, and the audience held its breath. It was clear that she had made a tremendous effort to participate in the event.[25]

On August 10 Mary sent the manuscript of the Spanish colonial arts book to Houghton Mifflin. Accompanying it was a completely coherent letter in which she stated, "I do not wish to crowd this book upon you. I really believe there will be a good and lasting sale for it.... I should like you to consider it seriously but you are not to feel any undue pressure for publication...."[26]

Two days later Mary suffered a final heart attack, and on August 13 she died quietly in her sleep.

Once in a poem she had posed the question, "What's dead, but set free from Time-space?"

And she had given her answer:

> ... This new concept of Time as the measure of
>   Consciousness
> Tracking its way through space...
> Death seems merely the notice of disembarcation,
> From which we find ourselves
> High on the coast of eternal Nowness.[27]

Epilogue

To the east of Casa Querida, on the edge of the Sangre de Cristo Mountains, stands a great pyramid of sand and rock called Mount Picacho. Below its lofty eminence, the valley of Santa Fe spreads in a luminous checkerboard of green and gold, and on the far horizon, multilayered mountains meet the sky. Near the summit of Picacho, sealed in the crevice of a cairn amid rough, granite boulders, are the ashes of Mary Austin. There they remain forever at one with the earth.[1]

She would have been pleased with her final resting place. She had written:

> Some day I shall go West,
> Having won all time to love it in, at last
> Too still to boast,
> But when I smell the sage,
> When the long, marching landscape line
> Melts into wreathing mountains,
> And the dust cones dance
> Something in me that is of them shall stir....[2]

Mary Austin's beloved house eventually became a privately owned art gallery of authentic western paintings. The work of the Indian Arts Fund has continued, achieving ever more of the goals that were closest to her heart. A part of the School of American Research, it has benefited from ownership of the copyrights to her writings. Best of all, her words live on, a testament to the undying quality of her country and of her spirit.

Not long before her death, she had reiterated her uncompromising belief: "I will be Mary. I will be forever Mary. And others will be themselves, those who have contributed something by the individuality of their lives and thought."[3]

Notes
to the Chapters

MARY AUSTIN: THE WOMAN AND THE WRITER

1. Mary Austin to Mr. Schroeder, February 20, 1919, Huntington Collection, Box 2.

2. Mary Austin, "The Mother of Felipe," *The Overland Monthly*, November 1892.

3. Mary Austin to Daniel Trembly MacDougal, July 5, 1920, The Carnegie Desert Laboratory, MacDougal Collection, University of Arizona Library, Special Collections.

4. Carl Van Doren, "Mary Hunter Austin: 1868–1934," *New York Herald Tribune*, August 26, 1934.

5. Mary Austin, *Christ in Italy* (Duffield & Company, New York, 1912), p. 2.

CHAPTER 1

The main source of material on Mary Austin's childhood and early womanhood is her autobiography, *Earth Horizon* (Houghton Mifflin Company, Boston, 1932).

1. *Earth Horizon*, p. 47.

2. Ibid., p. 41.

3. Ibid., p. 47.

4. Ibid., p. 25.

5. Ibid., p. 23.

6. Ibid., p. 22.

7. August 2, 1861.

8. D. J. McMillan to Mary Austin, April 10, 1929, Huntington Collection, Box 24b.

9. *Earth Horizon,* pp. 29, 31.

10. George Hunter completed his term of enlistment in 1864.

11. *Earth Horizon,* p. 30.

12. Ibid., p. 32.

13. Ibid., p. 42.

14. Ibid., p. 45.

15. Ibid., p. 45.

16. Ibid., p. 46.

17. Ibid., p. 47.

18. Ibid., p. 47.

19. Ibid., p. 54.

20. Ibid., p. 56.

21. Ibid., p. 14.

22. Ibid., p. 14.

23. Ibid., p. 15.

24. Ibid., pp. 19–20.

25. Ibid., p. 20.

26. Louis Jacques Mande Daguerre.

27. *Earth Horizon,* pp. 12–14.

28. Ibid., p. 15.

29. Thomas Matthews Pearce, *The Beloved House* (The Caxton Printers, Caldwell, Idaho, 1940), p. 36.

30. *Earth Horizon,* p. 34.

31. Ibid., p. 70.

32. Ibid., p. 3.

33. Ibid., p. 9.

34. Ibid., pp. 35–38, pp. 316–318.

35. Ibid., p. 11.

36. Ibid., pp. 43, 70, 75.

37. Ibid., p. 56.

38. Ibid., p. 5.

39. Ibid., p. 48.

40. Ibid., p. 79.

41. Mary Austin, *Experiences Facing Death* (The Bobbs-Merrill Company, Indianapolis, 1931), pp. 24–26.

42. Mary Austin, "How I Learned to Read and Write," *My First Publication,* edited by James D. Hart (The Book Club of California, 1961), p. 62; *Earth Horizon,* pp. 59–61.

43. Pearce, *Beloved House,* p. 37.

44. *Earth Horizon,* p. 72.

45. Ibid., p. 62.

46. Ibid., p. 70.

47. "How I Learned to Read and Write," p. 62.

48. *Earth Horizon,* p. 74.

49. Ibid., p. 78.

50. Ibid., pp. 17, 18, 20, 68.

51. Ibid., pp. 81–83.

52. Ibid., pp. 5, 55, 84, 85.

53. Ibid., p. 74.

54. Mary Austin to a Mr. Schroeder, February 18, 1919, Huntington Collection, Box 2.

55. *Earth Horizon,* p. 153.

56. Ibid., p. 75.

57. Ibid., p. 85.

58. Ibid., p. 86.

59. Ibid., p. 86.

60. Helen MacKnight Doyle, *Mary Austin: Woman of Genius* (Gotham House, New York, 1939), p. 34.

61. *Earth Horizon,* p. 87.

CHAPTER 2

1. *Earth Horizon,* p. 91.

2. Ibid., p. 94.

3. Ibid., p. 92.

4. Ibid., p. 94–95.

5. Ibid., p. 91–92.

6. Ibid., p. 96–97.

7. Ibid., p. 61.

8. Ibid., p. 103.

9. Ibid., p. 104.

10. Ibid., pp. 107–110.

11. Ibid., pp. 128–129.

12. Ibid., pp. 112–113.

13. Ibid., p. 114.

14. Ibid., p. 115.

15. Ibid., p. 163.

16. Ibid., p. 101.

17. Ibid., p. 163.

18. Ibid., p. 142.

19. Ibid., p. 116.

20. Ibid., p. 223.

21. Ibid., p. 105.

22. Ibid., p. 127.

23. September 1883.

24. *Earth Horizon,* pp. 116–117.

25. Ibid., pp. 153–154.

26. Ibid., pp. 154, 132–133.

27. Ibid., p. 135.

28. Ibid., p. 164.

29. Ibid., p. 135.

30. Ibid., pp. 151–152.

31. Ibid., pp. 157–158.

32. Ibid., p. 159.

33. Mary Austin, *A Woman of Genius* (Doubleday, Page, & Company, New York, 1912; Houghton Mifflin Company, Boston, 1917).

34. *Earth Horizon,* p. 172.

35. Ibid., pp. 162–164.

36. Ibid., p. 167.

37. Ibid., p. 168.

38. Ibid., pp. 170–172.

39. Ibid., pp. 173–174.

40. Ibid., pp. 175–176.

41. James Hunter to Effie Vancil, May 16, 1888, Blackburn College Collection.

42. *Earth Horizon,* p. 177.

43. Susanna Hunter to friends in Carlinville, September 23, 1888, Huntington Collection, Box 24a.

CHAPTER 3

1. Susanna Hunter to friends in Carlinville, September 23, 1888, Huntington Collection.

2. *Earth Horizon,* p. 182.

3. Ibid., pp. 182–186.

4. Susanna Hunter to friends in Carlinville, September 23, 1888, Huntington Collection.

5. Donald P. Ringler, "Mary Austin: Kern County Days, 1888–1892," *Southern California Quarterly,* Vol. XLV, No. I, pp. 32, 61, March 1963.

6. Ibid., p. 40.

7. Mary Austin, *One Hundred Miles On Horseback* (Dawson's Book Shop, Los Angeles, 1963), p. 3.

8. Ibid., p. 10.

9. Ibid., p. 8.

10. Ibid., pp. 11–14.

11. *Earth Horizon,* p. 187.

12. Ibid., pp. 190–191.

13. Ibid., p. 193.

14. Ibid., p. 194.

15. "The Tejon Notebook," Huntington Collection, Box 24c.

16. *Earth Horizon*, p. 194; "The Last Antelope," *Lost Borders* (Harper & Brothers, New York, 1909).

17. "The Tejon Notebook," Huntington Collection.

18. Ringler, p. 31.

19. *Earth Horizon*, p. 195.

20. Ibid., p. 192.

21. "The Tejon Notebook," Huntington Collection.

22. Ringler, pp. 34–37; Stephen Bonsal, *Edward Fitzgerald Beale, A Pioneer in the Path of Empire, 1822–1903* (Putnam, New York, 1912).

23. *Earth Horizon*, p. 197.

24. Doyle, p. 93.

25. Susanna Hunter to Bro. Kep (Keplinger), June 3, 1889, Huntington Collection, Box 24a.

26. Ringler, p. 33.

27. Susanna Hunter to Bro. Kep, June 3, 1889, Huntington Collection.

28. *Earth Horizon*, pp. 197–198.

29. Mary Austin, *The Flock* (Houghton Mifflin, Boston, 1906), p. 11.

30. Ringler, pp. 39–40.

31. *The Flock*, p. 227.

32. Ringler, pp. 38–39.

33. *The Flock*, pp. 239–249.

34. "The Tejon Notebook," Huntington Collection.

35. Mary Austin, *The Land of Little Rain* (Houghton Mifflin, Boston, 1903), p. 49.

36. Mary Austin, *Isidro* (Houghton Mifflin, Boston, 1905).

37. Mary Austin, *The Ford* (Houghton Mifflin, Boston, 1917).

38. *The Flock*, p. 12.

39. *Earth Horizon*, p. 201; "The Walking Woman," *Lost Borders*.

40. *Earth Horizon*, p. 198.

41. Doyle, p. 92.

42. Ibid., pp. 87–88.

43. *Earth Horizon*, p. 202.

44. Ibid., p. 202.

45. James Hunter to Effie Vancil, September 2, 1889, Blackburn College Collection.

46. *Earth Horizon*, p. 203.

47. Ringler, pp. 50–51; Susanna Hunter to Mrs. Kep (Keplinger), June 3, 1889, Huntington Collection, Box 24a.

48. James Hunter to Effie Vancil, September 2, 1889, Blackburn College Collection.

CHAPTER 4

1. *Christ in Italy,* p. ix.
2. "The Mother of Felipe."
3. Doyle, p. 110.
4. Ibid., pp. 112–113.
5. Ibid., p. 112.
6. Ringler, pp. 45–47.
7. Ibid., pp. 47–49; *Earth Horizon,* pp. 204–212.
8. Doyle, p. 120.
9. Ringler, p. 50.
10. James Hunter to Effie Vancil, September 3, 1890, Blackburn College Collection.
11. Ringler, p. 51.
12. Ibid., p. 57.
13. *Earth Horizon,* pp. 218–219.
14. James Hunter to Effie Vancil, September 3, 1890, Blackburn College Collection.
15. Doyle, p. 127.
16. Ringler, p. 56.
17. Stafford Wallace Austin to Mary Hunter, July 19, 1929, Huntington Collection, Box 24a.
18. Ringler, p. 55.
19. Doyle, p. 128.
20. Mary Austin, "Frustrate," *Century* Magazine, January 1912.
21. Ibid.
22. Ringler, pp. 53–54.
23. Doyle, p. 109.
24. Ringler, p. 57.
25. "Frustrate."
26. James Hunter to Effie Vancil, November 29, 1890, Blackburn College Collection; Ringler, pp. 56–57.
27. James Hunter to Effie Vancil, September 3, 1890, Blackburn College Collection.
28. *A Woman of Genius,* pp. 123–124.
29. *Earth Horizon,* p. 220.
30. Wedding invitation, Huntington Collection, Box 24a.
31. Doyle, p. 131; Ringler, p. 58.
32. Doyle, p. 132.
33. "Frustrate."

34. Ringler, p. 59.

35. *Earth Horizon*, p. 228.

36. Doyle, p. 134.

37. Ringler, p. 59.

38. Ringler, p. 53.

39. Doyle, p. 135.

40. *Earth Horizon*, p. 229.

41. Ibid., pp. 230–231.

42. *The Overland Monthly,* November 1892; also published by The Book Club of California in *The Mother of Felipe and Other Early Stories,* 1950.

43. Mary Austin, "The Conversion of Ah Lew Sing," *The Overland Monthly,* October 1896; also included in *One-Smoke Stories* (Houghton Mifflin, Boston, 1934).

44. *Earth Horizon*, p. 232.

CHAPTER 5

1. *The Land of Little Rain,* p. 183.

2. *Earth Horizon,* p. 234.

3. Ibid., p. 234.

4. Ibid., p. 235.

5. Ibid., p. 236.

6. Ibid., p. 236.

7. Ibid., p. 236.

8. Ibid., p. 242.

9. Ibid., pp. 242–243.

10. Ibid., pp. 237–238.

11. Mary Austin, *Lost Borders* (Harper & Brothers, New York, 1909).

12. *Earth Horizon,* p. 238.

13. Ibid., pp. 257–258.

14. Ibid., p. 239.

15. Ibid., p. 238.

16. Ibid., p. 239.

17. Ibid., p. 240.

18. Ibid., p. 240.

19. Ibid., pp. 241–243.

20. Ibid., pp. 243–245.

21. Mary Austin, *The Basket Woman* (Houghton Mifflin, Boston, 1904).

22. Mary Austin, "The Basket Maker," in *The Land of Little Rain; Earth Horizon,* p. 289.

23. *Earth Horizon,* pp. 246–247.

24. Ibid., p. 252.

25. Stafford Wallace Austin to Mary Austin, July 2, 1929, Huntington Collection, Box 24a.

26. *Earth Horizon*, p. 253.

27. *Christ in Italy*, p. 6.

28. *Earth Horizon*, p. 247.

29. Doyle, pp. 171–172.

30. Wallace Austin to Mary Austin, July 2, 1929, Huntington Collection.

31. *Earth Horizon*, pp. 251–252.

32. Ibid., pp. 248–251.

33. Ibid., p. 246.

34. Doyle, p. 171.

35. Ibid., p. 172; *Earth Horizon*, p. 256.

36. Ringler, p. 53.

37. *Earth Horizon*, p. 257.

38. Ibid., p. 257.

CHAPTER 6

1. Mary Austin to Daniel Trembly MacDougal, July 5, 1920, The Carnegie Desert Laboratory, MacDougal Collection, University of Arizona Library, Special Collections.

2. Mary Austin, *The Land of Journeys' Ending* (The Century Company, New York, 1924), p. 386.

3. *Earth Horizon*, pp. 268–269.

4. *The Land of Little Rain*, p. 87.

5. The Inyo *Register*, October 10, 1895.

6. Ibid.

7. Doyle, pp. 174–175.

8. *The Flock*, p. 13.

9. Doyle, p. 182.

10. The Inyo *Register*, December 19, 1895.

11. *Earth Horizon*, p. 294.

12. Ibid.

13. Doyle, pp. 181–182.

14. *Earth Horizon*, p. 268.

15. Doyle, p. ix.

16. The Indian teacher mentioned in Wallace Austin's letter to Mary Austin, July 2, 1929; also Mary Austin to Miss Williams, October 27, 1905, Huntington Collection, Box 2; and Mary Austin to Frances Douglas, January 7, 1901, University of Arizona Library, Special Collections.

17. *Earth Horizon*, pp. 266–267.

18. Doyle, p. 175.

19. *Earth Horizon,* p. 273.
20. Doyle, p. 176.
21. *Earth Horizon,* p. 273.
22. Ibid., p. 274.
23. Ibid., p. 276.
24. Mary Austin, *Can Prayer Be Answered?* (Farrar & Rinehart, New York, 1934), pp. 4–6.
25. Ibid., pp. 3–4, 7–10; *Earth Horizon,* pp. 275–277; *Experiences Facing Death,* pp. 126–128.
26. *The Black Cat.*
27. Inyo *Register,* October 29, 1896.
28. Ibid., October 8, 1896.
29. Doyle, p. ix.
30. Doyle, p. x.
31. Ibid.
32. Ibid.
33. Ibid., p. 180.
34. *Earth Horizon,* p. 269; Guy Phoenix Doyle, M.D.
35. Mary Austin, Foreword to *A Child Went Forth: The Autobiography of Helen MacKnight Doyle* (Gotham House, N.Y., 1934).
36. Doyle, p. 185.
37. Mary Austin, "The Walking Woman," *Lost Borders.*
38. Stafford Wallace Austin to Mary Austin, July 2, 1929, Huntington Collection; Mary Austin received a Grammar Grade County Certificate, County of Inyo, August 9, 1897, valid for six years.
39. *Earth Horizon,* p. 280.
40. "The Wooing of the Señorita," *The Overland Monthly,* 1897.
41. *Earth Horizon,* p. 270.
42. Ibid., p. 271.
43. Ibid., p. 271.
44. Ibid., p. 281.
45. Doyle, p. 193.
46. Wallace Austin to Mary Austin, July 2, 1929, Huntington Collection.
47. Annie Payson Call, *Power Through Repose* (Little, Brown, & Co., 1898).
48. *Earth Horizon,* p. 282.
49. *Earth Horizon,* pp. 282–283; *Experiences Facing Death,* p. 238.
50. Mary Austin to Henry James Forman, September 17, 1918, Department of Special Collections, University Research Library, University of California at Los Angeles, Number 278 V.

51. Ibid.

52. *Experiences Facing Death,* p. 238.

53. *Earth Horizon,* p. 289.

54. Ibid., pp. 289–290.

55. Ibid., p. 290.

56. Dudley Gordon, *Charles F. Lummis: Crusader in Corduroy* (Cultural Assets Press, Los Angeles, 1972).

57. Wallace Austin to Mary Austin, July 2, 1929, Huntington Collection.

58. *Earth Horizon,* p. 290.

CHAPTER 7

1. Adolph Francis Bandelier (1840–1914), archaeologist and authority on the Indian cultures of America.

2. Edwin R. Bingham, *Charles F. Lummis, Editor of the Southwest* (Huntington Library, San Marino, California, 1955).

3. Mary Austin to Eva Lummis, 1903, Huntington Collection, Box 1.

4. Mary Austin to Eva Lummis, January 9 and January 30, 1901, University of Arizona Collection; Frances Douglas De Kalb (Eva Lummis) to Mary Austin, August 7, 1929, Huntington Collection, Box 1; Dudley Gordon, p. 54; *Earth Horizon,* pp. 293–294.

5. Bingham, p. 21.

6. Doyle, pp. 216–217.

7. *Earth Horizon,* p. 291.

8. Augusta Fink, *Monterey: The Presence of the Past* (Chronicle Books, San Francisco, 1972), p. 220.

9. *Earth Horizon,* p. 291.

10. Mary Austin to Frederick Webb Hodge, November 5, 1899, Southwest Museum Collection.

11. *Earth Horizon,* pp. 292–293.

12. Bingham, p. 180.

13. *Women and Economics,* 1898.

14. Doyle, pp. 196–197; *Earth Horizon,* pp. 290–291.

15. *Earth Horizon,* p. 291.

16. Ibid., p. 292.

17. Ibid., pp. 290, 292.

18. "How I Learned to Read and Write," p. 63.

19. *Earth Horizon,* p. 294.

20. Ibid., p. 294.

21. Ibid., p. 294.

22. Mary Austin to Charles Lummis, December 28, 1918, Huntington Collection, Box 1.

23. *The Land of Little Rain,* p. 16.

24. *Earth Horizon,* pp. 284–285.

25. *The Land of Little Rain,* p. xi.

26. Doyle, pp. 197–198.

27. Mary Austin to Eva Lummis, January 7, 1901, University of Arizona Library, Special Collections.

28. Mary Austin to Charles Lummis, December 28, 1918, Huntington Collection.

29. "How I Learned to Read and Write," p. 64.

30. *Earth Horizon,* pp. 285–287.

31. Doyle, p. 196.

32. *Earth Horizon,* p. 288.

33. Doyle, pp. 206–207.

34. *Earth Horizon,* p. 295.

35. Bliss Perry to Mary Austin, February 25 and July 31, 1902, Huntington Collection, Box 3.

36. Mary Austin to Houghton Mifflin, November 25, 1902, in Grant Overton, *The Women Who Made Our Novels* (Moffat, Yard, & Company, New York, 1918), pp. 164–169.

37. Ringler, p. 53.

38. James Hunter married Mary Hutchins on June 25, 1901, in Bakersfield.

39. *Earth Horizon,* pp. 296–297.

CHAPTER 8

1. Ringler, p. 53.

2. *Earth Horizon,* p. 296.

3. Ibid., p. 297; Robert Righter, "A Dedication to the Memory of Theodore Henry Hittell, 1830–1917," *Arizona and the West,* Winter 1974.

4. Mary Austin, "George Sterling at Carmel," *The American Mercury,* Vol. 11, May 1927.

5. Donald R. Fleming, "The Last Bohemian," *Quarterly News-Letter of the Book Club of California,* Vol. 37, No. 4, Fall 1972.

6. Franklin Walker, *The Seacoast of Bohemia* (The Book Club of California, San Francisco, 1966), p. 28.

7. Oscar Lewis, *Bay Window Bohemia* (Doubleday, New York, 1956), p. 100.

8. *Earth Horizon,* p. 297.

9. Michael Orth, "Ideality to Reality: The Founding of Carmel," *The California Historical Society Quarterly,* Vol. 48, No. 3, Sept. 1969, p. 200.

10. *Earth Horizon,* p. 297.

11. Orth, pp. 200–201.

12. Fink, pp. 222–223.

13. "George Sterling at Carmel."

14. *Earth Horizon,* p. 298.

15. Austin, "Frustrate."

16. Mary Austin to Eva Lummis, 1903, Huntington Collection, Box 1.

17. Ibid.

18. Mary Austin to Ferris Greenslet, Houghton Mifflin, March 14, 1920, Bancroft Collection. Published by permission of the Bancroft Library.

19. Stafford Wallace Austin to A. R. Orr, February 4, 1904, Huntington Collection, Box 24a.

20. Mary Austin to Ferris Greenslet, March 14, 1920, Bancroft Collection.

21. *Earth Horizon,* p. 87.

22. Mary Austin to Sidney Parsons, December 26, 1903, Bancroft Collection.

23. *Earth Horizon,* p. 295.

24. Mary Austin to Mrs. Sidney Parsons, October 19, 1903, Bancroft Collection.

25. Mary Austin, *Santa Lucia* (Harper & Brothers, New York, 1908).

26. Ruth Austin's death certificate, dated October 6, 1918, signed by R. E. Osbourne, M. D., states that he attended her from January 15, 1904, to her death, and that she had been in residence for 13 years and 9 months.

27. *Earth Horizon,* p. 295.

28. Doyle, pp. 210–212.

29. William Booth to Mary Austin, October 10, 1905, Huntington Collection, Box 12.

30. Mary Austin to Miss Williams, October 27, 1905, Huntington Collection, Box 2.

31. W. A. Chalfant, *The Story of Inyo* (Chalfant Press, Bishop, 1933), and Remi Nadeau, *The Water Seekers* (Peregrine Smith, Inc., Salt Lake City, 1974).

32. Mary Austin to Miss Williams, October 27, 1905, Huntington Collection.

33. *Earth Horizon,* pp. 307–308.

34. Ibid., pp. 349–350.

35. Orth, p. 201.

CHAPTER 9

1. "George Sterling at Carmel."

2. Walker, p. 28.

3. Interview with Elsie Martinez, the wife of artist Xavier Martinez.

4. Fink, p. 241.

5. Interview with Harry Downey, early resident of Carmel.

6. Property description and agreement, Huntington Collection, Box 24a.

7. George Sterling diaries, March 11, 1906, Bancroft Collection.

8. Interview with Elsie Martinez.

9. *Earth Horizon,* p. 298.

10. Mary Austin, "A Poet in Outland," *The Overland Monthly and Out West* Magazine, November 1927.

11. *Earth Horizon,* pp. 298–299.

12. "George Sterling at Carmel."

13. Walker, p. 28.

14. *Earth Horizon,* p. 302.

15. Ibid.

16. Oscar Lewis, *San Francisco: Mission to Metropolis* (Howell-North Books, Berkeley, 1966), pp. 185–196.

17. Mary Austin, "Trembler and Fire," *The Argonaut,* 1906.

18. *Earth Horizon,* p. 303.

19. Ibid., p. 308.

20. Walker, p. 34.

21. Ibid., p. 37.

22. Ibid., p. 28.

23. Ibid., p. 37.

24. Mary Austin, *Outland* (John Murray, London, 1910; Boni and Liveright, New York, 1919).

25. *Earth Horizon,* p. 322.

26. *Lost Borders,* pp. 3–4.

27. Ibid., p. 10.

28. Ibid., p. 208–209.

29. Ibid., p. 208.

30. Mary Austin to Mr. Schroeder, February 20, 1919, Huntington Collection, Box 2.

31. *Experiences Facing Death,* p. 26.

32. Walker, pp. 38–39.

33. *Earth Horizon,* p. 303.

34. Andrew Sinclair, *Jack: A Biography of Jack London* (Harper and Row, New York, 1977), p. 116.

35. "George Sterling at Carmel."

36. Walker, p. 40.

37. *Earth Horizon,* p. 303.

38. "George Sterling at Carmel."

39. Doyle, p. 219.

40. Interview with Jean Kellogg Dickie, daughter of Vernon and Charlotte Kellogg.

41. Carol Green Wilson, *Herbert Hoover, a Challenge for Today* (Evans Publishing Company, New York, 1968).

42. Helen B. Pryor, *Lou Henry Hoover, Gallant First Lady* (Dodd, Mead & Company, New York, 1969).

43. Doyle, pp. 219–220.

44. *Earth Horizon,* p. 311.

45. Doyle, p. 251.

46. William Booth to Mary Austin, December 7, 1906, Huntington Collection, Box 12.

47. Mary Austin to William Booth, June 11, 1907, Huntington Collection, Box 1.

48. Doyle, p. 251.

49. Walker, p. 47.

50. Interview with Elsie Martinez.

51. *Can Prayer Be Answered?,* pp. 23–24.

52. Mary Austin, *The Arrow Maker* (Duffield and Company, New York, 1911).

53. *Earth Horizon,* p. 308.

54. Interview with Jean Kellogg Dickie.

55. Mary Austin to Vernon Kellogg, December 4, 1907, Huntington Collection, Box 1.

56. Mary Austin to Houghton Mifflin, September 10, 1907, Huntington Collection, Box 1.

57. Memo in Houghton Mifflin files written by William Booth: "She evidently needs a lesson....I should let her go...in a friendly polite letter...." Huntington Collection, Box 1.

58. Mary Austin to Houghton Mifflin, September 30 and October 1, 1907, Huntington Collection, Box 1.

59. *Christ in Italy,* pp. xv–xvi.

60. *Earth Horizon,* pp. 349–350.

61. Ibid., p. 309.

CHAPTER 10

1. Mary Austin to Vernon Kellogg, December 4, 1907, Huntington Collection, Box 1.

2. *Earth Horizon,* p. 309.

3. Mary Austin to Vernon Kellogg, December 4, 1907, Huntington Collection.

4. *Experiences Facing Death,* p. 129.

5. Ibid., p. 18.

6. Interview with Jean Kellogg Dickie.

7. *Christ in Italy,* pp. 70–72.

8. Ibid., pp. 72–73.

9. *Earth Horizon,* p. 310.

10. *Christ in Italy,* p. 3.

11. Ibid., pp. 11–12.

12. Ibid., pp. 31–32.

13. Ibid., pp. 34–35.

14. *Earth Horizon,* p. 309.

15. Doyle, p. 225.

16. *Earth Horizon,* p. 309.

17. Edward Craig, *Gordon Craig* (Alfred Knopf, New York, 1968).

18. *Earth Horizon,* p. 309.

19. Craig, p. 223.

20. *Earth Horizon,* p. 309.

21. Ibid., p. 328.

22. Ibid., p. 310.

23. *Can Prayer Be Answered?,* pp. 17–21.

24. *Earth Horizon,* p. 310.

25. *Experiences Facing Death,* p. 130.

26. *Can Prayer Be Answered?,* p. 25.

27. Mary Austin to Mr. Schroeder, May 22, 1919, Huntington Collection, Box 2.

28. *Earth Horizon,* p. 310.

29. Pearce, pp. 17–18.

30. Mary Austin to Daniel Trembly MacDougal, circa 1922, Huntington Collection, Box 2.

31. *Earth Horizon,* p. 198.

32. Ibid., pp. 310–311; also fragment from letter, probably from James Wilkinson to Mary Austin, Huntington Collection, Box 24a.

33. "A Poet in Outland."

34. Wilson, pp. 61–62.

35. Will Irwin, *Herbert Hoover: A Reminiscent Biography* (The Century Company, New York, 1928).

36. Eugene Lyons, *Herbert Hoover: A Biography* (Doubleday, New York, 1964), pp. 195–199.

37. *Earth Horizon*, p. 311.

38. Norman Mackenzie and Jeanne Mackenzie, *H. G. Wells* (Simon & Schuster, New York, 1973), p. 229.

39. Ibid., p. 92.

40. Ibid., p. 226.

41. *Earth Horizon*, p. 98.

42. Mary Austin to Ferris Greenslet, Houghton Mifflin, March 14, 1920, Bancroft Collection.

43. *Earth Horizon*, p. 311.

44. Ibid., pp. 311–312.

45. Doyle, p. 226.

46. *Christ in Italy.*

47. *Earth Horizon*, p. 312.

48. Mackenzie and Mackenzie, pp. 255–256.

49. *Earth Horizon*, p. 312.

50. Mary Austin to Ferris Greenslet, March 14, 1920, Bancroft Collection.

51. *Earth Horizon*, p. 313.

52. *The Memoirs of Herbert Hoover: Years of Adventure, 1874–1920* (Macmillan, New York, 1951), p. 121.

53. *Earth Horizon*, p. 313.

54. Doyle, pp. 226–228.

55. *Earth Horizon*, p. 315.

56. Mary Austin, "A New Medium for Poetic Drama," *Theatre Arts Magazine*, Vol. 1, No. 2, February 1917.

57. *Earth Horizon*, p. 315.

58. Walker pp. 89–90.

CHAPTER 11

1. Doyle, p. 239.

2. "The New York Notebook," Huntington Collection, Box 24c.

3. Lincoln Steffens to Laura Steffens, December 25, 1910, *The Letters of Lincoln Steffens*, Vol. I: 1889–1919 (Harcourt, Brace and Company, New York, 1938), p. 255.

4. Lincoln Steffens, "Mary Austin," *The American Magazine*, Vol. 72, No. 2, June 1911.

5. Walker, pp. 51–52, 61.

6. *Earth Horizon*, pp. 325–326.

7. Justin Kaplan, *Lincoln Steffens: A Biography* (Simon and Schuster, New York, 1974), p. 193.

8. Ibid., p. 166.

9. Ibid., pp. 168–169.

10. Lincoln Steffens to Laura Steffens, December 28, 1910, *The Letters of Lincoln Steffens*, p. 255.

11. Kaplan, pp. 118, 166, 168–169.

12. Lincoln Steffens to Mrs. Joseph Steffens, February 4, 1892, *The Letters of Lincoln Steffens*, p. 35.

13. Kaplan, p. 35.

14. Ibid., p. 11.

15. Ibid., p. 18.

16. Ibid., pp. 34–35.

17. Ibid., p. 169.

18. Ibid., p. 197.

19. Kaplan, p. 197.

20. Ibid., pp. 149–150.

21. Ibid., p. 153.

22. Interview with Elsie Martinez.

23. "The New York Notebook," Huntington Collection.

24. Produced February 27, 1911, with George Foster Platt as director.

25. *Earth Horizon*, p. 315.

26. *The American Magazine*, October 1911.

27. Allen Churchill, *The Improper Bohemians* (E. P. Dutton & Company, New York, 1959), p. 33.

28. *Earth Horizon*, p. 326.

29. Ibid., p. 327.

30. "The New York Notebook," Huntington Collection.

31. Ibid.

32. Mary Austin to Dr. Stivers, April 11, 1911, Huntington Collection, Box 2.

33. George Sterling to Mary Austin, May 9, 1911, Huntington Collection, Box 21.

34. Lincoln Steffens to Mary Austin, May 8, 1911, Thomas Matthews Pearce (editor), *Literary America 1903–1934, The Mary Austin Letters* (Greenwood Press, Westport, Connecticut, 1979). Reprinted by permission of Peter Steffens.

35. Interview with Elsie Martinez; also Kaplan, p. 198.

36. "The New York Notebook," Huntington Collection.

37. Kaplan, p. 196.

38. Lincoln Steffens to Laura Steffens, June 25, 1912, *The Letters of Lincoln Steffens*, p. 302.

39. *Earth Horizon*, p. 136.

40. *Mary Austin, A Memorial,* edited by Willard Hougland (Laboratory of Anthropology, Santa Fe, New Mexico, September, 1944), p. 21.

41. *A Woman of Genius,* 1912 edition, p. 495.

42. Harry Peyton Steger to Mary Austin, April 18 and May 2, 1912, Huntington Collection, Box 8.

43. George Sterling to Mary Austin, 1911, Huntington Collection, Box 21.

44. *Earth Horizon,* p. 355.

45. Gordon, p. 41.

46. Charles Lummis to Mary Austin, February 18, 1913, Huntington Collection, Box 14.

47. Russell Doubleday to Mary Austin, January 9, 1913, Huntington Collection, Box 8.

48. "The Garden Book, Carmel-By-The-Sea," Huntington Collection, Box 24c.

49. Walker, p. 118.

50. Fleming, p. 88.

51. Walker, p. 126.

52. Ibid., p. 123.

53. Ibid., p. 126.

54. *Earth Horizon,* p. 322.

55. Ibid., p. 321.

56. Interviews with Mr. and Mrs. Francis Duveneck and Mr. and Mrs. Frank Lloyd.

57. Walker, p. 119.

58. Doyle, p. 239.

59. Walker, p. 119.

60. Arnold Genthe, *As I Remember* (John Day in association with Reynal and Hitchcock, New York, 1936), p. 76.

61. *Earth Horizon,* p. 321.

62. Ibid., p. 320.

CHAPTER 12

1. Lincoln Steffens to Mary Austin, circa 1913, Huntington Collection, Box 21.

2. Mabel Dodge Luhan, *Movers and Shakers,* Vol. III of *Intimate Memories* (Harcourt, Brace and Company, New York, 1936), p. 68.

3. Emily Hahn, *Mabel* (Houghton Mifflin Company, Boston, 1977), pp. 1–50.

4. Churchill, pp. 38–39.

5. Kaplan, p. 187.

6. Hahn, pp. 67–71.

7. Luhan, p. 88.

8. Churchill, pp. 57–58.

9. Hahn, pp. 53–55.

10. Churchill, p. 18.

11. Luhan, p. 68.

12. Mary Austin, *Love and the Soul Maker* (D. Appleton & Company, New York, 1914); *Earth Horizon,* p. 319; Mary Austin to Mr. Schroeder April 8, 1919, Huntington Collection, Box 2.

13. Mary Austin to Ferris Greenslet, October 16, 1915, Bancroft Collection.

14. Daniel T. MacDougal to Mary Austin, March 14, 1914, Huntington Collection, Box 15.

15. "The Garden Book, Carmel-By-The-Sea," Huntington Collection.

16. Carrie Sterling to Mary Austin, December 16, 1914, Huntington Collection, Box 21.

17. Walker, pp. 119–120; Mary Austin to Phoebe Hearst, August 1, 1914, Bancroft Collection.

18. Elizabeth Jordan to Mary Austin, July 15, 1914, Huntington Collection, Box 10.

19. *Earth Horizon,* p. 322.

20. Summons to appear before the Superior Court of the State of California in and for the County of San Bernardino, October 21, 1914, Huntington Collection, Box 24a.

21. *Earth Horizon,* p. 350.

22. Property Settlement, October 22, 1914, Huntington Collection, Box 24a.

23. *Earth Horizon,* p. 351.

24. Thomas Matthews Pearce, *Mary Hunter Austin* (Twayne Publishers, Inc., New York, 1965), pp. 43–44.

25. Elizabeth Jordan to Mary Austin, December 23, 1914, Huntington Collection, Box 10.

26. Informal talk given by Mary Austin in Santa Fe, January 16, 1919, Cassidy Notes, Bancroft Collection.

27. Pearce, *Beloved House,* p. 195.

28. Mary Austin, *The Man Jesus* (Harper, New York, 1925), p. ix.

29. Jack London to Mary Austin, November 5, 1915. Huntington Collection, Box 14. Permission to reprint granted by The Trust of Irving Shepard.

30. Mary Austin to Houghton Mifflin, January 1, 1915, Bancroft Collection.

31. Ferris Greenslet to Mary Austin, May 5, 1915, Bancroft Collection.

32. *Earth Horizon,* pp. 352–353.

33. Mary Austin to Houghton Mifflin, July 15, 1915, Bancroft Collection.

34. *Earth Horizon,* p. 322.

35. Mary Austin to Houghton Mifflin, October 1915, Bancroft Collection.

36. Daniel T. MacDougal to Mary Austin, March 14, 1914, Huntington Collection, Box 15.

37. Mary Austin to Houghton Mifflin, October 1915, Bancroft Collection.

38. Mary Austin to Houghton Mifflin, October 16, 1915, Bancroft Collection.

39. Ferris Greenslet to Mary Austin, December 15, 1915, Bancroft Collection.

40. Mary Austin to Ferris Greenslet, January 7, 1916, Bancroft Collection.

41. Informal talk given by Mary Austin in Santa Fe, January 25, 1919, Cassidy Notes, Bancroft Collection.

42. Sheldon Cheney, "New York's Best Season," *Theatre Arts Magazine,* Vol I, No. 2, February 1917.

43. Pearce, *Literary America,* pp. 83–84.

44. Mary Austin to Grace Mason, December 22, 1915, Huntington Collection, Box HM 41078.

45. Katherine Leckie to Mary Austin, December 1, 1915, Huntington Collection, Box 14.

46. Mary Austin to John Hilliard, March 16, 1916, Huntington Collection, Box HM 41074.

47. Mary Austin to Houghton Mifflin, June 3 to October 30, 1916, Bancroft Collection.

48. Mary Austin to Houghton Mifflin, June 8 to August 12, 1916, Bancroft Collection.

49. Mary Austin to Houghton Mifflin, September 28, 1916, Bancroft Collection.

50. Mary Austin to Ina Cassidy, October 14, 1916, Cassidy Notes, Bancroft Collection.

51. Mary Austin to Ida Hilliard, December 5, 1916, Huntington Collection, Box HM 41071.

CHAPTER 13

1. Mary Austin to H. G. Wells, January 24, 1917, Huntington Collection, Box 2.

2. Herbert Hoover to Mary Austin, June 23, 1917, Huntington Collection, Box 11.

3. George Hunter to Mary Austin, July 29 and August 4, 1917, Huntington Collection, Box 24a.

4. *Earth Horizon,* pp. 355–356.

5. Mary Austin to Houghton Mifflin, September 1, 1917, Bancroft Collection.

6. Mary Austin to Sonya Levien, September 1, 1917, Huntington Collection, Box 1.

7. Mary Austin to Sonya Levien, September 4, 1917, Huntington Collection, Box 1.

8. George Hunter to Mary Austin, September 1917; Mary Hunter to Mary Austin, circa 1917, Huntington Collection, Box 24a.

9. Doyle, p. 245.

10. Mary Austin to S. E. Vermilyea, Attorney, February 24, 1919, Huntington Collection, Box 24a.

11. Mary Austin to Houghton Mifflin, January 8, 1918, Bancroft Collection.

12. Houghton Mifflin to Mary Austin, February 28, 1918, Bancroft Collection.

13. Mary Austin to Houghton Mifflin, January 8, 1918, Bancroft Collection.

14. Mary Austin to Houghton Mifflin, November 16, 1917, Bancroft Collection, Box 12.

15. Hougland (ed.) *Mary Austin, A Memorial,* p. 21.

16. George Hunter to Mary Austin, December 21, 1917, Huntington Collection, Box 24a.

17. Daniel T. MacDougal to Mary Austin, March 16, 1918, Huntington Collection, Box 15.

18. Mary Austin to Ina Cassidy, June 21, 1918, Bancroft Collection.

19. Interview with Peggy Pond Church; Pearce, *Literary America,* pp. 247–48.

20. Hahn pp. 108, 116.

21. *Earth Horizon,* p. 338.

22. Mary Austin to S. E. Vermilyea, June 11, 1919, Huntington Collection, Box 24a.

23. October 6, 1918.

24. Death Certificate signed by Dr. R. E. Osbourne.

25. Mary Austin to Charles Lummis, December 28, 1918, Huntington Collection, Box 1.

26. Mary Austin to Ferris Greenslet, November 11, 1918, Bancroft Collection.

27. "Mary Austin in Santa Fe," *El Palacio,* November 9, 1918.

28. *El Palacio,* December 7, 1918.

29. "Community Theater for Santa Fe," *El Palacio,* December 9, 1918.

30. *El Palacio,* February 5, 1919.

31. Mary Austin to S. E. Vermilyea, February 24, 1919, Huntington Collection, Box 24a.

32. Mary Austin to Ferris Greenslet, December 30, 1918, Bancroft Collection; also *El Palacio,* July 31, 1919.

33. Henry Holt to Mary Austin, January 21 and February 7, 1919, Huntington Collection, Box 11.

34. Mary Austin to Ferris Greenslet, November 11, 1918, Bancroft Collection.

35. Daniel T. MacDougal to Mary Austin, November 25, 1918, and January 18 and February 4, 1919, Huntington Collection, Box 15.

36. Ruth Kelsey to Ferris Greenslet, March 12, 1919, Bancroft Collection.

37. Mary Austin to Mr. Schroeder, February 18, 1919, Huntington Collection, Box 2.

38. Mary Austin to Mr. Schroeder, February 20, 1919, Huntington Collection, Box 2.

39. Mary Austin to Mr. Schroeder, n.d. (probably February or March 1919), Huntington Collection, Box 2.

40. Ruth Kelsey to Ferris Greenslet, March 12, 1919, Bancroft Collection.

41. Hahn, p. 34.

42. Mabel Sterne to Mary Austin, May 28, 1919, Huntington Collection, Box 14.

43. Hahn, p. 138.

44. Ibid., p. 127.

45. *Earth Horizon,* p. 340.

46. Mabel Sterne to Mary Austin, circa June 1919, Huntington Collection, Box 14.

47. Interview with Peggy Pond Church; also *El Palacio,* April–May 1919.

48. Mary Hunter to Mary Austin, June 8, October 23, and December 6, 1919, Huntington Collection, Box 24a.

49. Mary Austin to S. E. Vermilyea, June 11, 1919, Huntington Collection, Box 24a.

50. Mabel Sterne to Mary Austin, circa June 1919, Huntington Collection, Box 14.

51. *El Palacio*, May 24, 1919; also Mary Austin to Mr. Schroeder, May 22, 1919, Huntington Collection, Box 2.

52. Daniel T. MacDougal to Mary Austin, July 22, 1919, Huntington Collection, Box 15.

53. *El Palacio*, July 3, 1919.

54. Mary Austin to Ina Cassidy, September 12, 1919, Bancroft Collection.

55. Mabel Sterne to Mary Austin, circa 1920, Huntington Collection, Box 14; also Hougland (ed.), *Mary Austin, A Memorial*, p. 21.

56. *The New Mexican*, October 29, 1919.

57. Mary Austin to Daniel T. MacDougal, March 13, 1920, The Carnegie Desert Laboratory, MacDougal Collection, University of Arizona Library, Special Collections.

58. Mary Austin to Houghton Mifflin, March 2, 1920, Bancroft Collection.

59. Interview with Mr. and Mrs. Frank Lloyd.

60. Mary Austin to Mr. Schroeder, December 24, 1919, Huntington Collection, Box 2.

CHAPTER 14

1. Mary Austin to Ferris Greenslet, January 5 and 15, Bancroft Collection.

2. Daniel T. MacDougal to Mary Austin, January 14, 1920, Huntington Collection, Box 15.

3. Mary Austin to D. T. MacDougal, March 13, 1920, The Carnegie Desert Laboratory, MacDougal Collection, University of Arizona Library, Special Collections.

4. Ibid.

5. Mary Austin to John Hilliard, May 24, 1920, Huntington Collection, Box HM 41076.

6. *The Nation*, Vol. 110, February 21, 1920.

7. Mary Austin, "Hoover and Johnson: West Is West," *The Nation*, Vol. 110, May 15, 1920.

8. Churchill, pp. 235–237.

9. Interview with Mr. and Mrs. Francis Duveneck, and with Mr. and Mrs. Frank Lloyd.

10. D. T. MacDougal to Mary Austin, July 12, 1920, Huntington Collection, Box 15.

11. Mary Austin to D. T. MacDougal, July 5, 1920, The Carnegie Desert Laboratory, MacDougal Collection, University of Arizona Library, Special Collections.

12. Mary Austin to Ina Cassidy, August 16, 1920, Bancroft Collection.

13. Mary Austin to Ferris Greenslet, March 14, 1920, Bancroft Collection.

14. Mary Austin to Ferris Greenslet, December 23, 1920, and January 4, 1921, Bancroft Collection.

15. *Earth Horizon*, p. 331.

16. Marion K. Sanders, *Dorothy Thompson* (Houghton Mifflin, Boston, 1973), p. 112.

17. Mary Austin to Ferris Greenslet, March 14, 1920, Bancroft Collection.

18. *Earth Horizon*, p. 337.

19. Mary Austin to John Hilliard, May 24, 1920, Huntington Collection, HM 41076.

20. *Earth Horizon*, p. 341.

21. D. T. MacDougal to Mary Austin, March 21 and May 5, 1921, Huntington Collection, Box 15.

22. Mary Austin to Houghton Mifflin, April 2, 1921, Bancroft Collection.

23. *Ladies Home Journal* to Mary Austin, June 23, 1921, Huntington Collection, Box 14.

24. Mary Austin, "May Sinclair," manuscript, Huntington collection, Box 26.

25. *Earth Horizon*, pp. 341–342.

26. Mary Austin to Ferris Greenslet, July 26, 1921, Bancroft Collection.

27. Mary Austin, "My Fabian Summer," *The Bookman*, December 1921.

28. Kitty Muggeridge and Ruth Adam, *Beatrice Webb* (Alfred Knopf, New York, 1968), p. 73.

29. Lovat Dickson, *H. G. Wells, His Turbulent Life & Times* (Atheneum, New York, 1969), pp. 94–95.

30. "My Fabian Summer."

31. *Carmel Pine Cone*, August 10, 1922.

32. *Earth Horizon*, p. 344.

33. Ibid., p. 342; Mary Austin to Ina Cassidy, November 8, 1921, Bancroft Collection.

34. "My Fabian Summer."

35. Gérard Jean-Aubrey, *The Sea Dreamer, A Definitive Biography of Joseph Conrad* (Doubleday, New York, 1957).

36. *Earth Horizon,* p. 343.

37. Ibid., p. 342.

38. "My Fabian Summer."

39. *Earth Horizon,* p. 344.

40. *Earth Horizon* (first ed.), p. 343.

41. Mary Austin to Ina Cassidy, November 8, 1921, Bancroft Collection.

42. D. T. MacDougal to Mary Austin, January 2, 1922, Huntington Collection, Box 15.

43. D. T. MacDougal to Mary Austin, July 18, 1921, Huntington Collection, Box 15.

44. Mary Austin to D. T. MacDougal, December 31, 1921, Huntington Collection, Box 2.

45. Mary Austin to D. T. MacDougal, January 2, 1922, Huntington Collection, Box 2.

46. Ibid.

47. Mary Austin to D. T. MacDougal, January 9, 1922, Huntington Collection, Box 2.

48. Mary Austin to Ina Cassidy, January 10, 1922, Bancroft Collection.

49. Mary Austin to D. T. MacDougal, January 9, 1922, Huntington Collection.

50. Ibid.

51. Mary Austin to D. T. MacDougal, January 11, January 28, and February 12, 1922, Huntington Collection, Box 2.

52. D. T. MacDougal to Mary Austin, January 12, 1922, Huntington Collection, Box 15.

53. D. T. MacDougal to Mary Austin, February 20, 1922, Huntington Collection.

54. D. T. MacDougal to Mary Austin, March 3, 1922, Huntington Collection.

55. Mary Austin to D. T. MacDougal, January 14, 1922, Huntington Collection, Box 2.

56. Mary Austin to D. T. MacDougal, February 12, 1922, Huntington Collection.

57. Mary Austin to D. T. MacDougal, March 8, 1922, Huntington Collection.

58. D. T. MacDougal to Mary Austin, April 5, 1922, Huntington Collection, Box 2.

59. Mary Austin to Edwin E. Slosson, May 11, 1922, Huntington Collection, Box 2.

60. Mary Austin to William Ritter, May 18, 1922, Bancroft Collection.

61. Mary Austin to D. T. MacDougal, June 6, 1922, Huntington Collection, Box 2.

62. Mary Austin to D. T. MacDougal, June 14, 1922, Huntington Collection.

CHAPTER 15

1. Mary Austin, "Love Coming Late," *The Nation,* July 11, 1928.

2. D. T. MacDougal to Mary Austin, June 20, 1922, Huntington Collection, Box 15; interview with the Francis Duvenecks.

3. D. T. MacDougal to Mary Austin, October 21, 1922, Huntington Collection.

4. James Franklin Devendorf to Mary Austin, April 2, 1926, Huntington Collection, Box 6.

5. Interview with the Frank Lloyds.

6. "My Fabian Summer."

7. Interview with the Lloyds.

8. Interview with the Duvenecks.

9. Interview with the Lloyds.

10. *Carmel Pine Cone,* September 7, 1922.

11. George Hunter to Mary Austin, August 17, 1922, Huntington Collection, Box 24a.

12. Mary Austin to D. T. MacDougal, September 19, 1922, Huntington Collection, Box 2.

13. Mary Austin to D. T. MacDougal, October 11, 1922, Huntington Collection.

14. D. T. MacDougal to Mary Austin, October 21, 1922, Huntington Collection, Box 15.

15. D. T. MacDougal to Mary Austin, October 25, 1922, Huntington Collection.

16. D. T. MacDougal to Mary Austin, November 11, 1922, Huntington Collection.

17. Mary Austin to D. T. MacDougal, October 11, 1922, Huntington Collection, Box 2.

18. Mary Austin to Ina Cassidy, December 12 and 30, 1922, and January 20, 1923, Bancroft Collection. The Century Company chose John Edwin Jackson to illustrate *The Land of Journeys' Ending.*

19. Ina Cassidy to Mary Austin, January 12, 1923, Bancroft Collection.

20. Carl Van Doren, Century Company, to Mary Austin, December 27, 1922, Huntington Collection, Box 22.

21. Mary Austin to D. T. MacDougal, February 2, 1923, Huntington Collection, Box 2.

22. Mabel Sterne to Mary Austin, November 1922, Huntington Collection, Box 14.

23. January 17, 1923, Huntington Collection, Box 25.

24. Mabel Sterne to Mary Austin, November 11, 1922 and January 6, 1923, Huntington Collection, Box 14.

25. Mary Austin to D. T. MacDougal, January 18, 1923, Huntington Collection, Box 2.

26. Mary Austin to Ina Cassidy, February 20, 1923, Bancroft Collection.

27. Mary Austin to D. T. MacDougal, March 1, 1923, Huntington Collection, Box 2.

28. Frances Perkins to Mary Austin, March 5, 1923, Huntington Collection, Box 18.

29. Ina Cassidy's "Journal of the Desert Trip," Bancroft Collection.

30. Ibid.

31. Ibid.

32. Ina Cassidy, "I-Mary and Me, The Chronicle of a Friendship," *The New Mexico Quarterly,* November, 1939.

33. Cassidy, "Journal of the Desert Trip," Bancroft Collection.

34. *The Land of Journeys' Ending,* p. 231.

35. Mary Austin to D. T. MacDougal, April 29 and May 4, 1923, Huntington Collection, Box 2.

36. Mary Austin to D. T. MacDougal, May 8 and 9, 1923, Huntington Collection.

37. Mary Austin to D. T. MacDougal, May 13, 1923, Huntington Collection.

38. *The Morning Press,* Santa Barbara, June 8, 9, 10, 1923.

39. Mary Austin to D. T. MacDougal, May 30, 1923, Huntington Collection.

40. Mary Austin to D. T. MacDougal, June 23 and July 2, 1923, Huntington collection.

41. Mabel Luhan to Mary Austin, April 23, 1923, Huntington Collection, Box 14.

42. Mary Austin to D. T. MacDougal, July 2, 1923, Huntington collection.

43. Mary Austin to D. T. MacDougal, July 21, 1923, Huntington Collection.

44. Mary Austin to Ina Cassidy, July 1923, Bancroft Collection.

45. Mary Austin to D. T. MacDougal, August 15, 1923, Huntington Collection, Box 2.

46. D. T. MacDougal to Mary Austin, July 27 to August 26, 1923, Huntington Collection, Box 15.

47. Agnes de Mille, *Dance to the Piper* (Little, Brown and Company, Boston, 1952), pp. 17–18.

48. *The New Mexican,* August 30, September 8, 1923.

49. Mary Austin to D. T. MacDougal, October 12, 1923, Huntington Collection.

50. Mary Austin to D. T. MacDougal, October 22, 1923, Huntington Collection.

51. D. T. MacDougal to Mary Austin, October 21, 1923, Huntington Collection.

52. Mary Austin to D. T. MacDougal, October 27, 1923, Huntington Collection.

53. *The New Mexican,* October 29, 1923.

CHAPTER 16

1. Mary Austin to D. T. MacDougal, February 25 and March 9, 1924, Huntington Collection; Helen Barnes, Century Company, to Mary Austin, April 1924, Huntington Collection, Box 6.

2. Mary Austin, *Everyman's Genius* (The Bobbs-Merrill Company, Indianapolis, 1925), p. 223.

3. Mary Austin to D. T. MacDougal, May 27, 1924, Huntington Collection.

4. Mary Austin to Eva Lummis De Kalb, August 14, 1929, Huntington Collection, Box 1.

5. Mary Austin to Ina Cassidy, October 1924, Bancroft Collection.

6. Mabel Luhan to Mary Austin, October 1924, Huntington Collection, Box 14.

7. Mary Austin to Alice Waite, Dean of Wellesley College, April 9, 1924; Alice Waite to Mary Austin, May 6, 1924, Huntington Collection, Box 24a; also Katherine Raymond to Mary Austin, February 23, 1925.

8. Luhan, *Movers and Shakers.*

9. Interview with Peggy Pond Church.

10. Mary Austin to Ina Cassidy, December 18, 1924, Bancroft Collection.

11. Transfer of property to Carrie Horton Blackman, October 18, 1924, nine lots in City of Carmel, Records of Monterey County Recorder.

12. Mary Hunter to Mary Austin, March 19, 1925, Huntington Collection, Box 24a.

13. Interview with Kathryn Frazer.

14. Mary Austin, "Frank Applegate," *The New Mexico Quarterly,* 1932; also *Earth Horizon,* p. 357.

15. Oliver La Farge, *Santa Fe* (University of Oklahoma Press, Norman, Oklahoma, 1959), pp. 269–270.

16. Interview with Peggy Pond Church.

17. Mary Austin, "Life at Santa Fe," ms, Huntington Collection, Box 26.

18. Income Tax Report, 1924, Huntington Collection, Box 24a.

19. Royalty Statement, Century Company, March 31, 1925, Huntington Collection, Box 6.

20. George Hunter to Mary Austin, May 24, 1925, Huntington Collection, Box 24a.

21. Mary Hunter to Mary Austin, May 17, September 3 and 14, 1925, Huntington Collection, Box 24a.

22. Mary Austin to Ina Cassidy, December 23, 1925, Bancroft Collection.

23. "The Indian Arts Fund," in W. Hougland (ed.), *Mary Austin, A Memorial,* pp. 59–61.

24. La Farge, p. 289.

25. Mary Austin, "The Town That Doesn't Want a Chautauqua," *The New Republic,* July 7, 1926.

26. La Farge, pp. 288–294.

27. Interview with Peggy Pond Church.

28. Mary Austin to Dr. H. L. Brainerd, December 2, 1926, Huntington Collection, Box 24a.

29. Mary Austin to Houghton Mifflin, June 6, 1926, Bancroft Collection; Mary Austin to Ina Cassidy, September 24, 1926, University of New Mexico Collection; also Ina Cassidy, "Mary Austin's Casa Querida," *The New Mexico Daily Examiner,* June 18, 1939.

30. Mary Austin to Albert Bender, October 9, 1929, Mills College Collection; Mary Austin to Eva Lummis De Kalb, August 14, 1929, Huntington Collection, Box 1.

31. Interview with Peggy Pond Church.

32. Mary Austin to George Hunter, January 15 and April 15, 1927, Huntington Collection, Box 24a.

33. Mary Austin to Ina Cassidy, January 19, 1927, University of New Mexico Collection.

34. B. A. Botkins Papers, Interview with Alta Applegate, Bancroft Collection.

35. La Farge, pp. 308–309.

36. W. Hougland (ed.), *Mary Austin, A Memorial,* pp. 59–61.

37. Mary Austin, *The Lands of the Sun* (Houghton Mifflin Company, Boston, 1927).

38. Houghton Mifflin to Mary Austin, November 6 and 29, 1926, Huntington Collection, Box 11.

39. "George Sterling at Carmel"; "A Poet in Outland."

40. Mary Austin, "Three at Carmel," *The Saturday Review of Literature,* September 29, 1928.

41. Interview with Ansel Adams.

42. Nancy Newhall, *The Eloquent Light* (Sierra Club, San Francisco, 1963), p. 48.

43. Interview with Ansel Adams.

44. B. A. Botkin Papers, Interview with Dr. Foster, Bancroft Collection.

45. Ansel Adams and Mary Austin, *Taos Pueblo* (Grabhorn Press, San Francisco, 1930).

46. Oscar Lewis, *To Remember Albert M. Bender* (Grabhorn & Hoyem, San Francisco, 1973); also Monroe E. Deutsch, "Saint Albert of San Francisco," *The Menorah Journal,* Spring–Summer 1955.

47. Houghton Mifflin to Mary Austin, May 3, July 25, and September 19, 1927, Huntington Collection, Box 11.

48. De Mille, *Dance to the Piper,* p. 112. Reprinted by permission of Agnes de Mille and Harold Ober Associates Incorporated. Copyright © 1951, 1952, 1979, 1980 by Agnes de Mille.

49. Ibid, pp. 111–114.

50. *The New Mexican,* August 18, 1927.

51. Mary Austin, "The Colorado River Controversy," *The Nation,* November 9, 1927.

52. Mary Austin to Albert Bender, August 10, 1927, Mills College Collection.

53. Anna de Mille to Mary Austin, September 11, 1927, Huntington Collection, Box 8.

54. Ferris Greenslet to Mary Austin, October 24, 1927, Huntington Collection, Box 12.

55. Mary Austin to Albert Bender, November 5, 1927, Mills College Collection; also *The New Mexican,* December 23, 1927.

56. George Baker, Yale University, to Mary Austin, October 28, 1927, Huntington Collection, Box 4.

CHAPTER 17

1. Mabel Major, "Mary Austin in Fort Worth," *New Mexico Quarterly,* November 1934.

2. *Boston Evening Transcript,* October 1928, Huntington Collection, Box 48.

3. Mary Austin to Albert Bender, January 1928, Mills College Collection.

4. Mary Austin to Albert Bender, March 9, 1928, Mills College Collection.

5. Mary Austin, *The Children Sing in the Far West* (Houghton Mifflin, Boston, 1928).

6. Mary Austin to Henry Goddard Leach, May 22, 1928, Huntington Collection, Box 1.

7. *Experiences Facing Death*, p. 61.

8. Ibid.

9. Mary Austin to Albert Bender, June 9, 1928, Mills College Collection.

10. Ibid.

11. Newhall, pp. 51, 54.

12. Ferris Greenslet to Mary Austin, November 23, 1928, Huntington Collection, Box 11.

13. George Baker to Mary Austin, June 25 and August 13, 1928, Huntington Collection, Box 4.

14. *Can Prayer Be Answered?* pp. 44–45; also La Farge, pp. 369–371, and George Parmley Day, Treasurer, Yale University, to Mary Austin, March 1929, Huntington Collection, Box 8.

15. Pearce, *Beloved House*, p. 31.

16. Ferris Greenslet to Mary Austin, February 1, 1929, Huntington Collection, Box 12.

17. Mary Austin to Carey McWilliams, March 19, 1929, U.C.L.A. Collection.

18. Newhall, pp. 54, 60.

19. Ibid., p. 54.

20. Ansel Adams to Malcolm Davis, Yale University Press, April 14, 1929, Ansel Adams Collection.

21. Interview with Virginia Adams.

22. May 22–28, 1929, noted in Los Angeles *Times*, May 10, 1929.

23. Interview with Kathryn Frazer.

24. Mary Austin to Albert Bender, September 4, 1929, Mills College Collection.

25. Albert Bender to Mary Austin, September 14, 1929, Huntington Collection, Box 4.

26. Albert Bender to Mary Austin, September 1929, Huntington Collection, Box 4.

27. Mary Austin to Albert Bender, October 9, 1929, Mills College Collection.

28. Mary Austin to Albert Bender, October 27, 1929, Mills College Collection.

29. Mary Austin to Albert Bender, April 26, 1930, Mills College Collection.

30. Pearce, *Mary Hunter Austin,* pp. 59–60; also Mary Austin to Ray Lyman Wilbur, Secretary of the Interior, April 19, 1930, Huntington Collection, Box 2.

31. Mary Austin to Albert Bender, October 14, 1930, Mills College Collection.

32. Ibid.; also *Earth Horizon,* p. 365.

33. La Farge, pp. 325–326.

34. Agnes de Mille to Mary Austin, August 30, 1930, Huntington Collection, Box 8.

35. Don McDonagh, *Martha Graham* (Praeger Publishers, New York, 1973), pp. 76–77.

36. Newhall, p. 65.

37. Mary Austin to Albert Bender, January 16, 1931, Mills College Collection.

38. Frank Applegate died February 13, 1931.

39. Mary Austin to Ansel Adams, March 13, 1931, Ansel Adams Collection.

40. Mary Austin to Albert Bender, April 8, 1931, Mills College Collection.

41. Mary Austin to Ray Lyman Wilbur, January 7 and July 17, 1931, Huntington Collection, Box 2.

42. Mary Austin to Virginia Adams, June 25, 1931, Ansel Adams Collection.

43. Houghton Mifflin to Mary Austin, October 13, 1931, Huntington Collection, Box 12.

44. *The New Mexican,* October 14 and 22, 1931.

45. Mary Austin to Albert Bender, November 13, 1931, Mills College Collection.

46. *The New Mexican,* December 8, 1931.

47. Alta Applegate to Ansel Adams, December 31, 1931, Ansel Adams Collection; also Jane Baumann to Witter Bynner, January 9, 1932, University of New Mexico Collection.

48. Mary Austin to Albert Bender, February 22, 1932, Mills College Collection.

49. Ferris Greenslet to Mary Austin, February 24, 1932, Huntington Collection, Box 12.

50. Alta Applegate to Ansel Adams, February 24, 1932, Ansel Adams Collection.

51. Mary Austin to Virginia Adams, April 29, 1932, Ansel Adams Collection.

52. Mary Austin, *One-Smoke Stories* (Houghton Mifflin, Boston, 1934).

53. Houghton Mifflin to Mary Austin, October 10 and November 5, 1932, Huntington Collection, Box 12.

54. Houghton Mifflin to Mary Austin, October 31, 1932, Huntington Collection, Box 12.

55. *Earth Horizon* (first ed.), pp. 311, 312.

56. Houghton Mifflin to Mary Austin, October 31, 1932, Huntington Collection, Box 12.

57. Report of Cadis Phipps, M. D., to John Ames, M. D., November 5, 1932, Huntington Collection, Box 24a.

58. Mary Austin to Albert Bender, November 28, 1932, Mills College Collection.

CHAPTER 18

1. *The New Mexican,* December 7, 1932.

2. Pearce, *Beloved House,* pp. 15–20.

3. Ibid., p. 17.

4. *Earth Horizon,* p. vii.

5. Pearce, *Mary Hunter Austin,* p. 63.

6. Pearce, *Beloved House,* pp. 117–118.

7. Mary Austin to Albert Bender, December 17, 1932, Mills College Collection.

8. Mary Austin to Albert Bender, May 9, 1933, Mills College Collection.

9. *Experiences Facing Death,* pp. 22–23.

10. Ibid., pp. 23–24.

11. Mary Austin to Albert Bender, May 14, 1933, Mills College Collection.

12. Last Will and Testament of Mary Austin, October 20, 1933, files of the School of American Research.

13. Mary Austin to Albert Bender, October 16, 1933, Mills College Collection.

14. Ibid.

15. *Pasadena Star News,* October 24, 1933.

16. Mary Austin to Albert Bender, December 3 and 27, 1933, Mills College Collection.

17. Charlotte E. Dickinson to Mary Austin, December 21, 1933, Huntington Collection, Box 24a.

18. Ina Cassidy's Journal, December 13 and 17, 1933, Cassidy Materials, Bancroft Library.

19. Mary Austin to Albert Bender, November 9, 1933, Mills College Collection.

20. Cassidy Journal, January 1, 1934, Bancroft Library.

21. Mary Austin to Albert Bender, December 21, 1933, Mills College Collection.

22. *Can Prayer Be Answered?*, p. 55.

23. Mary Austin to Albert Bender, May 28, 1934, Mills College Collection.

24. Francis Wilson to Mary Hunter, July 23, 1934, Huntington Collection, Box 24a.

25. Pearce, *Mary Hunter Austin,* pp. 64–65; also Doyle, pp. 284–289.

26. Mary Austin to Houghton Mifflin, August 10, 1934, Huntington Collection, Box 1. The book was never published. Copies of the manuscript are in the Special Collections of the Zimmerman Library at the University of New Mexico, according to Pearce, *Literary America,* p. 217.

27. Mary Austin, "The Aged Poet Discourses," *The Saturday Review of Literature,* August 29, 1931.

EPILOGUE

1. Pearce, *Beloved House,* pp. 219–222.

2. Mary Austin, "Going West," *The Bookman,* September 1922.

3. Pearce, *Beloved House,* p. 205.

Bibliography

The principal collection of unpublished Mary Austin material, comprising correspondence, diaries, notebooks, and manuscripts, is in the Henry E. Huntington Library, San Marino, California. Other important material is housed in the Bancroft Library, University of California at Berkeley; and the Mills College Library, Oakland, California. There are smaller collections in the libraries of the University of California at Los Angeles; the University of Arizona, Tucson; the University of New Mexico, Albuquerque; Blackburn College, Carlinville, Illinois; and the Southwest Museum, Los Angeles.

BOOKS BY MARY AUSTIN

The American Rhythm. New York: Harcourt, Brace and Company, 1923; Boston and New York: Houghton Mifflin Company, 1930. Reprinted by Cooper Square Publishers (New York, 1970).

The Arrow Maker. New York: Duffield and Company, 1911; revised edition, Boston: Houghton Mifflin and Company, 1915. Reprinted by AMS Press, Inc., 1915 ed. (New York, 1969).

The Basket Woman. Boston and New York: Houghton Mifflin Company, 1904. Reprinted by AMS Press, Inc. (New York, 1969).

[295]

California, Land of the Sun. London: A. and C. Black Limited, 1914; New York: Macmillan Company, 1914; revised edition, *Lands of the Sun,* Houghton Mifflin Company, 1927.

Can Prayer Be Answered? New York: Farrar and Rinehart, 1934.

The Children Sing in the Far West. Boston and New York: Houghton Mifflin Company, 1928.

Christ in Italy. New York: Duffield and Company, 1912.

Earth Horizon: An Autobiography. Boston and New York, Houghton Mifflin Company, 1932. Reprinted by Folcroft (Folcroft, Pa.).

Everyman's Genius. Indianapolis: The Bobbs-Merrill Company, Inc., 1925.

Experiences Facing Death. Indianapolis: The Bobbs-Merrill Company, Inc., 1931. Reprinted by Arno Press (New York, 1977, Death and Dying Series).

The Flock. Boston and New York: Houghton Mifflin and Company, 1906. Reprinted by William Gannon (Santa Fe, 1973).

The Ford. Boston and New York: Houghton Mifflin Company, 1917.

The Green Bough. New York: Doubleday, Page and Company, 1913; also pp. 134–163 in *Christ in Italy.*

Indian Pottery of the Rio Grande. Pasadena, California: Esto Publishing Company, 1934.

Isidro. Boston and New York: Houghton Mifflin and Company, 1905. Reprinted by Literature House (Upper Saddle River, N. J., 1970).

The Land of Journeys' Ending. New York and London: The Century Company, 1924. Reprinted by AMS Press, Inc. (New York, 1969) and by University of Arizona Press (Tucson, 1983).

The Land of Little Rain. Boston and New York: Houghton Mifflin Company, 1903. Reprinted by University of New Mexico Press (Albuquerque, 1974) and by Gordon Press (New York, 1974).

Love and the Soul Maker. New York: D. Appleton and Company, 1914.

The Lovely Lady. New York: Doubleday, Page and Company, 1913.

Lost Borders. New York and London: Harper and Brothers, 1909.

The Man Jesus. New York and London: Harper and Brothers, 1915; revised edition, *A Small Town Man,* 1925.

No. 26 Jayne Street. Boston and New York: Houghton Mifflin Company, 1920.

One Hundred Miles on Horseback. Los Angeles: Dawson's Book Shop, 1963.

One-Smoke Stories. Boston and New York: Houghton Mifflin Company, 1934.

Outland (under the pseudonym of Gordon Stairs). London: John Murray, 1910; New York: Boni and Liveright, 1919, 1920.

Santa Lucia. New York and London: Harper and Brothers, 1908.

Starry Adventure. Boston and New York: Houghton Mifflin Company, 1931.

Taos Pueblo. Photographed by Ansel Adams and described by Mary Austin. San Francisco: Grabhorn Press, 1930. Reprinted by The New York Graphic Society (Boston, 1977).

The Trail Book. Boston and New York: Houghton Mifflin Company, 1918.

A Woman of Genius. New York: Doubleday, Page and Company, 1912; Boston and New York: Houghton Mifflin Company, 1917. Reprinted by Arno Press (New York, 1977, Recovered Fiction by American Women Series).

The Young Woman Citizen. New York: The Woman's Press, 1918. Reprinted by Designs Three Publishers (Fullerton, Calif., 1976).

ANTHOLOGIES

"How I Learned to Read and Write." *My Maiden Effort,* edited by Gelett Burgess for the Authors' League of America, 1921; reprinted in *My First Publication,* edited by James D. Hart, The Book Club of California, 1961.

Mother of Felipe and Other Early Stories. Collected and edited by Franklin Walker. Los Angeles: The Book Club of California, 1950.

ARTICLES, STORIES, AND POEMS

More than 125 of Mary Austin's writings appeared in more than 60 periodicals. A partial list may be found in *Mary Austin: Bibliography and Biographical Data,* California Library Research *Digest,* Monograph #2 (Berkeley, 1924). Four short pieces especially pertinent to her life story have been selected for listing in this volume.

"Frustrate." *Century* Magazine (January 1912).

"A Poet in Outland." *The Overland Monthly and Out West Magazine* (November 1927).

"George Sterling at Carmel." *The American Mercury,* XI (May 1927).

"Three at Carmel." *The Saturday Review of Literature* (September 29, 1928).

SECONDARY SOURCES

Bingham, Edwin R. *Charles F. Lummis, Editor of the Southwest.* San Marino, California: Huntington Library, 1955.

Bonsal, Stephen. *Edward Fitzgerald Beale, A Pioneer in the Path of Empire, 1822–1903.* New York: Putnam, 1912.

Brooks, Van Wyck. *The Confident Years, 1885–1915.* New York: E. P. Dutton and Company, 1952.

Cassidy, Ina Sizer. "I-Mary and Me: The Chronicle of a Friendship." *New Mexico Quarterly* (November 1939).

Chalfant, W. A. *The Story of Inyo.* Bishop, California: Chalfant Press, 1933.

Cheney, Sheldon. "New York's Best Season." *Theatre Arts Magazine,* I, 2 (February 1917).

Churchill, Allen. *The Improper Bohemians.* New York: E. P. Dutton and Company, 1959.

Craig, Edward. *Gordon Craig.* New York: Alfred Knopf, 1968.

de Mille, Agnes. *Dance to the Piper.* Boston: Little Brown and Company, 1952.

Deutsch, Monroe E. "Saint Albert of San Francisco." *The Menorah Journal* (Spring–Summer, 1955).

Dickson, Lovat. *H. G. Wells, His Turbulent Life and Times.* New York: Atheneum, 1969.

Doyle, Helen MacKnight. *Mary Austin: Woman of Genius.* New York: Gotham House, 1939.

Fink, Augusta. *Monterey: The Presence of the Past.* San Francisco: Chronicle Books, 1972; reprint edition, *Monterey County: The Dramatic Story of Its Past.* Fresno: Valley Publishers, 1978.

Fleming, Donald R. "The Last Bohemian." *Quarterly News-Letter of the Book Club of California,* XXXVII, 4 (Fall 1972).

Genthe, Arnold. *As I Remember.* New York: John Day, 1936.

Gordon, Dudley. *Charles F. Lummis, Crusader in Corduroy.* Los Angeles: Cultural Assets Press, 1972.

Hahn, Emily. *Mabel.* Boston: Houghton Mifflin Company, 1977.

Hoover, Herbert. *The Memoirs of Herbert Hoover: Years of Adventure.* New York: Macmillan, 1951.

Hougland, Willard, ed. *Mary Austin: A Memorial.* Santa Fe, New Mexico: The Laboratory of Anthropology, 1944.

Irwin, Will. *Herbert Hoover: A Reminiscent Biography.* New York: The Century Company, 1928.

Jean-Aubrey, Gérard. *The Sea Dreamer: A Definitive Biography of Joseph Conrad.* New York: Doubleday, 1957.

Kaplan, Justin. *Lincoln Steffens: A Biography.* New York: Simon and Schuster, 1974.

La Farge, Oliver. *Santa Fe.* Norman, Oklahoma: The University of Oklahoma Press, 1959.

Lewis, Oscar. *Bay Window Bohemia.* New York: Doubleday, 1956.

———. *San Francisco: Mission to Metropolis.* Berkeley, California: Howell-North Books, 1966.

———. *To Remember Albert M. Bender.* San Francisco: Grabhorn and Hoyem, 1973.

Luhan, Mabel Dodge. *Intimate Memories.* Vol. III, *Movers and Shakers.* New York: Harcourt, Brace, and Company, 1936.

Lyday, Jo W. *Mary Austin: The Southwest Works.* Austin, Texas: Steck-Vaughn Company, 1968.

Lyons, Eugene. *Herbert Hoover: A Biography.* New York: Doubleday, 1964.

MacKenzie, Norman, and MacKenzie, Jeanne. *H. G. Wells.* New York: Simon and Schuster, 1973.

McDonagh, Don. *Martha Graham.* New York: Praeger Publishers, 1973.

Muggeridge, Kitty, and Adam, Ruth. *Beatrice Webb.* New York: Alfred Knopf, 1968.

Nadeau, Remi. *The Water Seekers.* Salt Lake City, Utah: Peregrine Smith, Inc., 1974.

Newhall, Nancy. *The Eloquent Light.* San Francisco: The Sierra Club, 1963.

Orth, Michael. "Ideality to Reality: The Founding of Carmel." *The California Historical Society Quarterly,* XLVIII, 3 (September 1969).

Overton, Grant. *The Women Who Made Our Novels.* New York: Moffet, Yard, and Company, 1918.

Pearce, Thomas Matthews. *The Beloved House.* Caldwell, Idaho: Caxton Printers, 1940.

———. *Mary Hunter Austin.* Boston: Twayne Publishers, 1965.

Pearce, Thomas Matthews, ed. *Literary America, 1903–1934: The Mary Austin Letters.* Westport, Connecticut: Greenwood Press, 1979.

Powell, Lawrence Clark. "Mary Hunter Austin: 1868–1934." *Arizona and the West* (Spring 1968).

Powell, Lawrence Clark. "Mary Austin: The Land of Little Rain." *California Classics*. Los Angeles: The Ward Ritchie Press, 1974.

―――. "Mary Austin: The Land of Journeys' Ending." *Southwest Classics*. Los Angeles: The Ward Ritchie Press, 1971; Tucson: University of Arizona Press, 1982.

Pryor, Helen B. *Lou Henry Hoover, Gallant First Lady*. New York: Dodd, Mead and Company, 1969.

Righter, Robert. "A Dedication to the Memory of Henry Hittell, 1830–1917." *Arizona and the West* (Winter 1974).

Ringler, Donald P. "Mary Austin: Kern County Days, 1888–1892." *Southern California Quarterly*, XLV, 1 (March 1963).

Sanders, Marion K. *Dorothy Thompson*. Boston: Houghton Mifflin Company, 1973.

Sergeant, Elizabeth Shepley. "Mary Austin: A Portrait." *Saturday Review of Literature*, XI, 8 (September 8, 1934).

Sinclair, Andrew. *Jack: A Biography of Jack London*. New York: Harper and Row, 1977.

Starr, Kevin. "Mary Austin: Mystic, Writer, Conservationist." *Sierra Club Bulletin*, Vol. 61, 10 (November/December 1976).

Steffens, Lincoln. *The Letters of Lincoln Steffens*, edited by Ella Winter and Granville Hicks. Vol. I, *1889–1919*. New York: Harcourt, Brace, and Company, 1938.

Steffens, Lincoln. "Mary Austin." *The American Magazine*, LXXII, 2 (June 1911).

Van Doren, Carl. "American Rhythm: Mary Austin." *Many Minds*. New York: A. A. Knopf, 1926.

―――. "Mary Hunter Austin: 1868–1934." *New York Herald Tribune Books*, August 26, 1934.

Walker, Franklin. *Seacoast of Bohemia*. San Francisco: The Book Club of California, 1966.

Wilson, Carol Green. *Herbert Hoover: A Challenge for Today*. New York: Evans Publishing Company, 1968.

Wynn, Dudley. *A Critical Study of the Writings of Mary Austin*. Graduate School of Arts and Science, New York University, 1941.